The Currents of
Lethal Violence

SUNY Series in Violence
David F. Luckenbill, Editor

The Currents of Lethal Violence

An Integrated Model of Suicide and Homicide

N. Prabha Unnithan
Lin Huff-Corzine
Jay Corzine
Hugh P. Whitt

STATE UNIVERSITY OF NEW YORK PRESS

Published by
State University of New York Press, Albany

© 1994 State University of New York

Printed in the United States of America

For information, address State University of New York
Press, State University Plaza, Albany, N.Y., 12246

Production by E. Moore
Marketing by Fran Keneston

Library of Congress Cataloging-in-Publication Data

The Currents of lethal violence : an integrated model of suicide and
    homicide / N. Prabha Unnithan . . . [et al.].
        p.   cm. — (SUNY series in violence)
    Includes bibliographical references and index.
    ISBN 0-7914-2052-3 (pbk.). — ISBN 0-7914-2051-5
    1. Suicide—United States.   2. Homicide—United States.
    3. Violence—United States.   I. Unnithan, N. Prabha, 1952–   .
    II. Series.
    HV6548.U5C87   1994
    364.1'52'0973—dc20   93-39934
                                                                                          CIP

10 9 8 7 6 5 4 3 2 1

Contents

JAMES F. SHORT, JR.

Foreword

Research and theoretical traditions in the sciences are often spurred by an especially powerful empirical discovery or theoretical insight, by the introduction of an especially powerful analytic tool, or by the sheer persistence of a strong research program. This is no less true of the social and behavioral sciences than it is of the physical and biological sciences. Traditions may be neglected because no such stimulus occurs or because empirical inquiry fails to nourish a theory or somehow reaches a theoretical dead end. In this book Unnithan and his colleagues trace the uneven fortunes of the *stream analogy* of lethal violence—the theoretical view that suicide and homicide represent alternative extreme expressions of aggression.

When Andy Henry and I combined and added to research reported in Andy's Ph.D. dissertation on suicide and mine on crime— both focusing on relationships between these phenomena and the business cycle—we knew we were not the first to suggest that these behaviors might be alternative means of expressing aggression; but we were unaware of the rich theoretical tradition that is reviewed in the pages that follow. When we had completed our book, we felt we had begun to understand something very fundamental about the expression of aggression as revealed in suicidal and homicidal behavior. Yet despite considerable interest in the book, the tradition did not flourish. Andy's untimely death and my own preoccupation with studying juvenile delinquency may have contributed to the failure of the tradition to develop. But those were not the only reasons.

Perhaps the theory, as we developed it, left too many questions unanswered concerning why some people express aggression outwardly while others direct aggression toward themselves. Perhaps the concepts we used were too difficult to disentangle among either classes of individuals or social systems. External restraints, encompassing both position in the social order and strength of the relational system, vary not only in magnitude but in relationship to one another, within and among individuals. Identification and measurement of such differences are extremely difficult. Our measure of frustration—the business cycle—was also crude and variable in its impact on classes of individuals. In the end, Andy and I could only point to promising research that might aid in sorting out the complex relationships suggested by our theory.

The theoretical traditions upon which we based our work—frustration/aggression as well as the twin streams of aggression—did not die, of course, and research that contributed to both traditions continued. Among the contributors to these developments were the authors of this book, N. Prabha Unnithan, Lin Huff-Corzine, Jay Corzine, and Hugh P. Whitt—the latter among the few sociologists to pursue the stream analogy after the publication of *Suicide and Homicide* (Henry and Short 1954).

The Currents of Lethal Violence reviews the history of research and theory in the stream analogy tradition and adds considerably to it by making distinctions among different types of suicide and homicide, refined concepts and measures, and applications to international data that extend the tradition. The book closes with suggestions as to how the tradition might be further extended to explain some types of accidents and collective violence. The analysis focuses primarily on the macrosocial level of explanation, though insights from the social-psychological literature are also brought to bear.

The social and behavioral sciences have much to gain by further pursuit of the stream of violence analogy. While knowledge of both suicide and homicide has been advanced in their separate study under the rubrics of suicidology and criminology, satisfactory explanation of both has suffered by the failure to study them together. How shall we account for the volatility of rates of both suicide and homicide among African Americans, for example, and for observed increases in rates for most age groups relative to comparable rates for whites? (See Stafford and Weisheit 1988; Reiss and Roth 1993.)

Unnithan and his colleagues have made a promising start toward the revival of an important, but neglected, research tradition. Let us hope this revival will prosper.

Preface

This book has been literally decades in the making. That it is now completed is due most of all to the power of an idea. The idea that homicide and suicide constitute two alternative channels of a single stream of lethal violence has been around since the fifth century A.D. It first received scholarly attention in the formative years of the social sciences in the nineteenth century. This conceptualization more or less disappeared for several decades before it was resurrected in the mid-twentieth century; the circumstances of its rebirth are recounted by James F. Short, Jr., in the foreword. This book represents a third attempt, in the waning years of the twentieth century, to synthesize, revitalize, and move the idea forward. That this book has been completed is also due to patience and friendship. Among the four coauthors, Hugh P. Whitt first became interested in the stream analogy in 1964 while working on his masters thesis under the direction of the late Rupert B. Vance at the University of North Carolina at Chapel Hill. Whitt had collected census-tract data on suicide rates and various measures of social disorganization for Atlanta, his hometown, and was working on an ecological study in the Chicago school tradition of Ruth Shonle Cavan and Calvin S. Schmid. For reasons that escaped him at the time but now seem perfectly clear, he found that the relationship between suicide rates and social disorganization was curvilinear; rates were high both in the disorganized tracts in the zone in transition and those in the affluent suburbs, but they were lower in between. Moreover, the suicide rate correlated negatively across tracts with the homicide rate, one of his measures of social disorganization. Vance would not accept "I don't know" as an explanation for these seemingly anomalous findings, and Whitt grew more and more frustrated and less and less confident he would ever get his M.A.

Several weeks after reading the work of Henry and Short and Martin Gold and not finding them particularly relevant, he was three or four days into a period of studiously avoiding both his thesis and his adviser when he awoke late one night with the sudden realization that the suicide rate was the product of Gold's suicide murder ratio (SMR), $S/(S + H)$, and the sum of the suicide and homicide rates, $(S + H)$. Applying Gold's SMR (now the SHR) and what he called the lethal aggression rate or LAR [$(S + H)$, which we now label the LVR] to the implicit logical structure of Henry and Short's theory, he was able to complete his thesis and move on to pursue the idea in a doctoral dissertation.

Coincidentally and quite independently, the historian Sheldon Hackney had arrived at the same realization at about the same time. Hackney's paper using the suicide homicide ratio (SHR) and lethal violence rate (LVR) appeared in 1969. Thanks largely to the forbearance of James Short, then the editor of the *American Sociological Review*, Whitt, along with Charles C. Gordon and John R. Hofley, was able to publish a paper in 1972 using these same measures.

The climate of opinion in sociology in the late 1960s and early 1970s was not conducive to macrosociological studies of suicide. In 1967, Jack Douglas published his well-received monograph, *The Social Meanings of Suicide*, which argued persuasively against research strategies based on macrolevel theory and the use of official data. Then in 1974, Karl Schuessler chose Whitt, Gordon, and Hofley's article as an example of the difficulties inherent in using ratio variables.

Whitt's attempts during this period to publish follow-up studies were met by a barrage of theoretical and methodological criticisms and resounding rejections by journal reviewers and editors. Knowing he must publish or surely perish, Whitt, who had joined the faculty of the University of Nebraska at Lincoln in 1967, turned his attention to research with more immediate payoffs. It was not until the early 1980s that he again devoted attention to the stream analogy.

At about that time, N. Prabha Unnithan, a criminologist by training who had spent his early years in Malaysia and India, began doctoral studies at the university. Beginning with a vague notion that he would like to study homicide rates cross-nationally, Unnithan was slowly drawn to the stream analogy. He had read Henry and Short's work in India (ironically, for a class called "Social Disorganization") but had not thought much about it at the time. He became more interested after hearing Whitt speak on the intellectual lineage and possible contemporary applications of the stream analogy. Under Whitt's direction he completed a dissertation on comparative structural determinants of lethal violence using the LVR and SHR. Several departmental colloquia and endless noisy brainstorming sessions in Whitt's office accompanied the Unnithan-Whitt collaboration.

Whitt's office was (and is) next to Jay Corzine's. Corzine, also a faculty member at UNL, had long-standing research interests in lethal violence in the Southern regions of the United States. He had published research on lynchings, and he was aware of and dissatisfied with the protracted and bitter debate between proponents of structural and cultural explanations of Southern violence. Perhaps partly because he could not escape the noisy debates filtering through his office wall, Corzine came to see the pronounced differences between homicide and suicide rates in the North and South as one key to a resolution of the debate.

Lin Huff-Corzine, who had worked as a psychiatric nurse in what she calls her "past life," became a sociology undergraduate at UNL during the late 1970s. There she studied deviance with Hugh Whitt and began her collaboration with Corzine in studying Southern violence. Huff-Corzine's social psychological conceptualization, like Whitt's at the University of North Carolina, was primarily influenced by the late Harry J. Crockett, Jr., at UNL. They both feel especially indebted to him for helping them begin to think first about how locus of control (Whitt) and later attribution theory (Huff-Corzine) could be applied to the study of suicide and homicide. While at UNC, Harry convinced Whitt to replace Henry and Short's external restraints with locus of control as the basis for the choice between suicide and homicide. The change was an improvement, but, as we shall see in the pages that follow, it still left much to be desired. Later, at UNL, Harry became more deeply immersed in attribution theory, and especially the work of Harold H. Kelley, through the latter's participation in the 1967 Nebraska Symposium on Motivation. Harry's perspective influenced Huff-Corzine, along with Corzine and David C. Moore, another of his former students, to replace locus of control with social psychological attribution theory as a predictor of whether lethal violence will be channeled outward as homicide or inward as suicide. We sorely miss him.

The four of us are charter members, and, indeed, the only members (with the exception of David C. Moore, our methodological guru and collaborator), of the mythical Nebraska Center for the Study of Lethal Violence. Despite our common interest in the stream analogy and our many discussions of it while we were all at UNL, we did not come up with the idea for this book until much later.

By the early 1990s, while Whitt and Corzine remained at UNL, Unnithan had joined the sociology faculty at Colorado State University in Fort Collins and Huff-Corzine, who received her Ph.D. from Washington University in 1986, had taken a faculty position in the sociology program at Kansas State University in Manhattan. Spurred by an an-

nouncement inviting submission of manuscripts for the series on violence undertaken by the State University of New York Press and realiz-
ing that the climate of scholarly opinion was again becoming favorable
to perspectives such as ours, we decided the time was right to attempt
a resurrection of the stream analogy.

Because we were now scattered, we had our first planning meeting for the project in North Platte, Nebraska, roughly equidistant between our respective universities, on a gray and rainy day in May 1991.
This book was launched in a motel room and over a surprisingly excel-
lent dinner at the local Chinese restaurant. Since then the project has
taken shape by linking together four researchers at three campuses in
three different states. It was put together by fax and by computer disks
sent through the mail, and refined over the telephone and through elec-
tronic mail. The monograph has grown well beyond our initial chapter
outline as new leads and new insights have led us deeper into the literature on lethal violence and its directions.

Using a tradition borrowed from the natural sciences but seldom
seen in sociology, Whitt, the principal investigator and chief architect of
the integrated model, is listed as fourth author of the book as a whole.
Unnithan, who first suggested that we should collaborate on a monograph on the stream analogy, is listed first, and the ordering of Huff-
Corzine and Corzine is arbitrary.

Authorship of each individual chapter, however, indicates our involvement in each portion of the total project. Although each chapter
has its own author(s), all of us have done our best to ensure that the fin-
ished product hangs together as an internally consistent and coherent
treatment of the history of the stream analogy and the integrated model,
our operationalization of the analogy.

We gratefully acknowledge the help and interest of many professional colleagues who motivated us to move this project from a hazy
idea toward completion. Our first thanks are to the faculty, students,
and staff of the sociology departments at UNL, KSU, and CSU, both past
and present. UNL provided a place where four individuals with diverse
backgrounds could come together at a particular time in a supportive
environment to form the Nebraska Center for the Study of Lethal Violence. In particular, our thanks go to David C. Moore, an integral part
of our research team over the years. Without any implication that our
thanks exclude the many others at UNL to whom we are also indebted,
we wish to single out the contributions of present and former faculty
members Nicholas Babchuk, Alan P. Bates, Robert Benford, David
Brinkerhoff, Jerry Cloyd, David R. Johnson, Jennifer Lehmann, Helen A.
Moore, Suzanne T. Ortega, D. Wayne Osgood, and Lynn K. White.

They, along with the rest of the UNL sociology faculty, have listened patiently to our ideas over the years and made many cogent suggestions for improving them.

We have also received invaluable help from our colleagues Donald D. Jensen and Theo B. Sonderegger in the Department of Psychology at UNL. Don and Theo introduced us to the intricacies of the psychobiology of suicidal behavior and the possibility that 5-hydroxy-indoleacetic acid or the lithium content of drinking water might be somehow relevant to what we were doing. Brigitte Formentin-Humbert of the Department of Modern Languages helped with translations—convincing us, for example, to render a phrase from Despine as "dung-heap" rather than "pile of shit," which perhaps comes closer to the spirit of the original.

Our thanks go also to our students. UNL graduate students Cynthia Douglas, Phyllis Gerstenfeld, Maria Potenza, Scott Sasse, Christine Scott, and Jody Van Laningham, who participated in Whitt's seminar on lethal violence during the fall semester of 1992, read the first draft of the manuscript and put their stamp firmly on the final version. Phyllis, in particular, has our gratitude for making us aware of Karl Marx's 1853 article on suicide and homicide and suggesting the relevance of learned helplessness and hopelessness theory to our perspective.

Other students have also made contributions. Candice Nelsen, a former undergraduate at UNL who later received her M.A. at Kansas State University, has helped in many ways, ranging from providing social support and intellectual stimulation to acting as a courier between the two campuses. H. Wade German, a UNL Ph.D. candidate working on a time-series analysis of lethal violence in the United States using the integrated model, is already pushing us to develop additional extensions.

Outside UNL, David Luckenbill, editor of the SUNY series on violence, provided crucial initial support, while Rosalie Robertson and Chris Worden, editors at SUNY Press, showed patience and trust as the book took shape and the four of us sometimes missed deadlines. James F. Short, Jr., and Steven Stack reviewed the manuscript and made many valuable suggestions, which are now incorporated into the final product.

We owe a special debt of gratitude to Jim Short, the godfather of this project and our entire research program. Jim has contributed, perhaps more than anyone else now living, to this book's seeing the light of day. Jim's work with Andrew F. Henry during the 1950s provided a springboard for our ideas, and it is especially appropriate that this book appears on the fortieth anniversary of the publication of their classic monograph. But Jim's help has come again and again over the years in countless ways. In 1972, the first publication of our position might not have occurred if someone less willing to help with editorial revisions and grant journal space to a piece that ran counter to the temper of the times had been editor of the *American Sociological Review*. More recently, Jim has earned our thanks not only for his meticulous review of an earlier draft of our manuscript, but also for graciously agreeing to write the foreword and for organizing a session on the integrated model for the 1993 annual meeting of the American Society of Criminology in Phoenix, Arizona. He won't know it until he opens his copy of this book, but Jim has been named the first, and so far the only, honorary fellow of the Nebraska Center for the Study of Lethal Violence.

Each of us has incurred many personal debts in the process of writing this book. Unnithan thanks his parents, P. Neelakantan Unnithan and the late K. Ammini Unnithan, and his spouse, Shashikala Unnithan, whose support for his educational and career goals was always unwavering, and he dedicates this book to them. He also acknowledges the love, ready laughter, and childhood curiosity of his two daughters, Rachna and Ranjana, who make life and work worthwhile. He is grateful to his first mentor in social research, M. Z. Khan, now at Jamia Millia Islamia University in New Delhi, India, who taught him many invaluable lessons. On a collegial level, he thanks James D. Jones, now at Mississippi State University, who hired him for his first academic position. At CSU, the support of David M. Freeman and advice from D. Stanley Eitzen have helped and shaped his professional growth.

Together, Huff-Corzine and Corzine wish to thank David Pittman, who served as major adviser to each of them during their graduate careers at Washington University in St. Louis. Although they attended graduate school at different times, (Jay in the mid-1970s and Lin during the early 1980s), Professor Pittman gave them many of the same invaluable insights into the world of sociology. Among the more memorable are two facts that they use to guide their own careers in sociology, as well as those of their students. First, "sociology is what a sociologist does. If you are a sociologist, then your work is sociology." The topic of your research is of no real concern. And second, "look at your dissertation as the beginning of an exciting intellectual journey; not as an end to your journey. It should be good and show promise, but certainly not be the major work of your lifetime."

Huff-Corzine is grateful to her parents, Dean Huff and the late Marilyn (Huff) Baird, for socializing her to be strong (some would say stubborn), independent, and flexible in her approach to life. She is also indebted to her children, Heidi and Chris, and grandchildren, Chasady and Devlynn, for bringing joy and purpose to her life.

Beyond the family, friends, and colleagues she has already noted, Huff-Corzine gives special thanks to her colleagues at KSU, who listened as ideas for this book took form and offered professional advice as requested. Among those colleagues, the late George R. Peters was especially important from the first day she set foot on the KSU campus. Until his recent death, George was always there to discuss both professional and personal questions as well as to provide insight into social-psychological concepts related to homicide and suicide. He is now missed in body; but his spirit, strength, and ethical guidance live on.

Huff-Corzine dedicates her part in this book to her coauthor and best friend, Jay Corzine, whose undying emotional support and respect encourages her intellectual strengths, independence, and flexibility to take form in reality.

Corzine thanks his mother, Ann L. Smith, and his late uncle and aunt, Oliver and Emma McEvers, for early and persistent encouragement as he pursued his education. An ongoing debt of thanks is owed to his children, Heidi and Chris, and to his spouse and frequent collaborator, Lin Huff-Corzine, who is a constant source of support and also available to bounce intellectual ideas off at eleven o'clock at night. He dedicates this book to her.

When Corzine was an undergraduate at Illinois College, Dr. Malcolm Stewart and Dr. Ken Studer provided the role models that first made an academic career seem an attractive choice. In addition to the special thanks previously offered to David Pittman, he thanks the faculty and graduate students at Washington University in the mid-1970s. To the stimulating intellectual climate they collectively created and maintained he owes much of his success as a researcher. Special thanks are also extended to Robert Boguslaw, Barry Glassner, Murray Wax, and Rosalie Wax.

Whitt owes a debt of gratitude to the memory of many who are no longer with us. Chief among these are Rupert B. Vance, Harry J. Crockett, Jr., and Hubert M. Blalock, Jr., his chief mentors during the formative years in Chapel Hill when the integrated model began to assume a recognizable shape.

Among the living, he thanks Ernest Q. Campbell and Edward A. Tiryakian, who first awakened his interest in the study of suicide; Richard L. Simpson and Gerhard E. Lenski, former mentors and long-time friends who have nurtured his intellectual development by instruction and by example; and the members of his graduate student cohort at UNC. Those of us who occupied the bullpen in Alumni Building at UNC in the mid- to late 1960s bounced so many trial balloons off each other that it was impossible to tell who was responsible for which idea. In particular, he thanks Charles C. Gordon and John R. Hofley, his first collaborators in extending his dissertation research, and Nancy Diefenbach, Gay Kitson, Colin Loftin, Charles F. Longino, Jr., the late Alden D. Miller, and Donald R. Ploch, any one of whom may just be responsible for planting the seed that eventually became the integrated model.

Whitt dedicates this book to the memory of his parents, Brigadier General Hugh Whitt and Jewel B. Whitt, who encouraged him to pursue the life of the mind, and to his best friend and recent bride, Susan Louise Brailey, for her love, for all she has patiently put up with during the writing of the manuscript, and for simply being there.

We present this book to the reader both as a document in the history of ideas and in the hope that it will act as a catalyst for future research to clarify, extend, and evaluate the integrated model of homicide and suicide presented in these pages. Finally, because the overall objective of our work is to develop a clearer theoretical and empirical understanding of violent interpersonal death, we dedicate this book to *Life*.

Acknowledgments

Sections of two chapters originally appeared in previous publications by the authors. We thank E. J. Brill, Leiden, The Netherlands, publishers of the *International Journal of Comparative Sociology*, for permission to use portions of N. Prabha Unnithan and Hugh P. Whitt, "Inequality, Economic Development and Lethal Violence: A Cross-National Analysis of Suicide and Homicide" (33 [1992], 182–96) in chapter 7; and the University of North Carolina Press, publishers of *Social Forces*, for permission to use portions of Lin Huff-Corzine, Jay Corzine, and David C. Moore, "Deadly Connections: Culture, Poverty, and the Direction of Lethal Violence" (69 [1991], 715–32) in chapter 8.

Our appreciation is also extended to Karl Schuessler and the University of Chicago Press, publisher of the *American Journal of Sociology*, for permission to reprint material from Karl Schuessler, "Analysis of Ratio Variables: Opportunities and Pitfalls" (80 [1974], 379–96); to Sheldon Hackney for permission to reprint material from "Southern Violence," *American Historical Review* 39 (1969), 906–25; and to Stuart Palmer for permission to reprint material from "Murder and Suicide in Forty Non-Literate Societies," *Journal of Criminal Law, Criminology and Police Science* 56 (1965), 320–24, originally published by the Northwestern University School of Law.

JAY CORZINE
LIN HUFF-CORZINE
HUGH P. WHITT
N. PRABHA UNNITHAN

1

To Every Good Thing There Must Be a Beginning

Sandwiched between the typical headlines, local features, announcements of births and deaths, weather and sports news typical of major metropolitan newspapers in the United States, the *Denver Post* on Sunday, 22 March 1992 ran separate stories on the violent deaths of two young Colorado girls. A fifteen-year-old had hung herself in a jail cell in Weld County, Colorado, on the previous Wednesday and had died the next day (*Denver Post*, 1992a). Her death was discussed as an unfortunate suicide. The second story told of a ten-month-old girl who had allegedly been beaten to death by a worker in a day-care center in Arapahoe County, Colorado, some three months earlier (*Denver Post*, 1992b). The newspaper was refocusing on a possible homicide that by itself was old news. Recent allegations, however, claimed that earlier accusations against the woman held in the death of the ten-month-old had been mishandled by the authorities. It will not surprise the reader to know that the day-care worker was being charged with criminal conduct or that the girl's death had been officially labeled as a murder. There was little that was unique in the *Denver Post* stories, and most readers of other major newspapers on 22 March 1992 would have been only momentarily shocked to discover accounts of similar violent deaths in or near their own communities.

Citizens of the United States in the late twentieth century may not have learned to accept the body count associated with violence in their society, but they have nonetheless become accustomed to it. In fact, the stories in the Denver newspaper were located in section C, well off the front page, and both stories were relatively short. Some characteristic surrounding a violent death has to be particularly startling for the story to appear on the front page of a major newspaper.

The *Kansas City Star* ran such a story on 22 March 1992, concerning a Sullivan, Missouri, man who killed himself in his basement with a twelve-gauge shotgun after taking the lives of five family members spanning three generations (*Kansas City Star* 1992). Greatly increasing the newsworthiness of this violent episode was the protagonist's standing in the Sullivan area. He was a community leader who owned a construction company and served as a county commissioner. Actually, high social status is not uncommon among the perpetrators of murder-suicides involving family members, but members of the affected community may find such events shocking (West 1967).

The public's emotional reaction to these three types of violent deaths ranges from sorrow to bewilderment for suicides, especially those involving younger persons, to fear and outrage at the killing of innocent victims by murderers. On a more cognitive level, people are often interested in obtaining answers to three types of questions. The first is linked to the common reaction of disbelief and addresses the issue of how "normal" people can commit such acts. For example, it was suggested that the county commissioner in Sullivan, Missouri, had become depressed because of a recent change in prescription medication, and a surviving relative declared, "It was not him there" (*Kansas City Star* 1992, 1) when the murders of kin were carried out. The second question asked by the public is whether the violent death could have been foreseen, an inquiry that implies that the tragic episode was a surprise. A Weld County District Court judge who had seen the teenage girl shortly before her suicide was reported to have stated, "I've seen some of them down and depressed. . . . She wasn't one of them. . . . I didn't see her as a suicidal person" (*Denver Post* 1992a, 3C). Related to the second question, which focuses on prediction, is the third one about the potential for prevention. The major implication of the follow-up story of the day-care center death in Colorado is that the tragedy could have been prevented if only local authorities had made a proper response to an earlier charge of child abuse.

The public's concern with the ability to predict and the potential to prevent violent deaths overlaps with the professional (and personal) interests of sociologists, criminologists, psychologists, and investigators from other fields (such as psychiatry, anthropology, history) who study homicide or suicide at either the individual or aggregate level. Most academics who conduct research on violent deaths have put aside the question of whether normal people commit these acts. The sheer volume of lethal human violence in the United States—22,909 homicides and 30,232 suicides in 1989 (National Center for Health Statistics 1992)—is compelling evidence that, at most, we are dealing with typical people who sometimes commit abnormal, or atypical, acts.

Although much will be said about homicide and suicide in the following pages, the focus of this book is only secondarily on individual or aggregate events of lethal violence. Instead, this volume is primarily about how professionals (and, to a lesser degree, the public) think about or conceptualize homicidal and suicidal behaviors. On one basic point, lay and professional definitions of these causes of death are in agreement. Namely, although homicide and suicide share the common component that a death occurs because of the purposeful actions of a human agent, they are perceived as fundamentally different in nature. Suicide and attempted suicide are considered public health or mental health problems and are thought of as tragedies for the deceased and often for surviving family members. Homicide and attempted homicide are also seen as tragedies and health issues; but depending on the surrounding circumstances, they are also viewed as crimes or offenses against society to be handled by criminal justice agencies. The perceived seriousness of criminal homicide—that is, murder or manslaughter—is exemplified by the fact that it is currently the only crime for which capital punishment is a potential penalty in the United States.

The distinction between homicide and suicide found in public and professional thought is also reflected in the social organization of research directed at their understanding and prevention. Most investigations of lethal violence focus on either homicide or suicide, but not on both at the same time. Many of the studies that are concerned with both conceive of them as separate indicators of anomie, disorganization, or other underlying problems in the social fabric. Research on homicide and suicide is frequently funded by different agencies, and the results usually appear in separate monographs or specialty journals such as *Criminology* and *Suicide and Life-Threatening Behavior*. Finally, the pools of experts on homicide and suicide called on by the media to provide appropriate insights and comments often have few common members. In brief, homicide and suicide are seen as distinct, unrelated behaviors.

There is, however, a second way of examining homicide and suicide that sees them as connected, representing alternative expressions of the same underlying motivations and social forces. While we will be concerned primarily with the scientific version of this perspective, it is important to note that a similar mode of conceptualizing homicide and suicide was once prevalent in the public mind, at least in Western societies. Early Christian thought made no distinction between suicide and homicide in regard to their moral and religious implications, and the same word or closely related ones were used to name both types of deaths in the Germanic and Scandinavian languages. The serious punishments, including death, imposed for unsuccessful attempts to end one's life in some European nations were invoked precisely because attempted suicide was viewed as equivalent to attempted murder.

In the social sciences, the idea that homicide and suicide are alternate expressions of the same underlying phenomenon was first suggested in the 1830s but was not systematically developed until the late 1800s with the work of the Italian scholars Enrico Ferri and Enrico Morselli. Although their ideas were influential in guiding research in Europe, their position was strongly criticized by Emile Durkheim, who believed that homicide and suicide were distinct acts with particularistic sets of causes. Of course, it was Durkheim's *Suicide* that more than any other single volume influenced sociologists and other social scientists in the United States, and the theoretical position outlined by Ferri and Morselli received little attention on this side of the Atlantic. Like Ferri and Morselli, Sigmund Freud viewed suicide as homicide turned inward toward the self. His work was known in the United States, but it had little impact on the social sciences until after World War II.

Following in the footsteps of the European moral statisticians, Austin Porterfield's empirical investigations of the spatial juxtaposition of homicide and suicide rates in the late 1940s paved the way for the development of a model stressing linkages between the two forms of lethal violence. In 1954, Andrew F. Henry and James F. Short, Jr., constructed a theoretical explanation of the relationship between homicide and suicide on the foundation provided by Freud and the frustration-aggression hypothesis developed by John Dollard and his associates at Yale University in 1939. Their book, *Suicide and Homicide*, was well received upon release and is now considered a classic in criminology. Its publication stimulated some attention to the common sources of homicide and suicide, as well as attempts at further specification (for example, Gold 1958). Attention to Henry and Short's thesis gradually waned, however, and articles by Sheldon Hackney (1969) and Hugh Whitt, Charles Gordon, and John Hofley (1972) marked the end of a period when the possibility that homicide and suicide should be studied together was given serious consideration by more than a handful of scholars. Research on lethal violence has not abated in the 1980s and 1990s, but it has once again been almost exclusively focused on either homicide or suicide. Hypotheses suggesting a connection between the two are rarely tested, and investigators in each area often appear to be unaware of developments occurring in the other.

Our basic argument in this book is that although there are dissimilarities between homicide and suicide, there is much to be gained from revitalizing the theory developed by Henry and Short. Specifically, there are numerous issues related to lethal violence that can be better addressed—and, in some cases, understood—by working from an integrated model that emphasizes the similarities between self-directed and other-directed lethal violence. These include the peculiar nature of Southern violence in the United States; continued differences in the patterns of lethal violence between blacks and whites; and the relationships between homicide, suicide, and economic development in a cross-national context. We are not, however, advocating a cessation of research that views homicide and suicide as distinct behaviors. Depending on the topic of investigation, this approach may be entirely appropriate and reasonable. Our contention is that for many research questions related to human violence, the goal of explanation will be better served by a theoretical model that explicitly takes into account the connections between homicide and suicide. In the following chapters, we attempt to establish our case to the reader's satisfaction.

OVERVIEW OF CHAPTERS

Chapter 2 reviews the early history of the stream analogy, the idea that homicide and suicide are linked, as it was developed in Europe by the moral statisticians; and it discusses Durkheim's criticism of the analogy. The same theme is traced in the works of Freud and Dollard and his collaborators. As the title of chapter 2, "Old Theories Never Die," implies, there have been two previous incarnations of the stream analogy, and the present volume represents the third. Chapter 3, "Old Wine in New Wineskins," examines the revival of interest in the stream analogy, which lasted from the late 1940s through 1972.

In chapter 4, we review the literature on lethal violence circa 1972–92. A basic premise of this chapter is that although interest in human violence is not lacking either among the general public or scholars, the study of suicide and homicide have become separate enterprises. In addition, a high percentage of investigations that do examine both homicide and suicide lack a unifying theoretical model. Finally, we address the question of whether accidental deaths should be studied along with those from homicide and suicide.

Chapter 5 focuses on recent developments in social psychology, which, though they do not directly address suicide and homicide, seem to us to resolve some of the issues raised in chapter 3 and left unresolved in chapter 4. In particular, we identify a version of attribution theory that provides linkages between the individual level of analysis and the more macrolevel perspective that guides our own research.

In chapter 6, we specify an integrated model of self- and other-directed lethal violence that is, in essence, a modified and updated version of the theoretical perspective developed by Henry and Short. The definition and measurement of two synthetic variables, the lethal violence rate (LVR) and the suicide-homicide ratio (SHR) are explained, and their connection to the stream analogy is detailed. Implications that should not be, but frequently are, drawn from the stream analogy (for example, that homicide and suicide rates are by necessity inversely related) and relevant methodological questions (such as the ratio variables issue) are discussed. Finally, a strategy for testing the model across multiple levels of analysis, using logic derived from Gayl Ness's 1985 work on comparative cross-national research, is proposed.

Chapters 7 and 8 present empirical analyses derived from the model. Chapter 7 examines the effect of inequality and economic development on lethal violence measurements—suicide and homicide rates, the LVR and the SHR—in the cross-national context. Following the approach outlined by Ness, chapter 8 focuses on the United States, which, not surprisingly, emerges as an outlier in many cross-national analyses. This chapter offers a new understanding of Southern violence, one that focuses on regional differences in the SHR instead of high homicide rates. A major advantage of this perspective is that it transcends the ongoing debate between proponents of structural and cultural explanations of Southern homicide.

The concluding chapter, "Charting the Currents of Lethal Violence," provides a recapitulation and evaluation of the strengths and weaknesses of the stream analogy. In addition, we suggest further avenues for research on lethal violence and raise the issue of whether the model can be expanded to include collective violence, such as riots and wars, as a third branch in the stream of lethal violence.

2

Old Theories Never Die

Old soldiers never die; they simply
fade away.
— J. Foley, 1920

INTRODUCTION

For almost a century, the sociological study of suicide has drawn heavily upon Emile Durkheim's *Suicide* (1897). But Durkheim, too, had his sources. Our book will begin with ideas expressed in some of the books and articles in Durkheim's bibliography—the work of Andre Michel Guerry (1833), Alfred Maury (1860), Prosper Despine (1868), and especially Durkheim's Italian rivals Enrico Ferri (1883–84, 1895) and Enrico Morselli (1879a, 1879b). All these scholars suggested that there are statistical regularities in the relationship between suicide and homicide, which they regarded as alternative manifestations of the same underlying phenomenon.[1] Durkheim likened their conceptualization of suicide and homicide to two currents of a single stream of violence fed from a single source (Durkheim 1897, 340; see also Halbwachs 1930; Verkko 1951; Wolfgang and Ferracuti 1967 for discussions of the stream analogy).

At the time Durkheim wrote *Suicide*, he was embroiled in a running three-way academic battle with Gabriel Tarde and the Italian criminologists Morselli and especially Ferri. The two Frenchmen were constantly sniping at each other, but they joined forces in opposing the more biologically based position of Ferri, Morselli, and the other members of Cesare Lombroso's Italian school of criminal anthropology (see Tarde 1883, 1884, 1886a, 1886b, 1890). Durkheim's intellectual conflict

7

with Tarde, whose imitation theory he attacks mercilessly in *Suicide*, is well known (Clark 1969; Lukes 1973); but their uneasy alliance in the debate with the Italian school has received little attention.

This book documents how sociologists, beginning in the mid-twentieth century, resurrected parts of the theoretical system which guided Ferri and Morselli, stripping it of the Darwinian and Lombrosian baggage that led Durkheim and Tarde to oppose it. Ferri, though apparently not Morselli, took the extreme position that the sources of suicide and homicide can be found in an atavistic reversion to an earlier stage in the evolutionary process, citing the violent behavior of "savages" and animals as documentation (Zimmern 1896). In the first salvo of the debate, Tarde (1883, 663, our translation) chided Ferri for seriously suggesting that "horses and dogs" commit criminal homicide and that "the beasts kill for vengeance, for love, in order to steal, etc., just like humans; and all the categories of human murders seem to be derived from the twenty-eight varieties of zoological murders conscientiously distinguished by Monsieur Ferri."

The French sociologists' rejection of the hypothesis that suicide and homicide are causally related undoubtedly stemmed from what they viewed as wretched excess in such extreme statements of Ferri's Lombrosian evolutionism. But instead of simply rejecting a biological interpretation of the body of statistical data showing the existence of a relationship between suicide and homicide that had been accumulating since the early 1830s (Guerry 1833; Maury 1860; Despine 1868), both Durkheim (1897) and Tarde (1883, 1886a, 1886b, 1890) also refused to accept either the reality of the statistical patterns or the utility of the stream analogy.

While Tarde concentrated on attacking Ferri, Durkheim deemphasized both imitation and the link between suicide and homicide in favor of his own theories. His position eventually won out, largely because of the force of his arguments rather than because of an empirically demonstrated superiority over its competitors in explaining suicide (Douglas 1967; Lukes 1973). The positions taken by Tarde and Ferri in the debate largely passed from the scene, and the sociological study of suicide has had a distinctly Durkheimian cast ever since.

The outcome of scientific debates, however, sometimes has an uncanny way of not being final, especially when the winning side's theoretical position cannot adequately deal with some enduring aspect of physical or social reality that its losing competitors can easily accommodate. Both the stream analogy and Tarde's imitation theory have been revived in recent years precisely because they can deal effectively with findings that cannot be easily explained by Durkheim's perspective. We shall deal with the revival of Tarde's position only in passing, but its status is similar to that of theorizing based on the stream analogy—both can better accommodate a particular set of empirical findings than can theories in the Durkheimian tradition.[2]

The medical historian Sir William Osler (1922) once remarked that the philosophies of one age have become the absurdities of the next and the foolishness of yesterday has become the wisdom of tomorrow. Similarly, Thomas Kuhn (1970) tells us that theories that are swept under the rug in scientific debates are often eventually accepted long after their initial rejection. The process of conversion to a new point of view, however, can drag on well beyond the lifetimes of the parties to the original dispute. Max Planck (1949, 34) suggests that because of the vested professional and personal interests of those working in the dominant tradition, "a new scientific truth does not triumph by convincing its opponents and making them see the light, but rather because its opponents eventually die, and a new generation grows up that is familiar with it."

For Kuhn (1970), the progress of science is usually characterized by *normal science* within a particular paradigm—a taken-for-granted picture such as Durkheim's—of the broad outlines of how things work. Normal science is a puzzle-solving enterprise in which scientists attempt to fit their findings into the paradigm that guides their work. Occasionally, however, someone, usually a young researcher or an outsider with little vested interest in the prevailing paradigm, encounters an anomaly—a datum that cannot be fitted into the existing puzzle. Because of their considerable personal and professional investments, established scholars attempt to accommodate the anomaly within their theoretical system; but sometimes, try as they may, the anomaly stubbornly refuses either to fit into the puzzle or to disappear.

After his removal as supreme allied commander in the Korean conflict, General of the Army Douglas A. MacArthur made his farewell with the poignant statement, misquoted from an old post-World War I song, that "old soldiers never die; they just fade away" (MacArthur 1951, 150). Many old theories, including Morselli's and Ferri's, are a bit like MacArthur's old soldiers. They never really die because the anomalies on which they are based stubbornly refuse to go away. Even though it looked like Durkheim had killed off the currents of violence conceptualization of suicide and homicide in the 1890s, the "stream analogy" reemerged in the mid-twentieth century precisely because of the continued existence of patterns of statistical association between suicide and homicide that researchers working in the Durkheimian tradition found difficult to understand. Ferri and Morselli might have suggested, if they were alive today, that the resurrection of their ideas was accomplished by a Dr. Frankenstein, for there are major differences between the suicide-homicide theories of the twentieth century and their nineteenth-century ancestors. These differences, however, are chiefly confined to matters such as which variables should be used to explain the size of the stream and its diversion into two separate channels. While modern researchers have replaced biological with social factors as the variables that affect the amount of water in the stream as well as the direction in which the water flows, the basic logical structures of the newer theories are identical to those of Durkheim's competitors; and Ferri and Morselli would undoubtedly recognize their offspring as having a strong family resemblance. The major premise remains the image of two divergent channels in a single stream of violence.

EARLY HISTORY OF THE IDEA

The idea that suicide and homicide are different expressions of the same phenomenon has been around for a very long time—at least since the fifth century—as a part of the implicit culture of the Western world. This conceptualization can be traced back to Augustinian thought (Augustine c. 426 A.D.; see also Giddens 1970). In *The City of God*, St. Augustine explicitly argues that those who commit suicide "murder themselves." Their act is equivalent to the murder of another because "God's command, 'Thou shalt not kill,' is to be taken as forbidding self-destruction, especially as it does not add 'thy neighbor' " (Augustine c. 426 A.D., bk. 1, ch. 20).

Indeed, until 1662, when the word *suicide* apparently first entered the English language (Westcott 1885), this sense of equivalence was captured by the term *self-murther* then in general use (Hey 1785). Even today, the German *Selbstmord* and cognate terms in the Scandinavian languages retain a similar connotation. Blackstone's *Commentaries on the Laws of England* (1862, 4:189–90) retains the earlier usage, categorizing suicide (or, more correctly, *felo de se*) as a variety of felonious homicide:

> Felonious homicide is . . . the killing of a human creature, of any age or sex, without justification or excuse. This may be done either by killing one's self or another man. Self-murder . . . , though the attempting of it seems to be countenanced by the civil law, yet was punished by the Athenian law with cutting off the hand which committed the desperate deed. And, also, the law of England wisely and religiously considers that no man hath a

power to destroy life but by commission from God, the author of it; and as the suicide is guilty of a double offense, one spiritual, in evading the prerogative of the Almighty, and rushing into his immediate presence uncalled for; the other temporal, against the king, who hath an interest in the preservation of all his subjects, the law has, therefore, ranked this among the highest crimes, making it a peculiar species of felony, a felony committed on one's self.

Thus, Western cultural traditions in religion, language, and law for centuries conveyed an image of suicide and homicide as morally, ethically, and legally equivalent. Self-murder was distinguished from other felonious homicides only by the fact that the victim was also the perpetrator.

THE FIRST MORAL STATISTICIANS

It was within this cultural context that the earliest empirical treatments of the relationship between suicide and homicide began to be produced by members of an intellectual movement known as the cartographic school of criminology, or, more informally, as the moral statisticians. Durkheim's chief sources on the topic, Ferri and Morselli, came late in the development of this school and are usually identified as members of Cesare Lombroso's positive school of criminal anthropology rather than as moral statisticians. Jack Douglas (1967) argues persuasively that Durkheim's work is best understood as a part of the moral statistics tradition and that his greatest contribution was to synthesize its ideas rather than to develop entirely new theoretical insights.[3]

Moral statistics had its beginnings in the 1820s and 1830s. Both the origins of the cartographic school and the earliest empirical treatments of suicide, homicide, and their relationship to one another can be traced to the work of two Frenchmen whose names and careers are so remarkably similar that they are often confused in the literature on the cartographic school.

Andre Michel de Guerry de Champneuf, the French minister of justice in the late 1820s, was instrumental in establishing the first official national statistics on crime, the *Compte générale de l'administration de la justice*. Commissioned in 1825, the annual *Comptes généraux* report on criminal charges of various types brought by local public prosecutors in each district (Morris 1958).

De Guerry de Champneuf was apparently removed from office when King Charles X was deposed by the Revolution of 1830, and the task of analyzing and writing up the results fell to Andre-Michel Guerry, who is often confused with his predecessor. According to Terence Morris (1958), the two were apparently unrelated; and it is Andre-Michel Guerry, not Andre Michel de Guerry de Champneuf, whose early study of suicide and crime is remembered.[4] It is this latter Guerry whom Durkheim (1897) cites and whose contributions to the empirical study of suicide and homicide concern us here.

Guerry had been in charge of gathering data for the *Compte générale* for the city of Paris. In 1829, he teamed with Adriano Balbi to produce a statistical map showing the relationship between educational attainment and crime in France. His book, *Essai sur la statistique morale de la France* (1833), though sometimes attributed to de Guerry de Champneuf (for example, Elmer 1933), has been called "the first to utilise relatively accurate criminal statistics to test . . . hypotheses . . . in the light of the facts. . . . Guerry . . . raised . . . inquiry . . . to a level approaching . . . scientific enlightenment" (Morris 1958, 50).

Guerry used the methods of what is today called human ecology in an effort to uncover the causes of crime. He prepared shaded maps of the geographical distribution of "moral facts" such as crime, educational levels, illegitimacy, charitable donations, and suicide based on the *Comptes généraux* and other contemporary data sources. Darker colors represented high rates. Guerry's maps created a brief academic sensation. He took them on tour and displayed them with pride. As the *Westminster Review* noted at the time, the two maps showing rates of suicide and crimes against persons indicated that "the ignorant portion, in the center of France, attack other people's throats, but take special care of their own. On the subject of suicide they represent a great white patch" (quoted in Morris 1958, 50).

On the basis of this analysis, Guerry argued that suicide and crimes against persons were comparable phenomena and that a clear geographical relationship between their rates could be shown. Guerry noted that the northern departments of France, which had few murders and crimes against persons, were afflicted with very high suicide rates. On the other hand, suicide was a comparative rarity in the southern departments, but murder and other crimes against persons ran rampant.

Crime rates were soon being systematically compiled for nations in much of continental Europe. As the nineteenth-century passion for comparative moral statistics accumulated longer and longer series for various European countries, Guerry's early observations, virtually unnoticed in his own time (Durkheim 1897; Elmer 1933), began to attract attention among a number of French and Italian scholars. For example, Cazauvielh (1840, cited in Durkheim 1897; Tarde 1890; Verkko 1951) attempted to show that contrary to Guerry, suicide and homicide figures vary together over time.

Cazauvielh's position, however, was in the minority. In 1860, for example Alfred Maury pointed to an antagonism between suicide and homicide (1860, 469, our translation):

> The contrast between homicide and suicide is by no means inexplicable. Is not the first-mentioned crime the consequence of the feeling of selfishness brought to its climax? Man sacrifices to his lust, hatred, jealousy the life of his neighbour. The contrary state exists in voluntary death, where love of self is completely extinguished. Tiredness of life dulls the feeling of desire.

The physician and criminal psychologist Prosper Despine, another of Durkheim's sources, replicated Guerry's study using data from the *Comptes généraux* for 1852 and 1867. Although Despine is widely cited (see Durkheim 1897; Tarde 1890; Verkko 1951), we had never found his work directly quoted. After locating a copy of his three-volume work, *Psychologie naturelle: Etude sur les facultés intellectuelles et morales dans leur état normal et dans leur manifestations anomales chez les aliéns et chez les criminels* (Despine 1868), we now understand why. Despine's explanation of the relationship between suicide and homicide is extremely racist, even by the standards of Durkheim's day. His work is certainly not value-free social science. Nonetheless, his statement of his theory of suicide and homicide, Japan-bashing and all, is offered for the historical record:

> The suicide of the man in a state of sanity always finds its birth in the natural passions of humanity. If the base and egoistic passions push toward suicide, it is more often found that this act is determined by passions which are given birth in the noble and generous sentiments. "In suicides," says Ferrus, "ideas of generosity somewhat commonly predominate. It is precisely in those epochs when civilization is most advanced, where the customs are the most peaceful, the political virtues most widespread, that they are most frequent." The passions which produce homicide being the opposite of the generous passions, there is an antagonism between the instinctive elements which produce suicide and those which produce homicide, an antagonism which has the effect of rendering suicide rare indeed where homicide is most frequent, and *vice versa*. This is in fact what observation demonstrates. In studying the *Compte* report of criminal justice published in Octo-

ber, 1852, I have seen that this antagonism is real, and that, in general, the departments which have furnished the most homicides have been those which consistently have the fewest suicides, and *vice versa*. For example, if we take the fourteen departments which have contributed the most crimes against persons out of 100 [total] accusations, we see that they have produced fourteen suicides per 460,658 inhabitants during one year, while the fourteen departments which have contributed the fewest crimes against persons out of the same number of accusations, have contributed fourteen suicides over only 170,670 inhabitants.[5] But it is above all in the two extreme departments, that of the Seine and that of Corsica, that this antagonism between suicide and homicide is remarkable. Thus, in the department of the Seine, where, out of 100 accusations, only 17 were brought for crimes against persons, we find one suicide per 2,341 inhabitants, while Corsica, where out of 100 accusations, 83 were brought for crimes against persons, produced one suicide per 55,336 inhabitants. In addition, the *Compte* of criminal justice published in March, 1867, which shows for this latter department an important diminution in the number of attacks committed against persons, at the same time shows an increase in the number of suicides, so that one no longer finds one suicide per 55,366 inhabitants, but one per 28,098. It is not only in France that the antagonism between homicide and suicide has been established. The suicide statistics for the Austrian Empire given by Dr. Mayer, of Ansbach, demonstrates that in the non-German regions of the Empire of Austria suicides are more rare and murders are more frequent than in the German parts of the Empire.

The nature of the sentiments propelling toward suicide explains why this act is more frequent among the superior races and among educated persons of these races than among the inferior races and among the ignorant and uncultured classes of the superior races. Humanity, essentially imperfect in nature, always manifests its imperfection through acts contrary to morality. Only where its imperfection is least, its immoralities are less great and less repulsive. The man animated by noble and generous sentiments will tend to take upon himself the effects of his passions and his miseries rather than cause his fellow beings to suffer from them by indulging in immoral acts on their persons or their property. The ignorant, egoistic and perverse man, devoid of moral sentiments, thinks only of himself and [if he has] needs and desires inspired by his perversity, he will satisfy them through theft and even homicide rather than allow himself to suffer. "The unhappiest man in the world," says Monsieur Saint-Marc Girardin, "the one most cast down into Job's dung-heap, if he has not tasted of the tree of science, if he has not added to his sufferings the torment of thought, this man will not think of killing himself. Suicide is not a sickness of the simple of heart and spirit; it is a sickness of the refined, of philosophers, and if, in our day, even the artisans have been struck down by the sickness of suicide, it is because their intelligence is incessantly embittered by science and modern civilization."

If certain peoples of the inferior races, the Japanese, for example, kill themselves with great ease, this is in no way a result of generous and elevated motives associated with this act. They easily adopt suicide because of certain prejudices with which they have been nourished ever since infancy, because of the little power feelings tying them to life have over them, and also because of a certain ferocity of character that makes them punish themselves. For weak motives, they kill themselves and their fellow beings (Despine 1868, 3:77–80, our translation).

While the theories advanced by the criminal anthropologists of the 1880s continued to stress the importance of biological factors, the emphasis after Despine shifted toward the biological inferiority of suicidal and homicidal individuals rather than entire races.

FERRI, MORSELLI, TARDE, AND THE CONGRESS OF ROME

By 1880, the moral statisticians had mapped the distributions of rates for several European countries and had begun to develop analyses of fairly long time series. They had concluded that homicide was more common in southern Europe and in the southern parts of the nations they studied, while suicide predominated in northern latitudes. Over time, they argued, homicide rates had fallen and suicide rates increased with "the progress of civilization" (Maury 1860; Masaryk 1881).

These empirical studies and others like them formed the basis for a theory of suicide and homicide that emerged in the 1870s and 1880s from the research of Enrico Morselli (1879a 1879b) and Enrico Ferri (1883–84; see also Ferri 1894, 1895, 1925, 1926). The two criminal anthropologists worked largely independently of one another, but their views were similar. Ferri was able to examine longer time series than his predecessors, while Morselli drew ecological maps, replicating findings such as Guerry's and Despine's and extending them to include data for minor civil divisions for virtually the whole of Europe. Despite differences in methodology and emphasis, both characterized the relationship between homicide and suicide as involving parallelism in their underlying causes but contrast in their modes of expression. Their laws of parallelism and inversion combine to form the "dual law" (Morselli 1879a 1879b).

Morselli and Ferri both spoke at the First International Congress of Criminal Anthropology in Rome in November 1885, a gathering of about a hundred scholars from as far away as Russia (*Actes du premier congrès d'anthropologie criminelle: Biologie et sociologie* 1886–87, 202–6; Durkheim 1897; Tarde 1890; Ferri 1925; Verkko 1951). One of the major topics of the Congress of Rome, as it was called, was the relationship between suicide and homicide. Eleven speakers addressed the question "Do suicides increase in inverse proportion to crimes against life?" Morselli gave the keynote address and then responded to questions. The debate in the halls must have been spirited, as Ferri crossed verbal swords with "his good friend" Gabriel Tarde,[6] who denied that the alleged pattern was real in a book review in the *Revue philosophique* (Tarde 1884) and a then-unpublished paper circulated at the Congress of Rome (Tarde 1886b; see the 1912 translation of Tarde 1890 for a later version of his argument in English).

Because available translations of material from the Congress of Rome (for example, Verkko 1951) are fragmentary and fail to capture the richness of the various arguments, we have pulled together material from several contemporary sources to try to convey the flavor of the debate.

Morselli's remarks before the Congress of Rome echo his 1879 monograph. As the session begins,

> Monsieur Moleschott [Doctor Commander Jac. Moleschott, senator of the Kingdom of Italy and Professor of Physiology at the University of Rome] calls the assembly to order for the day and gives the floor to Monsieur Morselli to speak on the fourth thesis: if the number of suicides increases in inverse relationship to the number of homicides.
> M. MORSELLI: Gentlemen,
> A double phenomenon can be seen before our eyes in civilized countries. To the extent that civilization grows, the number of suicides increases while that of homicides decreases.
> Man's destructive activity against his neighbor turns on itself and is directed against himself.

Is there an antagonism between suicide and homicide? According to certain indications, one can believe it. Let us look at the pretty maps which our colleague, Monsieur Bodio [Luigi Bodio, Director General for Statistics of the Kingdom of Italy] has exhibited in our chambers, those in which the more or less dark shadings give us, in the most evident fashion, the intensity of suicide and the intensity of homicide in Italy. If we superimpose one on the other, we see that the dark colors on the one correspond to the light colors on the other, and that if we content ourselves with a superficial answer to the question, we would say that there exists an antagonism between suicide and homicide.

This would be to go too fast and to speak in too absolute a manner. The statement to which we are led based on the examination of Monsieur Bodio's maps is justified if we limit its scope, but it would be false were we to generalize too much. The truth is that between suicide and homicide there is sometimes antagonism and sometimes parallelism, depending on whether one or the other of the two phenomena is considered in relation to social conditions or to individual conditions. Now, the study of this subject precisely demonstrates this dual law: the tendency toward homicide and the tendency toward suicide are in antagonism with one another in the body social, within which the latter tends to substitute itself for the former; the two tendencies, on the contrary, are parallel within the individual, within which they are born and develop under the influence of the same causes. Let us examine what the statistics can teach us.

One might say that, but for easily explicable exceptions—the great cities, for example, where the artificial agglomeration gives social life an abnormal intensity—with respect to race, to topography, suicide and homicide are in antagonism. The north and center of Europe give us a marked predominance of [suicide].[7] Such is a fact, whose causes are numerous and complex—some evident and others obscure and poorly understood, some from the ethnic and social order, others from the cosmic, natural, and climatic order. The same fact is verified if we turn from the examination of a vast region to that of a single country: we have seen [this] in Italy, where the northern part gives a predominance of suicides and the southern part a predominance of homicides.

The antagonism between homicide and suicide is also observed with respect to ethnicity and demographics. The white race, for example, is the one that gives the most considerable contingent to suicide. It is also the one in which blood crimes—homicide in its varied forms—are relatively more rare. Among savages, on the contrary, suicide is very rare, homicide very frequent.

From the anthropological point of view, the antagonism between suicide and homicide is no less striking. Brunettes, for example, have a stronger affinity for homicide, a lesser affinity for suicide. The converse holds for blondes. I mean to speak of European brunettes and blondes.

A curious phenomenon is that which presents itself in mixed or crossbred populations, among whom one notices a large number of both suicides and homicides. It is sufficient to look at the statistics of the Austrian Empire.

We turn to social conditions.

The number of suicides increases [and] that of homicides decreases with education. From the point of view of individual cultivation there is, therefore, antagonism between the two facts. Homicide marches in tandem with illiteracy. To the extent that education gains ground, homicide loses it; in contrast, the number of suicides increases.

From the point of view of religion, one notices this dual fact: Catholics give the greatest contingent to homicides, and Protestants to suicide. Catholicism and Protestantism, it is superfluous to remark, equally reprove suicide and homicide.

This observation, however, has but relative value: differences of dogma and of rite generally coincide with differences of climate and of race.

From the point of view of social caste or class conditions, there also exists a marked antagonism between homicide and suicide. The upper classes contribute the larger number of suicides and the fewer number of homicides. The lower classes contribute a fewer number of suicides and a greater number of homicides.

[There is] the same antagonism in the professions. Those which contribute the greater number of suicides contribute the lower number of homicides, and *vice versa* (*Actes du premier congrès d'anthropologie criminelle; Biologie et sociologie* 1886–87, 202–6; our translation).

Thus, Morselli stressed the inverse relationship between suicide and homicide in ecological data. In particular, in his day as now, suicide predominated in northern and central Europe and homicide in the southern part of the continent. Similar north-south variations could be seen within individual countries (Morselli, 1879a, 1879b). Morselli suggested several possible explanations for these patterns, including variations in ethnicity and race, "cosmic" factors such as climate, and social factors such as the sense of duty, which he linked to suicide (cf. Durkheim 1897). Nonetheless, he lamented that many of the reasons for the pattern were "obscure and hardly suspected" (*Actes du premier congrès d'anthropologie criminelle; Biologie et sociologie* 1886–87, 204).

Ferri spoke only briefly at the congress. When his turn came to speak, he pointed out that he had noted two years before (Ferri, 1883–84) that the inverse pattern noted by Morselli also held in both short- and long-term time series, based on suicide and homicide statistics from 1827 through 1880 for Ireland, Italy, France, England, Prussia, Belgium, and Spain. Ferri's position comes through clearly in his lengthy polemical response to the charges made by Tarde in his review of *L'Omicidio-Suicidio* (Tarde 1884) and by the Spanish scholar C. Silió Cortés. Ferri (1925) provides a much-expanded argument in the later editions of his monograph:

> It yet remains for me to examine the statistical objection made by Tarde and repeated by Silió, in which is disputed the inverse development, in relationship to time, between suicide and homicide, established by me and that others have demonstrated in its ethnic and geographical aspects. "Illusions," says Tarde. "While suicide has tripled in France, crimes against persons have not diminished in any way. A glance at the official statistics is enough to convince oneself of it. In this, Ferri has been too optimistic."[8]
>
> If Tarde's affirmation had corresponded to the facts, I would have been an inexact and rash observer. I believe, on the contrary, to have proof positive of my affirmation, which, because it is based on facts rather than syllogisms, I believe it is now opportune to lay out, with the greatest bulk of statistical data that are at my disposition.
>
> Let us begin by establishing with precision that the antagonism is between suicide and homicide, not a connection with offenses or crimes against persons, the most numerous of which, like assaults, have too many other determining motives external to the individual to allow us to establish statistically a law of reciprocal, analogical, or inverse development. By homicide, we mean here the sad death of a man under a variety of headings: infanticide, simple homicide, or murder in the first degree.
>
> In the second place, the antagonism, in relation to time, is double, regardless of whether one considers the annual movement or the general movement of suicide and of homicide. That

is, as a general rule, the growth of suicide corresponds with a diminution of homicide, not only with the growth of civilization but also from year to year—but, naturally, with more frequent exceptions (Ferri 1925, 280–81; our translation from the Spanish edition).[9]

Thus, Morselli and Ferri saw suicide and homicide as contrasting phenomena in the social body, within which one strives to replace the other; but their causes in individuals are parallel if not identical. As disciples of Cesare Lombroso, founder of the then-dominant positive school of criminology in Italy, Ferri and Morselli found the common cause of both in biological factors such as the degeneration, impotence, or decay of the organism. Because of this physical decay and biological inferiority, both murderers and suicides find it difficult to compete successfully in life's struggles or to play a useful part in society. Their predisposition toward violence does not in itself prefer either form of expression at the expense of the other, but conditions in the environment can push the individual toward one form of expression or the other. Because individual factors do not vary on the average from time to time or place to place, suicide and homicide should always vary inversely in ecological data (Morselli) and in short- and long-term time series (Ferri).

According to Morselli (1879b, 114), "the psychical life of the individual is but the reflex of the nature and characteristics of that social aggregate in the midst of which it thinks, wills and acts." From this, he argued, it follows that where customs are generally peaceful and where violence is generally abhorred, impotent individuals will develop an aversion to violence against others and will be likely to withdraw from life's struggles by committing suicide. On the other hand, in societies with a robust and lusty culture, defective individuals will be more favorably disposed toward striking out against others, and indeed against society itself, by committing murder. The basic impulse is to kill not oneself but someone else. When this impulse finds no resistance from the social environment, the impotent individual commits murder; but when outward violence is blocked by the pressure of the public conscience, the impulse to kill is turned inward upon oneself.

Ferri's summary of his position establishes that he viewed the two aspects of the dual law as dealing with different causal processes:

Between suicide and homicide, therefore, the antagonism with respect to the ethnic, geographical, and annual aspects corresponds to a parallelism in relationship to the changing seasons and to age.[10] And this is easily explained if one thinks of the antagonism as having to do with the *direction* of forces and of the parallelism, on the contrary, as dealing with their *production*. And suicide being as much as homicide an act of personal violence, it is natural that it should be determined in its general outlines by the same cause and, as a consequence, to manifest itself with analogous frequency, while the direction of this violence, against self or against others, must manifest itself inversely (Ferri 1925, 281; our translation from the Spanish edition; emphasis in the original).

As we shall see in chapter 6, the theory that guides our own research adopts Ferri's and Morselli's notion that lethal violence, whether suicide or homicide, is a function of two separate causal processes, one of which leads to the production of violence while the other affects its direction. In the abstract, the logical structure of our theory is thus identical to Ferri's and Morselli's. Durkheim's 1897 stream analogy applies equally to both. But, like Durkheim, we reject the Italian scholars' contention that the causes underlying the production of violence are rooted in biological inferiority and decay or other strictly individual factors such as age. In essence, Ferri and Morselli hit upon a model that remains useful today, but they chose the wrong independent variables.

Tarde, however, remained unconvinced. In the paper that Ferri circulated for him at the Congress of Rome (Tarde 1886b), he raised a number of objections to the interpretations given by Morselli and Ferri to their data. First, though he acknowledged the existence of north-south geographical patterning of suicide, blood crimes, and crimes against property in both Europe and the United States, he suggested that there were notable exceptions and that the geographical distribution of homicide was due to the greater progress of civilization in the north rather than to climate per se. While admitting that his disagreement with Ferri was "more apparent than real" (Tarde 1886b, 15), he pointed to a number of exceptions to the temporal component of the law of inversion in Ferri's 1883–84 data. Indeed, he could find periods in all countries except the "insular exception" (Tarde 1886b, 16) of Ireland in which the two rates ran in the same direction. The existence of exceptions to the temporal and geographical patterns stressed respectively by Ferri and Morselli was, he argued, highly significant.

Tarde argued that suicide rates vary directly with rates of divorce and insanity, in essence sarcastically suggesting that the stream analogy could just as well include these phenomena instead of or in addition to suicide as "safety valve[s] against crime" (1886b, 16). According to him, the maps and time series of divorce and suicide for Swiss cantons and

French departments "resemble each other, right down to their details" (1886b, 22–23).

> This is singular, all the more so since . . . the imaginary inverse relationship between homicide and suicide must exist as well between homicide and divorce. Divorce, therefore, finds itself to be the substitute for homicide. How bizarre! (Tarde 1886b, 23; our translation).

In the case of insanity, he maintained that both suicide and mental disorder had been increasing "with fearful rapidity and regularity" while the homicide rates of European societies remained "more or less stationary" (1886b, 16).

> In this, as well as in other features, the development of suicide is analogous to that of madness. To tell the truth, there are the same statistical reasons to establish the indicated relationship between madness itself and homicide. But taken to this extreme, the thesis demonstrates its untruth. What does this parallel signify? That insanity is a safety valve against crime? It would be strange that this involuntary safety valve should develop at the same pace and in the same manner as suicide, in large part a voluntary act (Tarde 1886b, 16; our translation).

Tarde was *not* arguing against the possibility that different behaviors might represent alternative responses to social conditions. In Ireland, the one country in which he granted that the theories of the Italian criminologists appeared to him to fit the facts, the inverse relationship between homicide and suicide was "truly remarkable" (1886b, 16),[11] and both seemed to vary inversely with emigration. All three responded to "the situation so much a part of this unhappy country, where misery is so great and mutual hatred so exalted that an annual quota of the population is condemned to leave by one of its three doors: emigration, suicide, and murder. If one is restricted, the others ought therefore to expand" (Tarde 1886b, 16; our translation).

Tarde noted that an inverse relationship between emigration and suicide could also be seen in cross-national comparisons and time series in individual countries (1886b, 17–18):

> In Denmark, suicide diminishes year to year as emigration increases. Emigration is very strong in England, suicide very weak. In France, it is just the opposite. In Germany, the exceptional

growth in suicides from 1872 to 1878 coincided with a progressive drop-off in emigration. Now *that* . . . is an easy correlation to understand. . . . If an unhappy person at the extreme of privation or torment emigrates so as not to kill himself or kills himself lacking the ability to emigrate, nothing is more understandable (Tarde 1886b, 18; our translation).

In general, Tarde argued, the way to tell whether an inverse relationship between social phenomena is "non-accidental" is whether, like emigration and suicide, the phenomena are "complementary to one another, which is to say, responding to the same need by different paths" (1886b, 18). He used crime as an example, explicitly drawing on the analogy of currents in a river of crime (1886b, 19) to characterize the relationships between different offenses:

In a nation where the criminal instincts hypothetically remain of constant strength, there will undoubtedly be among the various branches of criminal offenses, for example, between murder, crimes against property, swindling, and moral outrages, a . . . joint relationship such that the increase in one would be immediately compensated for by a proportional decrease in all the others. Why? Not only because the types of misdeeds are derived from the same immoral source distributed among them, but also because the goal pursued is, in a general sense, the same for all. The murderer, like the thief, the swindler, or the elderly satyr, seeks either illicit enjoyment or the means for obtaining enjoyment. They proceed differently only in that the murderer kills, the thief scales a window or shatters a pane of glass, the molester violates a child. From this point of view, one may regard the thief, the swindler, the fixer, the abuser and violator of confidence, and criminal outrages against modesty as the true safety valves against manslaughter and murder. In other words, if the opportunity for theft, swindling, forgery, or sexual violations were suddenly made more rare in a given nation, it is probable that the murder rate would increase. Reciprocally, if these opportunities were suddenly to increase, people would commit fewer murders. It would be thus because, this change in social conditions being rapid, the strength of criminal tendencies ought to be considered as remaining constant. But when this transformation operates slowly, criminal energies have time to grow so as to mask the play of the safety valve. . . . From this we may draw the following conclusion: . . . the incessant flow of these derivative channels of . . .

criminality, among which we may name theft, swindling, commercial fraud, offenses against morals, is in no way sufficient to lower the numerical level of the principal current, . . . crimes against persons, which is where the river has become strongest (Tarde 1886b, 18–19; our translation).

"But," Tarde asked rhetorically, "what would be the common need satisfied by suicide and homicide? Would it be the need, experienced by who knows whom, to see a certain predetermined number of people perish either by their own hand or by the hand of another?" (1886b, 18). The goal of suicide, he argued, is totally unlike that of murder; suicide is the result of "intolerable despair," while homicide stems from "antisocial egoism" (1886b, 19). One might just as well try to link suicide and theft.

Like Durkheim's a decade later, Tarde's reaction to the theories of Moselli and Ferri was colored by his goal of establishing a point of view. His position, though more psychological than Durkheim's, was nonetheless far more sociological than the biological views of the criminal anthropologists. The increase in suicide, he believed, was due to the weakening of traditional religious beliefs and to the spread of new ideas, a process of imitation or contagion aggravated by the advances in transportation and communication that accompanied the growth of civilization, and by the spread of alcoholism (Tarde 1886b, 21–24).

EMILE DURKHEIM ON SUICIDE AND HOMICIDE

In rejecting Ferri's and Morselli's theses in favor of the view that suicide and homicide are opposing social currents, Durkheim followed a stategy similar to Tarde's (1886b), focusing primarily on exceptions to the law of inversion drawn from an array of European sources. He noted that the relationship between suicide and homicide can take many forms: "suicide sometimes coexists with homicide, sometimes they are mutually exclusive; sometimes they react under the same conditions in the same way, sometimes in opposite ways, and the antagonistic cases are the most numerous" (Durkheim 1897, 355).

A great mass of suicide and homicide data has been accumulated since Durkheim's day. More recent research suggests that Durkheim's statement is correct. Suicide and homicide rates do seem usually to be inversely related. But there are clear exceptions, such as the tendency for both rates to increase during times of economic downturn[12] and to decrease during popular wars (Durkheim 1897; Halbwachs 1930; Marshall 1981; Porterfield 1952a); a positive relationship reported by Palmer

(1965) for preliterate societies; tendencies for the rates to run in the same direction in Finland during and after Prohibition (Verkko 1951); and a positive relationship over time in the recent history of the United States (Klebba 1981; Seiden and Freitas 1980).

These exceptions to the law of inversion are theoretically interpretable within the context of the very analogy of two diverging currents in a single stream which Durkheim first proposed to describe the work of Morselli and Ferri. The stream itself represents the combined total of suicide and homicide; each of the two channels that it feeds corresponds to one of these two forms of violent death. Or in Ferri's (1925, 281) own terms, the size of the stream responds to variations in the *production* of personal violence, while the relative sizes of the two channels is a function of forces affecting the *direction* of violence—against the self or against others.

Given the stream analogy, the task of theory and research is to identify the variables that affect (1) the volume of the water in the stream and (2) the proportions of that water flowing into each of its two channels. In his critique of Ferri and Morselli, Durkheim, like the Italian scholars themselves and most suicide-homicide researchers until quite recently, focused primarily on the division of water into the two channels (what Henry and Short [1954] call the choice between suicide and homicide) while ignoring the possibility that the volume of the stream itself might ebb and flow in response to social factors. If the stream itself grows, as Ferri (1925) suggests is possible by pointing to the forces of production, suicide and homicide may without contradiction be positively rather than negatively related. In positing the law of parallelism, Ferri and Morselli were clearly aware that suicide and homicide shared causes in common, but their treatment of forces of production is confined exclusively to the effects of such individual factors as organic decay as the source of both forms of lethal violence. Social factors are introduced only as explanations for inverse relationships in ecological and time series data. The possibility eluded Ferri and Morselli that social factors might increase or decrease the overall propensity to violence as well as affecting its mode of expression.

Indeed, Durkheim (1897, 1900) suggests what some of these social factors might be. According to him, the only way to reconcile the seemingly contradictory facts "is by admitting that there are different sorts of suicide, some of which have a certain kinship to homicide, while it is repugnant to others. . . . The suicide which varies in the same proportion with murder and that which varies inversely with it cannot be of like nature" (Durkheim 1897, 355).

Durkheim argues that three of the four types of suicide he identifies[13] stand in different relationships to homicide (1897, 356–59). Homicide, being "a violent act inseparable from passion," is incompatible with egoistic suicide, the most common type. But it gets along well with altruistic suicide in primitive societies and with anomic suicide at certain points in the economic development of industrial civilization.

Durkheim's types of suicide have been the subject of considerable discussion and debate. His monograph is still by far the most influential single work in the sociological literature on suicide. It is nonetheless one of the least understood, largely because Durkheim's depth as a theorist is not matched by comparable clarity of presentation and definition. Someone once said that Talcott Parsons's writings are like a Rorschach test. This is no less true of Durkheim. For example, compare the interpretations of his types of suicide in Alpert (1939), Dohrenwend (1959), Douglas (1967), Johnson (1965), LaCapra (1972), Lukes (1973), Parsons (1937), Selvin (1958), and Wallwork (1972). All these varied interpretations and the many others that have been offered cannot possibly be completely accurate to both the letter and spirit of what Durkheim meant to say. Indeed, at least one of his interpreters insists that egoism and anomie are really the same thing (Johnson 1965). As Lukes (1973, 3) points out, Durkheim has been called "a materialist and an idealist, a positivist and a metaphysician, a rationalist and an irrationalist, a dogmatic atheist and a mystic, as well as a 'scholarly forerunner of Fascism', a late-nineteenth-century liberal, a conservative, and a socialist."

This is not the place for a lengthy discussion of all the complexities of *Suicide* or its place in the larger corpus of Durkheim's thought;[14] but a brief exposition of *our* interpretation of his concepts of anomie, egoism, altruism, and fatalism is necessary if the conclusions we draw from Durkheim's discussions of homicide and its relationship to suicide are to be understood. Part of the confusion over what Durkheim meant stems from his writing style, which is highly polemical and calculated to defend his paradigm against all competing positions. In particular, Durkheim's rejection of psychological interpretations is so strongly stated that it obscures his basic underlying social-psychological premises. But the social psychology is nonetheless there. *Suicide*, like his earlier discussion of self-destruction in *The Division of Labor in Society* (Durkheim 1893, 233–54), implicitly conceptualizes suicide as a response to disturbances of individual happiness and psychological well-being (Whitt 1968; Lukes 1973).

Durkheim (1897, 213, 319–20) drew a distinction between two analytically distinct aspects of the self, one biologically based and concerned with the individual as individual, the other grounded in society and identified with the sacred, the soul, or the spiritual self (cf.

Tiryakian 1962, 47–64). While the individual self involves strictly individual appetites and passions, the Durkheimian social self arises from the incorporation into the individual of external society, which gains thereby an inner existence.[15] It includes identification with others, the subordination of individual goals to those of the group, and a sense of duty and obligation. Durkheim believed that unless a harmonious balance could be struck between these two components of the self, there would be negative implications for psychological well-being and unhappiness would result.

Durkheim's egoism, altruism, anomie, and, by implication, fatalism are social conditions in which one component of the self suffers relative to the other (Whitt 1968). Egoism and altruism are opposite conditions, as are anomie and fatalism. The two sets of bipolar opposites represent the end points of two independent dimensions— integration and regulation (cf. Johnson 1965). Egoism results when the insufficient integration of individuals into social groups "throw[s] them on their own resources" (Durkheim 1897, 210) as "the masters of their destinies" (Durkheim 1897, 209) but simultaneously pushes them into a sense of meaninglessness and isolation. In altruism, a state of excessive integration, individual passions and desires are overwhelmed by an excessive sense of duty, obligation, and commitment to group goals. Anomie is a condition of too little regulation, in which expectations are unclear and unrestrained individual passions and desires exceed any possibility of realization. Finally, in fatalism, individual desires are ruthlessly choked off by external authority. Under none of these conditions can individuals be happy because a harmonious balance between individual and social aspects of the self is a prerequisite for true satisfaction.

In Ferri's words, all four conditions represent "forces of production" because they all disturb the necessary balance between individual egos and social egos, the two essential parts of Durkheim's "homo duplex." Thus, all else being equal, viewing Durkheim in the context of the dual law would lead us to expect that he would predict that both suicide and homicide rates should increase at either extreme of the continua based on integration and regulation. This is indeed what he claims for the excessive integration of altruism and the unregulated state of anomie, but, as noted previously, Durkheim (1897) argued that suicide varies directly and homicide inversely with egoism. In a separate discussion of homicide published three years later (Durkheim 1900), he links the slow but steady decline in European homicide rates during the nineteenth century to the increasing importance of the individual relative to the group (for example, the state) that accompanied the growth of civilization. Anything that increases collective passions and reduces reflection—holidays, wars,[16] religious fervor, the "cult of the State"—increases homicide (Durkheim 1900, 110–20).

Durkheim's discussion of egoism in *Suicide* (1897) and his treatment of homicide in *Professional Ethics and Civic Morals* (1900) are closely related. They seem to us to point toward Ferri's forces of direction as well as those of production, since the same conditions that Durkheim views as increasing suicide rates—individualism, reflection and free inquiry, and the weakening of collective ties—are seen as reducing homicide rates. Indeed, Durkheim links egoism to suicide in two ways: "Excessive individualism not only acts in favoring the action of suicidogenic causes, but it is itself such a cause" (Durkheim 1897, 210).

Durkheim's intention is, of course, not to support the stream analogy but to refute it. He is correct in rejecting the proposition offered by Morselli and Ferri that forces of production are always individual. The social conditions underlying egoism, altruism, anomie, and fatalism all actively impel individuals toward violence by making them dissatisfied. But egoism also affects direction. Durkheim believed that *something* about excessive individuation favors suicide over homicide. Looking back after nearly a century, in the context of much later theoretical developments, it is tempting to focus too tightly on words and phrases that support one's own position. Nonetheless, Durkheim (1897, 209–10) mentions that egoism throws individuals on their own resources, making them masters of their own destinies. As we look at this particular ink blot, we see in it the hazy outline of the idea that suicides choose themselves as victims because they have no one to blame but themselves. This tendency for suicidal individuals to attribute blame to themselves is central to our own theoretical position.

Perhaps we read too much into Durkheim. After all, his strategy was not to build on the work of the Italian criminologists but to replace it with his own paradigm. His success in doing so was so great that little more was heard from sociologists about the relationship between suicide and homicide until after World War II. In the meantime, theoretical developments in psychology were laying the groundwork for a resurgence in interest in the topic. The central figure in these developments was Sigmund Freud.

THE CONTRIBUTIONS OF
SIGMUND FREUD AND THE FREUDIANS

Although he dealt it a serious blow, Durkheim was unable to destroy the notion that suicide and murder are different manifestations of the same basic phenomenon. Sigmund Freud probably never heard of Morselli, Ferri, and the currents of violence, but he nonetheless shared with the Italian scholars the conceptualization of suicide and homicide as two channels in a single stream of violence. Indeed, the equivalence of suicide and homicide was a central tenet of Freud's theorizing on aggression, which has had considerable influence on clinical perspectives on both suicide (Menninger 1938; see also the theoretical articles in Shneidman and Farberow 1957) and homicide (see, for example, McCord and McCord 1956, 1964). When sociologists returned to a consideration of the relationship between suicide and homicide in the 1950s, much of their writing (for example, Straus and Straus 1953; Henry and Short 1954; Gold 1958) drew heavily on Freudian ideas.

Early in this century, Freud (1915, 1917, 1920), in his clinically based analyses of sadism, masochism, and aggression, suggested that suicide is an impulse to commit murder turned inward upon the self. Although he had two completely different theories of aggression—the earlier linking aggression to sexual frustrations and the later tying suicidal behaviors to the operation of the death instinct—both theories are consistent with this interpretation.

Prior to 1920, Freud believed human behavior in general to be determined by the interplay between ego instincts and sexual instincts. Aggression, according to this theory, results from the frustration associated with sexual repression. Hostility and aggression are seen as "primordial reactions" (Freud 1915) directed primarily against the source of frustration (assumed by Freud to be external) but secondarily displaced against other objects (Freud 1915) or turned inward against the self (Freud 1917). Aggression against the self is assumed to take place when the characteristics of a loved object are introjected into the self. Hate, Freud theorized, is originally directed against all external objects, but these objects may become endowed with love and hence become ambivalently cathected and symbolically incorporated into the self. By incorporating the object, however, the subject introjects the original hate along with the love.

According to Freud (1917), intropunitive acts are actually attacks on a lost ambivalently cathected love object introjected into the subject's ego. When the external object is withdrawn through death or departure, the aggression that would otherwise be directed against it is brought back against the self in the form of self-blame, masochism, or suicide. Freud argues that suicide results from this blocked desire to commit murder:

> No neurotic harbors thoughts of suicide which he has not turned back upon himself from murderous impulses against others redirected upon oneself. . . . The ego can kill itself only if, ow-

ing to the return of the object-cathexis, it can treat itself as an object—if it is able to direct against itself the animosity which relates to an object and which represents the ego's original reaction to objects in the external world (Freud 1917, 252).

With the publication of *Beyond the Pleasure Principle* in 1920, Freud elevated the urge to destroy oneself to a full-fledged instinct, Thanatos. The death instinct seeks the elimination of the tension caused by life itself: according to Freud, "the goal of all life is death" (1920, 38). Were Thanatos allowed free rein, all life would annihilate itself as quickly as possible; but Thanatos is countered by Eros, the libidinal life instinct. Eros can turn the self-destructive tendency outward against inanimate objects or other persons. This process, however, can produce a fusion of the life and death instincts and a consequent erotization of the self-destructive drive. Destructiveness and aggressiveness then become inherently pleasurable.

Freud maintained that sadism and masochism both result from this fusion of life and death instincts. Thus assertiveness, aggressiveness, and ultimately homicide follow when the diversion of the death instinct against the outer world goes unchecked. When the outward flow of destructive energy is overly repressed, it returns to its source and mingles with the residuum of the death instinct held within the organism. Under these circumstances, masochism, one expression of which is suicide, results.

In *Civilization and Its Discontents*, Freud (1929) argues that modern society creates excessive repression, thus contributing to the hyperdevelopment of the supergo—roughly the conscience plus internalized behavioral rules (the *ego ideal*). The more one conforms to the superego's demands, the more guilt-ridden one becomes: "the more virtuous a man is the more severe and more distrustful is its [the superego's] behaviour, so that ultimately it is precisely those people who have carried saintliness furthest who reproach themselves with the worst sinfulness" (Freud 1929, 125–26).

Freud's instinct theory of aggression, like his earlier formulation, stresses the central hypothesis that suicidal persons fail to express their aggressive impulses outwardly, instead turning them inward upon themselves (cf. Zilboorg 1936). Some psychoanalytically oriented suicide researchers, most notably Karl Menninger (1938), who spoke of the fusion of the wish to die, the wish to kill, and the wish to be killed, incorporated the death instinct into their work. Others (for example, Zilboorg 1937; Berkowitz 1962) rejected it as teleological or as simply an elaborate way of saying that people kill themselves. Thus both theories continued to be used side by side within the psychoanalytic community. Indeed, as Douglas (1967) notes, there are many different psychoanalytic theories of suicide, all loosely tied to Freud in one way or another. Several such theories are reviewed in Shneidman and Farberow (1957).

One psychoanalytic theory with particular relevance for research on suicide, homicide, and their relationship suggests that whether aggression will be intropunitive or extrapunitive depends upon the strength of the superego. McCord and McCord (1956, 1964), for example, suggest that psychopathic killers lack a superego because of physical punishments administered in cold and hostile childhood environments. Wood (1961a, 1961b) found that a strong conscience was common among a sample of suicide victims in Ceylon (Sri Lanka). Indeed, a large body of literature (for example, Miller and Swanson 1960; Whiting and Child 1953; Sears, Maccoby, and Levin 1957) has documented the relationships between childhood socialization practices, superego strength, and the later handling of aggression by the child. Three types of factors affecting the amount and kind of aggression expressed by the child had been specified by the 1950s. These included (1) the severity of punishment, (2) the permissiveness of parents, and (3) the type of punishment, whether physical or love-oriented (i.e., symbolic). While the amount of permissiveness and the severity of punishment affect the amount of overt aggressive behavior by the child, the type of punishment affects superego strength and whether aggression will be intropunitive or extrapunitive. Love-oriented techniques of punishment such as ostracism, denial of love, denial of reward, and disapproving gestures appear to produce a strong and punishing superego and the internalization of parental rules. Because of strong feelings of guilt, persons who received love-oriented punishment in childhood tend to be intropunitive. On the other hand, children disciplined by physical punishment tend to develop weak superegos and to express aggression more extrapunitively (Heinicke 1953; Whiting and Child 1953).

There is also evidence that the type of punishment affects the child's choice of defense mechanism and means of controlling aggressive impulses. Swanson (1960) has shown that the Freudian defense mechanisms of turning against the self, isolation, reaction formation, and undoing are related to love-oriented punishment, while projection results when parental discipline has been physical in nature. Swanson (1960) suggests that the symbolic nature of love-oriented punishment communicates to the child that his or her actions are the direct cause of punishment, and Whiting and Child (1953) reason that love-oriented techniques produce a tendency to ascribe responsibility to the self.

One reason for why there are so many different Freudian theories is that Freud's discussion of aggression is in no sense systematic. Scattered through his voluminous writings and obscured by a fog of highly questionable speculations on the nature of instincts, it suffers from a lack of clarity and precision that is, if anything, even worse than Durkheim's. Nonetheless, his ideas remain central to the study of aggression in general and suicide and homicide in particular. Their most direct link to the theory underlying this book runs through the frustration-aggression hypothesis (Dollard et al. 1939), a clarification and systematization of some of Freud's ideas, and the highly psychoanalytic approach of Henry and Short (1954) to the psychology of suicide and homicide.

THE FRUSTRATION-AGGRESION HYPOTHESIS

In 1939, an interdisciplinary team of scholars at Yale University— John Dollard, Leonard W. Doob, Neal E. Miller, O. H. Mowrer and Robert R. Sears—undertook the task of systematizing Freud's ideas on aggression and integrating them with materials from empirical psychology. Their collaboration led to the formulation of the frustration-aggression hypothesis (Dollard et al. 1939; Miller et al. 1941), which implicitly or explicitly guides most recent thinking on the relationship between suicide and homicide.

Simply stated, the frustration-aggression hypothesis states that "frustration produces instigations to a number of different types of response, one of which is the instigation to some form of aggression" (Miller et al. 1941, 338). The primary target of the action tendency toward aggression is the agent perceived to be the frustrator; but if the direct expression of aggression against the frustrator is inhibited by the anticipation of punishment, the frustrated individual will attack some secondary target. For example, the office worker frustrated by a supervisor may go home and kick the dog. In Freudian terms, this is the phenomenon of displacement.

The Yale group, like Freud, regarded suicide as primarily a displaced homicide, arguing that "other conditions being constant, self-aggression should be a relatively non-preferred type of expression which will not occur unless other forms of aggression are even more strongly inhibited" (Dollard et al. 1939, 48). Nonetheless, they suggested that aggression against the self should be more likely when the self rather than some external agent is perceived to be the source of frustration. Thus, they allowed for the possibility that not all suicides are merely displaced homicides.

Modern theoretical work on suicide and homicide has been closely tied to the frustration-aggression hypothesis. Researchers in this tradition begin with the assumption that suicide and homicide are alternative responses to frustration. Freud's perspectives and the frustration-aggression hypothesis are theories of individual behavior. They were developed in psychology, and it was some time before their relevance for studies of the relationship between rates of suicide and homicide was realized.

THE POST-DURKHEIMIANS

In sociology, work linking suicide and homicide went into a fifty-year hibernation after the appearance of Durkheim's *Suicide*. Only Ferri, who continued to argue for his theory in later editions of *L'Omicidio-suicidio* (Ferri 1925) and other publications (such as Ferri 1926), and Durkheim's student Maurice Halbwachs kept interest in the topic alive.

Halbwachs' monograph, *Les Causes du suicide* (1930), does not slavishly follow his mentor in every respect. After considering updated data on European suicide and homicide rates, however, he substantially agrees with Durkheim's 1897 conclusions. Suicide and homicide usually vary inversely across time and space, but there are exceptions in both ecological and time-series data.

Halbwachs' analysis of ecological patterns emphasizes the differences between Germany and France. In Germany's Protestant north, suicide rates near the end of the nineteenth century were high and rates of crimes involving severe injuries low. But in the Catholic southern provinces of the German Empire, serious injury crimes far exceeded suicides. The inverse relationship, he concluded, was "very close to the . . . [statistically possible] maximal opposition. This rather remarkable result supports Morselli to the extent that severe injuries result from homicidal intentions" (Halbwachs 1930, 194).

The situation in France, however, was different. Rates of suicide and homicide across departments during the period 1891–95 were totally independent of one another. The inverse patterns reported by Guerry, Despine, and Morselli had completely disappeared. There were departments with either high or low rates of both suicide and homicide as well as those showing inverse patterns. The progression from north to south was (1) high suicide rates, low homicide rates; (2) low rates of both; (3) low suicide rates, high homicide rates; and (4) high rates of both in the southeast coast of the Mediterranean Sea, but high rates of both also in the Paris Basin. Paris and its contiguous departments had changed over time from a low homicide to a high homicide area.

Aside from the contributions of Ferri and Halbwachs, the sociological study of suicide in the interval between Durkheim and the mid-twentieth century was largely dominated by Chicago-school ecological studies of suicide in individual cities. Members of this school such as Calvin Schmid (1928, 1933), Ruth Shonle Cavan (1928), Stuart A. Queen and Lewis F. Thomas (1939), Robert E. L. Faris (1955), Peter Sainsbury (1956), and P. M. Yap (1958) linked suicide to social disorganization. When they dealt with homicide at all, they treated high rates as indicative of—and indeed, in some cases, as measuring—social disorganization. Thus, they expected and generally found a positive relationship between suicide and homicide rates in the metropolitan spatial structure.[17] They define social disorganization enumeratively in terms of such indicators as population density, social mobility, anonymity, impersonality, and instability, suggesting that these factors reduce the effectiveness of social control. The parallel with Durkheim's concepts of anomie and egoism is obvious.

As Albert K. Cohen (1959, 474) notes, "Few terms in sociology are so variously and obscurely defined as social disorganization." Although the post-Durkheimians' theory suggests that social disorganization leads to deviant behavior of all kinds, it is, as Cohen points out, "difficult to determine what, if anything, is the line of demarcation between social disorganization and deviant behavior" (Cohen 1959, 474). Schmid (1928), for example, uses rescue missions, pawnshops, employment agencies, houses of prostitution, and homicides as indices of social disorganization. Similarly, Sainsbury (1956) discovers that of his three indices of social disorganization—divorce, illegitimacy, and juvenile delinquency—only the first two are related to suicide rates in London. He then concludes that juvenile delinquency is measuring poverty rather than social disorganization.

And there the matter rested until a series of events converged after World War II to produce a major rekindling of interest in the connection between suicide and homicide. The unfolding of these events and their implications for research on lethal violence are treated in the following chapter.

HUGH P. WHITT

3

Old Wine in a New Wineskin

The report of my death was an
exaggeration.
　　　　—Mark Twain

As World War II came and went and the Cold War began, virtually nothing had been said about the usual inverse relationship between
suicide and homicide for many years,[1] and the findings of post-
Durkheimian studies of the distribution of deviance and social disorganization seemed to suggest that the two forms of violence vary together
within the spatial structure of individual cities. As mid-century approached, however, Austin Porterfield rediscovered Enrico Ferri and
Enrico Morselli in Emile Durkheim's 1897 references, and Hans
von Hentig deduced a similar position from a study of suicide and
homicide in Pennsylvania by Walter Lunden (1932; cf. Lunden 1955).

Von Hentig was a latter-day criminal anthropologist (he called
what he did "sociobiology," but it bears little resemblance to modern
sociobiology). He is best known today for his pioneering work in victi-
mology and his now-dated theories linking left-handedness and red
hair to criminality. According to von Hentig,

> Suicide is an introverted act of destruction. Whether this is
> turned on the perpetrator himself or bursts forth against another
> being depends partly on the disposition of the individual, includ-
> ing racial traits; partly on the pattern of circumstances. . . . Murder
> and suicide are complementary phenomena: the total amount of
> available destructiveness is discharged in two psychologically
> similar, socially distinct *Gestalten* (von Hentig 1948, 389–90).

He also speculates on the significance of suicide pacts and murder followed by suicide: "In a suicide pact murder and suicide enter into a still more intimate integration. All shades of interaction may be woven together in an act in which the husband kills his wife, the children, dog and canary, and finally himself. European tradition calls it a broadened suicide" (von Hentig 1948, 390).

Von Hentig's brief discussion is in the context of the victim's contribution to the genesis of crime. In sociology, his work seems to have been largely ignored, but Marvin Wolfgang (1958b; 1959; Wolfgang and Ferracuti 1967) cites him in connection with his thesis that victim-precipitated homicide may be thought of as an extended suicide (see chapter 4).

Porterfield's first mention of the inverse relationship between suicide and homicide was in a thin volume intended for a non-sociological audience, *Suicide, Crime and Social Well-Being in Your City and State*, which he published for the Leo Potisham Foundation with his coauthor Robert H. Talbert in 1948. The following year, he reworked much of the material as a scholarly article that appeared in the *American Sociological Review*. Porterfield's findings, which ran counter to what the post-Durkheimians of the Chicago school had been saying since 1928, touched off a rekindling of interest among sociologists in the relationship between suicide and homicide. For a while, a new publication on the topic became an annual event in the major journals in sociology.

Porterfield's 1949 *ASR* article reported on a study contrasting indices of suicide and homicide for American cities and states. His findings include a clear-cut inverse relationship between suicide and homicide rates across states and a similar but weaker relationship across 105 cities. Cities in the South tend to have high homicide rates and low suicide rates, while the reverse is true outside the South.

Porterfield notes a tendency in time-series data from 1910 through 1946 for the two time series "to run in opposite directions when there is no crisis and in the same direction when there is a crisis" (Porterfield 1949, 487). Both rates, he points out, fell during the two world wars and both increased during the Great Depression (cf. Durkheim 1897; Halbwachs 1930).[2]

Noting that similar patterns had been reported for European countries by Durkheim, Halbwachs, Ferri, and Morselli,[3] Porterfield (1949) laid out a program of research to explore the implications of his findings.[4] Several of the questions he asked became an agenda for suicide-homicide researchers during the 1950s and 1960s. He began by suggesting the frustration-aggression hypothesis as an avenue to be explored:

First, how may we account for the observed opposite tendencies in indices of suicide and homicide? Are these acts opposite types of response to frustration? If so, why do the trends for the two not always run in opposite directions? Are these responses both forms of aggression differing principally only as overt manifestations of resentments?" (Porterfield 1949, 488).

For Porterfield, other issues that needed to be addressed include the South–non-South differences; cultural and structural factors responsible for differential responses to frustration by whites, who are more prone to suicide, and blacks, who more often commit murder; and the implications of child rearing as a determinant of whether the direction of later behavior will be a suicidal or homicidal response. How, Porterfield asked, do these findings relate to social disorganization theory, which dominated the sociology of deviance and especially the sociological study of suicide at the time? If both are supposed to be caused by social disorganization—essentially a state of normlessness in which social control breaks down—why do they vary inversely with one another? Why does suicide vary directly and homicide inversely with rates of alcoholism and divorce? And finally, what about murderers who kill themselves in a combination murder-suicide? Can they shed any light on the inverse relationship between suicide and murder?

Porterfield's article opened the floodgates for a new wave of interest in the currents of lethal violence. Within a year, Harry Alpert (1950) had added a footnote to Porterfield's findings by calling the attention of sociologists to an article in a trade journal of the Institute of Life Insurance, which presents death rates due to suicide and homicide separately for policyholders carrying ordinary life policies and those holding industrial life insurance. Ordinary life policyholders, who were higher in socioeconomic status than owners of industrial life policies, had high suicide rates but were seldom murder victims. In contrast, industrial life policyholders, who seldom committed suicide, had a higher probability of being murdered. Thus, one additional finding was added to the list of empirical generalizations about the relationship between suicide and homicide.[5]

In 1951, Durkheim's 1897 *Suicide,* previously inaccessible to the English-speaking reader unacquainted with French, appeared in an English translation by John A. Spaulding and George Simpson. Thus, Durkheim's discussion of the nineteenth-century debate over suicide and homicide became more widely available. That same year, the Finnish scholar Veli Verkko (1951) published in English a book called

Homicides and Suicides in Finland and Their Dependence on National Character, which explicitly uses the stream analogy to link both suicide and homicide to alcohol consumption:

> In Finland . . . suicides and homicides flow from one and the same source, viz. alcohol, where the Finn's poor ability to hold his liquor is concerned. But although one of the canals [*sic*] dries up, there is no sympathetic draining of the other, as the law [of inversion] presupposes. In Finland both outlets fill together when the alcohol situation is poor (Verkko 1951, 156).

Verkko (1951) includes a chapter titled "The Theories of Morselli and Ferri on Homicides and Suicides and the Attitude to Them of Tarde and Durkheim," which remains one of the few sources in English on the content of the nineteenth-century debate over the relationship between suicide and homicide involving Durkheim, Tarde, Ferri, and Morselli. Verkko, however, apparently did not fully understand the position of either Ferri or Tarde, and his criticism of all parties to the dispute is unreasonably severe.[6]

Porterfield, whose 1949 article had touched off the rekindling of interest among sociologists in the relationship between suicide and homicide, published two articles on the topic in 1952. An ecological study of suicide and crime data from Fort Worth showed, contrary to earlier studies of individual cities, high rates of suicide in high-status census tracts (Porterfield 1952a). The cities in earlier studies in which suicide and homicide were found to vary together were all non-Southern—Chicago (Cavan 1928), Seattle (Schmid 1928), Minneapolis (Schmid 1933), and St. Louis (Queen and Thomas 1939)—and Porterfield speculates that Fort Worth's location in the South is responsible for his different findings. Porterfield (1952a; cf. Gibbs and Porterfield 1960) suggests that homicides and other crimes against persons result from conditions involving rifts in personal gemeinschaft relationships, while white collar crime results from rifts in more impersonal gesellschaft mechanisms of connection and control.

> Murder, like sex, is rather personal, except as both become a business. But suicide may be related to factors emerging either from the personal or impersonal world. Thus, any city with a greater proportion of its population connected by interpersonal relations of a primary character, everything else being equal, might have a larger homicide rate than if its people were controlled to a greater degree by relations of impersonality. In the lat-

ter situation, it might be suicide. Perhaps Fort Worth belongs more to the former category, while the other cities named belong more to the latter; and perhaps the contrast holds for certain of their ecological zones which are expected to be pathological (Porterfield 1952a, 348).

Porterfield (1952b) continued his interest in aspects of the gemeinschaft-gesellschaft distinction in a paper that links both his data for states and his Fort Worth findings to the distinction between folk and secular societies. He argues that highly secularized states and census tracts, especially those with upper-class populations, tend more toward suicide, while high crime rates, including high rates of homicide, are found in areas resembling depressed folk society.

In 1953, Jacqueline H. Straus and Murray A. Straus reported on the relationship between suicide and homicide in Ceylon (now Sri Lanka), the first such study we have found using data from the Third World. Their findings are surprisingly similar to those for Europe and the United States. Suicide and homicide rates vary inversely with one another across provinces and ethnic groups. Suicides predominate in the north and homicides in the south. Their interpretation of these patterns is in terms of a distinction between *closely* and *loosely* structured social systems. They argue that suicide rates are high in closely structured societies that stress normative conformity, while the greater individual variation permitted in loosely structured systems is accompanied by high homicide rates. Because they have in mind something closely resembling altruistic suicide, the Straus and Straus explanation is undoubtedly more applicable to Sri Lanka than to the Western world, but the parallels in their data are nonetheless suggestive.

The period 1949–53 was dominated by the inductive phase of theory building. New and seemingly new empirical regularities, many of them well known to the nineteenth-century moral statisticians, were being "discovered"; and scholars such as Porterfield and Straus and Straus were casting about for a conceptual framework to explain the recurring patterns. Straus and Straus (1953) toyed with and rejected a Freudian explanation; Porterfield (1949) suggested the relevance of the frustration-aggression hypothesis but then moved on to conceptualize the problem in terms of the folk-urban continuum. Most of the theoretical paths they followed turned out to be blind alleys, but Porterfield's 1949 conceptualization of suicide and homicide as alternative responses to frustration has had considerable staying power. He asked the right questions, and in 1954 Andrew F. Henry and James F. Short, Jr., went a long way toward providing some of the answers.

HENRY AND SHORT

Henry and Short (1954; see also Henry and Short 1957) proposed a theory of suicide and homicide based on the frustration-aggression hypothesis (Dollard et al. 1939). Their monograph is an attempt to integrate sociological, psychological, and economic perspectives on suicide and homicide into a common theoretical framework.

Henry and Short's central underlying assumption is that suicide and homicide are alternative aggressive responses to frustration. They understand both concepts in the same way as John Dollard and his associates, who define aggression as any act the intent of which is to injure some object, target, or victim (Henry and Short 1954, 56; Dollard et al. 1939). As alternative forms of aggression, suicide and homicide are seen as differentiated from one another only in that the self is the target in the case of the former and another person in the case of the latter. The two forms of aggression "cannot be differentiated with respect to the source of the frustration generating the aggression" (Henry and Short 1954, 15).

Frustration, as conceptualized by Dollard et al. (1939, 1) is "that condition which exists when a goal response suffers interference." More simply, a frustration is a blockage of any kind in one's path toward a goal. In Ferri's 1925 terms, frustration is the "force of production" in Henry and Short's 1954 theory.

Henry and Short examine the impact of economic frustrations generated by fluctuations in the business cycle on suicide and homicide. While their treatment of the economic correlates of suicide and homicide is ingenious, it is nonetheless unsatisfactory. Henry and Short's data show that for the total population suicide varies inversely and homicide directly with economic cycles. The strength of the relationship between economic conditions and suicide varies by social status, however, and in the case of homicide, even the direction of the relationship is a function of status attributes.

According to Henry and Short, the correlation between suicide and the business cycle is higher for males, whites, persons in their economically productive years, and the economically privileged than it is for females, non-whites, persons past retirement age, and those with low incomes. "In each of our four cases, the group with higher status position reacts more violently to fluctuations of business than does the subordinate category with which it is compared" (Henry and Short 1954, 41). In short, the increase in suicide during recession is greatest for those groups with the most to lose.

Turning to the relationship of homicide and crimes against persons to the business cycle, Henry and Short find that the correlation between homicide and economic fluctuations is strongly negative for whites and strongly positive for blacks (1954, 48). They interpret their findings as suggesting that blacks gain status relative to whites during economic contractions, which narrows the status gap between races, and lose status during economic growth, when the lion's share of the new prosperity devolves upon whites (1954, 60–62). Thus blacks, especially those who are economically deprived, are actually less frustrated in times of depression than in times of prosperity, when their homicide rate increases as a consequence. Henry and Short speculate that blacks who commit suicide come from the black upper class, which has a stake in prosperity in some ways similar to that of whites (Henry and Short 1954, 124; cf. Prudhomme 1938).

Henry and Short having established to their satisfaction (but not to ours) that both suicide and homicide rates vary directly with economic frustration, conclude that suicide and homicide are "undifferentiated acts of aggression in the sense that they react in the same way to the same objective frustrating source" (1954, 101). But why do persons in some social groups kill themselves while others commit murders instead? Through an examination of the sociological correlates of suicide and homicide rates—social class, age, race, sex, marital status, region, rural-urban residence, location in the urban spatial structure—Henry and Short isolate two factors, status and strength of the relational system (the degree of involvement in primary relationships with others). They suggest that status is positively related to and strengh of the relational system negatively related to the tendency to "choose" suicide over homicide. These two factors are similar to those proposed by Prosper Despine (1868), Durkheim (1897, 1900), and others during the nineteenth century. They then argue that both low status and strong relational systems involve high levels of external restraint over behavior. Thus, they tentatively conclude that "suicide varies negatively and homicide positively with the strength of external restraint over behavior" (Henry and Short 1954, 97).

At the level of individual psychology, Henry and Short suggest that external restraints increase the legitimization of other-directed aggression:

> As the degree to which behavior is determined by the demands of others increases, the share of others in responsibility for the consequences of behavior also increases. . . . As the role of oth-

ers in the determination of behavior increases, the right to blame others for unfortunate consequences also increases. When the role of self in determining behavior is great relative to the role of others, the self must bear responsibility for the consequences of the behavior (Henry and Short 1954, 103).

Henry and Short also suggest that child-rearing practices affect the legitimization of other-directed aggression and the choice between suicide and homicide. Drawing on theories of the sources of superego strength such as those cited previously, they suggest that the legitimation of other-directed aggression is a function of the extent to which childhood aggression threatens nurturance and love.

Since 1954, most investigations of the relationship between suicide and homicide have been based implicitly or explicitly on Henry and Short's 1954 conceptualization. Soon after the appearance of their monograph, however, a number of critics suggested that their tests of their theory were inadequate and that the theory needed fine tuning. Martin Gold (1958) and Hugh P. Whitt (1966, 1968) proposed measurement strategies designed to permit more accurate mapping of Henry and Short's verbal theory than they themselves had accomplished; and several critics, most significantly Leonard Berkowitz (1962; see also Gold 1958; Whitt 1968; Hackney 1969), suggested minor but nonetheless significant theoretical retooling.

Methodological Fine Tuning

Methodologically, the modifications to Henry and Short's 1954 theory of suicide and homicide proposed during the 1950s and 1960s represent an explicit attempt to reformulate it in terms of the nineteenth-century stream analogy (Whitt 1968). Explaining these methodological innovations will take us far afield, introducing us to another of Thomas Kuhn's 1970 anomalies, this time a *positive* relationship between suicide and homicide across tribal societies uncovered in anthropological studies. Given that sociologists at the time were so accustomed to looking for inverse relationships that they were unable to grasp the theoretical relevance of a positive relationship, it is fortunate that anthropologists were working in a tradition in which a positive relationship made sense.

A bit of background is perhaps necessary. As Whitt (1968) notes, the logical structure of Henry and Short's 1954 theory is identical to that of Ferri's (1925) and Morselli's (1879a, 1879b). Frustration plays the same role in Henry and Short's perspective that biological decay and degeneration did for the two criminal anthropologists—it is a force of production. Changes in frustration should be accompanied by parallel increases or decreases in both suicide and homicide. On the other hand, Henry and Short treat status, strength of the relational system, the degree of external restraint, the type of child rearing, and the legitimization of other-directed aggression in the same way as the nineteenth-century scholars dealt with social factors such as education and ethnicity—as forces of direction. Any change in these variables should increase either the suicide rate or the homicide rate at the expense of the other. As D. J. West puts it: "Henry and Short recognized that two sets of factors were at work; the first (which they identified with various stresses and social frustrations) by provoking aggression might be expected to generate both suicide and homicide. The second set of factors determined the choice between homicide and suicide, that is between outward and inward directed violence" (West 1967, 138).

Modeling forces of direction came first and was fairly straightforward because it flowed smoothly from the long tradition in sociology and psychology of assuming that suicide and homicide are normally inversely correlated. On the other hand, it took more than a decade and the impact of a series of findings from anthropology to alert sociologists to the possibility that forces of production could also be modeled in a complementary way.

Gold (1958) was the first to recognize that hypotheses about the choice between suicide and homicide cannot be tested by examining the behavior of suicide or homicide rates in isolation from one another. If persons in one category have a higher suicide rate than those in another, it *may* be because they have a greater preference for suicide over homicide; but the alternative hypothesis that they are simply more frustrated cannot be rejected. If so, they would be expected to have a higher homicide rate as well.

To correct this logical error, Gold suggested a measure of preference that he calls the suicide-murder ratio, or SMR, which is obtained by dividing the suicide rate of a category by the sum of its suicide and homicide rates.[7] The SMR taps the proportion of the total number of suicides and homicides which is expressed intropunitively rather than extropunitively.

The SMR and its variant, the homicide-suicide ratio (HSR; homicide divided by the combined total) have been widely adopted as a measure of the preference for or choice between suicide and homicide—in short, as a measure of direction (see, for example, West 1967; Whitt 1968, 1985; Hackney 1969; Whitt et al. 1972; Unnithan 1983; Huff-Corzine, Corzine, and Moore 1991). Indeed, we use it as one of the two major dependent variables in the research reported in this book. We call it the

SHR, or suicide-homicide ratio, because the data we use are for homicides, a somewhat broader category than murders, but our measurement is identical to Gold's.[8]

Although Gold was clearly aware that Henry and Short's theory could be used to interpret positive relationships in terms of variations in levels of frustration, he stopped short of arguing that the degree of frustration should increase the combined rate of suicide and homicide. Perhaps Gold went no further because the vast majority of sociological writing about suicide and homicide since the nineteenth century had emphasized the usual inverse relationship between them. Except for Ferri's (1925) and Morselli's (1879a, 1879b) misguided attempts to locate the common sources of suicide and homicide in biological degeneracy and Durkheim's (1897) equally unconvincing argument linking both forms of violence to altruism and anomie, the few instances of positive relationships in industrialized nations had generally been taken by sociologists as evidence against a theoretical connection. Von Hentig (1948) was a notable exception.

Anthropologists, operating within a different research tradition, wore no such blinders. Studies of tribal societies had conditioned anthropologists to take positive relationships between suicide and homicide more or less for granted. This tendency was strengthened by their greater intellectual debt to von Hentig, who saw the possibility of parallelism more clearly than Henry and Short (1954). Von Hentig's different slant results from his using something very close to the stream analogy in the quote cited at the beginning of this chapter, in which he emphasizes *"the total amount of available destructiveness"* discharged into *"two psychologically similar,* but socially distinct *Gestalten"* (von Hentig 1948, 389–90; our emphasis).

The ethnographic literature on suicide and homicide is perhaps most fully developed for tribal societies in India and Africa, though Margaret Mead's well-known 1935 study in New Guinea found higher rates of both among the Mundugumor than among the Arapesh. Studies by Verrier Elwin (1950) and A. B. Saran (1974) of tribal societies on the Indian subcontinent also indicate a degree of cross-tribal parallelism between suicide and homicide. The African tribes surveyed in Bohannan's 1965 compilation show a varied mix of relationships.[9]

The sociologist Stuart Palmer deserves credit for bringing the anthropological and sociological traditions together. In 1965, Palmer, intrigued by the inverse relationship between suicide and homicide in cross-national studies of modern societies, collected data for a sample of forty tribal groups from the Human Relations Area Files to determine whether a similar pattern held across preliterate societies. Instead of an inverse relationship, he found a tendency for suicide and murder to vary together much as it does in the comparisons of rates for much smaller numbers of societies, such as those in New Guinea and India. Both suicide and homicide increased with the consistent use of such severe forms of punishment as execution, torture, total ostracism of the offender, and banishment from the society.[10]

Palmer's interpretation of his findings is especially significant:

> The finding that there is a considerable positive relationship between frequencies of murder and suicide in these nonliterate societies casts grave doubt on the contention that if murder is relatively uncommon then violent aggressive tendencies will be directed by individuals toward themselves and that as murder is more common suicide will be resorted to less. It is unlikely that practically all societies tend to have similarly sized reservoirs of aggression that under certain circumstances result in the behavior of murder and that under quite different circumstances eventuate in suicidal behavior.
>
> Rather, it is likely that societies generate various levels of drives toward violent aggression in their populations. Given that, which form of killing the drive may take will depend on many variables (Palmer 1965, 323).

Thus, Palmer suggests that societies are subject to variations in those factors that produce violent aggression as well as those that influence its direction. Similarly, Jack P. Gibbs contends that "it is improbable that progress will be made in examining the association between suicide and homicide without considering the source and total volume of aggression. . . . If the volume of aggressive tendencies is low in a population, both the homicide and the suicide rate will be low " (Gibbs 1968, 204).

The hypothesis that societies' reservoirs of aggression come in varying sizes suggests both a solution to the anomaly of positive relationships and a way of modeling the forces of production in Henry and Short's theory. Henry and Short (1954) suggested that suicide and homicide are undifferentiated from one another in the sense that both are generated by frustration. Thus, frustration should affect the size of the reservoir of aggression, or, in the quite similar metaphor of the stream analogy, the size of the stream of violence.

Whitt (1966, 1968, 1985; Whitt et al. 1972) suggested that the size of the stream of violent aggression could be measured by what he then called the lethal aggression rate (LAR). This measure—which we have renamed the LVR, or lethal violence rate, following current convention (Unnithan 1983; Huff-Corzine, Corzine, and Moore 1991)—is the sum of the suicide rate and the homicide rate. The LVR measures the size of the stream of violence, while Gold's 1958 suicide-murder ratio gauges the proportion of the total which is expressed as suicide rather than as homicide. The LVR is the complement of the SHR, because:

$$SHR = S/(S + H) \tag{3.1}$$

and

$$LVR = S + H. \tag{3.2}$$

From this, Whitt (1966, 1968) argued, it follows that an adequate test of Henry and Short's 1954 theory could be accomplished by using the SHR and the LVR instead of suicide and homicide rates themselves as dependent variables. He also suggested an alternative interpretation, which views both the suicide rate and the homicide rate as multiplicative functions of (1) frustration and (2) the various factors, such as status, strength of the relational system, external restraint over behavior, and child-rearing practices, which Henry and Short link to the choice between suicide and homicide. The multiplicative hypothesis flows from equations (3.3) and (3.4):

$$S = (SHR)(LVR) \tag{3.3}$$

and

$$H = (1 - SHR)(LVR). \tag{3.4}$$

A flurry of studies appearing in the late 1960s and early 1970s used the SHR, and, less often, the LVR, to explore the relationship between suicide and homicide. For example, D. J. West (1967) used the SHR in his study of murder-suicides in England. Murder-suicide, as Wolfgang (1958b, 1959) and others had already pointed out, may be conceptualized as an extended suicide in which a person kills first others and then himself or herself. The victims are usually family members, and the profile of the offender more closely resembles that of the typical suicide victim than that of the typical murderer. Indeed, West (1967) finds that national rates of murder-suicide vary directly with the SHR.

The historian Sheldon Hackney (1969) used both the SHR and the LVR in a study of violence in the American South, a region with a long cultural tradition of violence against others but relatively few suicides.[11] The SHRs of Southerners, both whites and non-whites, are lower than those of persons outside the South. Using multiple regression techniques, Hackney shows that the regional differences in SHRs of whites cannot be explained away by such structural variables as urbanization, education, income, unemployment, wealth, or the age distribution. After controlling for these variables, a significant contribution of residence in the South remains.

Hackney makes less of his statistical analysis than he might have. For example, neither the structural variables nor region do a very good job of explaining non-white SHRs; the only significant variable is income. As non-white income at the state level increases, non-whites in the state are increasingly likely to choose suicide over homicide. The LVRs of both whites and non-whites increase significantly with Southern residence after controls for structural variables. Thus, Hackney's 1969 statistical analysis suggests that the stream of violence is greater in the South, for both whites and non-whites, than the structural variables in his analysis would lead us to expect, and that income levels rather than region itself account for the tendency for non-white Southerners to choose homicide over suicide.[12]

Finally, Whitt, Gordon, and Hofley (1972) used the SHR and the LVR in a cross-national analysis of data from forty-seven nations. They find that the SHR varies directly with level of economic development and that the SHRs of Protestant nations are higher than those with Catholic or non-Western religious traditions. Religion and economic development have an interactive effect on the LVR, which decreases with economic development in Protestant nations, increases with economic development in non-Western nations, and is unrelated to economic development in Catholic nations.

The development of the LVR and the SHR represented methodological innovations designed to tap the effects of the two types of variables in Henry and Short's theory—Ferri's and Morselli's forces of production and direction. At the same time and often in the same studies, a number of theorists were suggesting ways of improving upon Henry and Short's 1954 theoretical specification.

Theoretical Fine Tuning

Theoretical criticisms of Henry and Short's 1954 theory during the 1950s and 1960s (as opposed to the methodological critiques involving the SHR and the LVR) focused on clarifying the variables affecting the choice between suicide and homicide and attempting to flesh out Henry and Short's rather meager treatment of the social sources of frustration.

Gold (1958), who first proposed the use of the SHR, also suggested minor changes in the specification of the sources of the choice between suicide and homicide. He argued, in essence, that the relationship between low status and external restraint posited by Henry and Short does not exist, because high-status persons experience restrictions on their behavior that are no less restraining than those experienced by persons of lower status. External restraints, he points out, are exerted not only by persons but also by norms, and norms may impinge more heavily upon persons higher in the status hierarchy. He suggests that the link between status and the choice between suicide and homicide can better be explained by class differences in the socialization of aggression. Henry and Short, of course, also recognized the importance of child-rearing practices, but Gold chose to emphasize the distinction between physical and psychological punishments rather than whether socialization practices threaten the flow of nurturance and love. This, frankly, is hair-splitting, for the literature on child-rearing practices cited in chapter 2 suggests that symbolic punishments are generally love-oriented. Love-oriented punishments tend to be used by persons higher in the status hierarchy while physical punishments are more often used by those who are less advantaged. Gold's 1958 point about the normative restraints on higher-status persons is well taken, but his attempt to substitute one child-rearing theory for another constitutes at best a minor addition to Henry and Short's basic theoretical model.

Another set of criticisms, which appears on the surface to be equally minor but that considerably simplifies Henry and Short's theory, involves recasting their psychology in less Freudian terms. In the 1960s, a number of scholars suggested, in effect, the replacement of both external control over behavior and the legitimization of other-directed aggression with a single variable tapping the attribution of responsibility for frustration. For example, Leonard Berkowitz (1962) argues that Henry and Short's reliance on external restraint seems forced. Although he does not entirely reject their external restraint argument, he points to class differences in the emphasis on self-reliance and individual accomplishment as perhaps of greater importance. If middle-class people "generally regard themselves as masters of their own fate," he maintains, "they must also blame themselves for their social and economic failures. In extreme cases such self-blame can lead to suicide" (Berkowitz 1962, 326). Similarly, Jack D. Douglas reformulated Henry and Short's 1954 model in such a way as "to make the frustration-aggression theory of suicide as strong as [he] can" (Douglas 1967, 133). Douglas, whose intended goal was not simply to build on earlier approaches to the study of suicide, including Henry and Short's, but to replace them with his own social contructionist theory (Douglas 1967, viii), replaces the legitimization of other-directed aggression with the "imputation of generalized responsibility" as the direct cause of the choice between suicide and homicide. Although this is an inaccurate reading of what Henry and Short actually said, we agree with Douglas that his rendering of their theory constitutes an improvement.

Whitt (1968) proposed a similar modification, arguing that external control over behavior is a less important factor than external control over outcomes in the direction of aggression against self or others. Drawing on Julian B. Rotter's 1966 concept of "internal vs. external locus of control" (for reviews of research on locus of control, see Lefcourt 1982, 1983) and Melvin Seeman's (1959, 1975; Rotter, Liverant, and Seeman, 1962) parallel construct, "alienation as powerlessness," he suggests that persons develop generalized tendencies to attribute responsibility for their outcomes either to themselves or others. Those who characteristically attribute responsibility to themselves tend to choose suicide over homicide, while those with external locus of control are more likely to kill someone else.

A cross-cultural study by Boor (1976) suggests precisely the opposite of what Whitt (1968) argued—suicide rates vary directly with the *externality* of locus of control as measured by social surveys in six industrial nations. In defense of Whitt, we should point out that Boor's sample is extremely small and the range of variation in locus of control is limited. Moreover, Whitt suggests that the SHR rather than the suicide rate itself is influenced by locus of control. Nonetheless, at least one study of persons who had recently made suicide attempts (Melges and Weisz 1971) suggests that suicidal thoughts were accompanied by a shift toward external control prior to the attempt, and another (Lester 1991a) finds that suicidal ideation is associated with external locus of control in a student sample. Indeed, David Lester's (1989b, 1991a) depression paradox theory of suicide maintains that "people who have high depression scores and who feel helpless (that is, have an *external* locus of control) would be more prone to suicide" (Lester 1991a, 1254; our emphasis).

An association between suicidal behavior and external locus of control in individual data *is* a problem for Whitt's 1968 position. Indeed, several studies (Abramowitz 1969; Miller and Seligman 1973) find that externality as measured by Rotter's 1966 IE scale is positively related to depression as Lester (1989b, 1991a) suggests. This finding, which parallels Melges and Weisz's (1971) and Lester's (1991a) for suicidal ideation and behavior, was generated as part of an ongoing research program designed to test the theory of learned helplessness developed by Martin E. P. Seligman and his associates (see, for example Abramson, Seligman, and Teasdale 1978). This theory and its successor, the stress-diathesis theory of hopelessness depression (Abramson, Alloy and Metalsky 1988; Abramson, Metalsky and Alloy 1988, 1989; Alloy, Abramson, Metalsky, and Hartlage 1988; Alloy, Kelly, Mineka and Clements 1990; DeVellis and Blalock 1992), resolve the apparent paradox by drawing distinctions between positive and negative outcomes and between interpretations of past and present outcomes (attributions or causal explanations) and expectancies for the future. From a learned helplessness-stress diathesis perspective, which replaces Rotter's locus of control in our current thinking about the stream analogy, both clinical depression and the choice of suicide over homicide combine self-blame for negative events (an internal causal explanation) with helplessness or hopelessness (an external expectancy for the future).

But we are getting ahead of ourselves. Learned helplessness and stress-diathesis theory represent fairly recent developments in cognitive psychology and attribution theory. For now, we must leave Whitt dangling in thin air with a clearly inadequate conceptualization that views locus of control as central to the choice between suicide and homicide. We shall return to learned helplessness and stress-diathesis theory in chapter 5, where we review developments in attribution theory and cognitive psychology over the last two decades that serve as the psychological underpinnings of the integrated model, laying out a more adequate conceptualization than the one Whitt (1968) proposed.

Less work was done on the LVR than the SHR during the 1949–72 revival of the stream analogy, though some effort was devoted to the development of ways of assessing the frustration levels of populations. Whitt (1968), Palmer (1972), and Palmer and Linsky (1972), for example, drew an explicit parallel between the frustration-aggression hypothesis and Robert K. Merton's 1957 theory of anomie. As Merton uses the term, anomie is a socially patterned disjunction between culturally approved goals and the opportunity to reach them by institutionalized means. According to Merton, the first consequence of such a situation is frustration for a segment of the population. Whitt (1968) and Whitt, Gordon, and Hofley (1972) had suggested the relevance of Pitirim A. Sorokin's 1937–41 concept of logico-meaningful integration, suggesting that incompatibilities between the value premises of religion and industrialization might increase lethal violence in societies outside the Judeo-Christian tradition.[13] Meanwhile, the work of political scientists such as

Ivo K. Feierabend and Rosalind L. Feierabend (1966, 1972) on the relationship between *systemic frustration* and political violence also seemed potentially relevant.

It seemed in 1972 as if the stream analogy might be on the edge of joining the Durkheimian perspective as an enduring approach to the study of suicide. Some researchers, of course, had rejected it. Richard C. Quinney (1965), later to become better known as a critical criminologist, concluded that suicide and homicide are causally separate phenomena on the basis of his finding that suicide varies directly and homicide inversely with economic development. Nonetheless, the frustration-aggression approach appeared in 1972 to hold promise for integrating research on suicide and homicide under the umbrella of a single theory, and developments in political science seemed to be moving in a direction that suggested that collective violence might also be incorporated as a third current in the stream.

But this promise was not fulfilled. After 1972, research in the currents of violence tradition fell off to a trickle. The sudden disappearance of the frustration-aggression paradigm from the scene was due largely to theoretical and methodological criticisms advanced by Karl Schuessler (1973, 1974), Herbert Hendin (1964), and Jack Douglas (1967). Schuessler's critique of ratio variables, which used the LVR and the SHR as an example, was widely misinterpreted until the mid-1980s as precluding the use of ratios in regression analysis. Hendin argued that it is impossible to apply *any* general theory of suicide cross-nationally because the meanings and motives of suicide are culturally and probably subculturally specific. The general explanations proposed by sociologists impose a set of categories that may have no meaning in the lives of the real people who commit suicide. Douglas's 1967 theoretical critique is in some ways similar: both he and Hendin stress the necessity of examining how suicide is socially constructed by actual victims. For Douglas, this necessitates building theory from the bottom up rather than from the top down, as theorists since Durkheim have usually done. One must examine the *situated* meanings of suicide rather than impose generalized explanations or even looking up meanings in a cultural catalog as Hendin does. Moreover, because the official statistics used to test general theories are also socially constructed, they may be subject to systematic biases of just the sort that will tend incorrectly to appear to support these theories.

We shall have more to say about these criticisms in chapter 6, but first we turn in chapter 4 to a consideration of the few studies linking suicide and homicide that have appeared in the twenty years since Douglas's 1967 promise to replace all previous approaches was almost fulfilled.

LIN HUFF-CORZINE
JAY CORZINE
HUGH P. WHITT
N. PRABHA UNNITHAN

4

Reinventing the Wheel

During the past two decades, scholarly and lay interest in violence-related topics has expanded significantly. With the emergence of spouse abuse as a public issue in the 1970s, family violence has become an important focus of research in psychology and sociology and a major social issue for the women's movement. Articles reflecting the ongoing debate between proponents of structural and cultural explanations for high homicide rates in the Southern states regularly appear in the leading sociology and criminology journals. In the last two decades, the heightened academic interest in lethal violence has been exemplified by the founding of the specialty journals *Suicide and Life-Threatening Behavior*, *Journal of Family Violence*, *Journal of Interpersonal Violence*, *Violence and Victims*, and *Child Abuse and Neglect* and by the founding of the Homicide Research Working Group at the annual meeting of the American Society of Criminology in 1991.

The billing by Home Box Office, a United States cable television network, of two movies, *Manhunter* and *Silence of the Lambs*, as the "Hannibal the Cannibal Double Feature" in early 1992 illustrates the general public's continued and perhaps growing fascination with mass murder and serial killers. After a period of dormancy, the 1992 riot in Los Angeles and lesser disturbances in other cities following the Rodney King verdict reawakened public, academic, and governmental interest in collective violence. There are signs that the early 1990s are the beginning of a period, reminiscent of the 1960s, when concern about violence is near the top of the public and political agendas. The National Research

Council Panel on the Understanding and Control of Violence released its report summarizing much of what is known about interpersonal violence and supporting increased funding for research to fill in the gaps (Reiss and Roth 1993). There is also evidence that violence research is becoming more politicized than in past years. The National Rifle Association flexed its political muscle in opposition to the Centers for Disease Control's research on gun-related violence (Taubes 1992). And the Congressional Black Caucus launched a successful campaign to cancel a National Institutes of Health-sponsored conference on genetic factors in crime because of fears it would promote the view that violence by blacks is genetically based (Stone 1992).

Although there has been no lack of research, recent theoretical advances in the area of lethal violence have been modest at best. From our viewpoint, a major shortcoming in much current work is that the study of homicide and suicide have become separated, and research on each type of lethal violence has progressed independently of the other. For the nineteen-year period between 1974 and 1992, *Sociological Abstracts* lists an average of fifty-six articles on suicide and eighteen articles on homicide, but only six articles on suicide *and* homicide per annum.

A second trend in studies of lethal violence is that much current research focuses on psychological interpretations. Not surprisingly, sociology journals, as well as criminology and criminal justice journals, publish macrolevel studies; but the specialty journals in the field, *Violence and Victims, Journal of Interpersonal Violence,* and *Journal of Family Violence,* are dominated by theoretical perspectives and research designs that search for the etiology of lethal violence in intrapsychic processes or personal relationships. These views are not deficient in themselves, and some progress on important issues—such as the treatment of family violence perpetrators—has been made. But research in the tradition of the stream analogy and Andrew F. Henry and James F. Short, Jr. (1954) has become scarce. We contend that a macrolevel approach that views homicide and suicide as related behaviors affected by group- and societal-level structures and processes offers distinct advantages for understanding lethal violence. We want to emphasize, however, that our purpose is not to denigrate theorizing or research at the psychological level.

In this chapter, we review the work appearing during the two decades from 1972 to 1992 that is directly related to the development of a comprehensive explanation of homicide and suicide. Many of these studies are atheoretical, however, with an emphasis on presenting trend data for violent deaths or comparing the rates of homicide and suicide among demographic groups such as men and women. The discussion of theoretical perspectives often occurs in a post hoc fashion in order to offer an explanation for observed patterns rather than for prediction. In many ways, research in this area has returned to a period of inductive theory building characteristic of the years prior to the publication of Henry and Short's *Suicide and Homicide*. Early advances by the European moral statisticians, including the concept of the dual law and the distinction between forces of production and forces of direction, have disappeared from the literature. Interest in the stream analogy idea has been conspicuous by its absence in research between Hugh Whitt's studies in the early 1970s and Unnithan and Whitt (1992).

Notably, we do not attempt a comprehensive review of studies on homicide and suicide in this chapter. The interested reader may find useful discussions of the empirical literature for this time period, or a significant portion of it, evaluated from different disciplines and theoretical perspectives in reviews by Dane Archer and Rosemary Gartner (1984) and Martin Daly and Margo Wilson (1988) for homicide and by David Lester (1983) and Steven Stack (1982) for suicide. A short but interesting overview of violence, both homicide and suicide, is presented by Jean-Claude Chesnais (1992).

The remainder of the chapter is divided into five sections. The first reviews the handful of recent attempts to expand the model of homicide and suicide developed by Henry and Short. In the second section, we discuss comparative studies of lethal violence at the national or cross-national level. In the third section, we examine research that compares homicide and suicide rates among social and demographic groups—such as whites and blacks—or tests the importance of explanatory variables using data from the United States. A fourth section briefly examines recent studies of suicide and interpersonal aggression in the fields of biology and medicine. Although these ideas have arisen independently of and to some extent in opposition to sociological traditions, they are nonetheless more consistent with the stream analogy than they appear at first glance. Finally, a body of research, much of it based in the public health field, which examines commonalities between homicide, suicide, and accidents, the third external cause of deaths, is reviewed.

THEORETICAL DEVELOPMENTS

In sociology, a persistent advocate of the frustration-aggression hypothesis as a framework for explaining homicide and suicide is Stuart Palmer, who has also attempted to integrate the concept of anomie into the theory. Robert K. Merton's highly influential 1938 theory of social structure and anomie conceptualizes seemingly unrelated forms of deviance as alternative responses to structural strains. These patterned disjunctions or discontinuities in the sociocultural structure exert pressures on certain categories of individuals—those most affected by the strains—to engage in nonconforming behavior. Anomie occurs when the opportunity to reach culturally approved goals (such as financial or any other type of success) by the means normatively institutionalized as legitimate (such as education and hard work) is blocked by the system of social arrangements. Under such conditions, normal individuals may be expected to adapt to their anomic situations in any of five alternative ways—conformity, innovation, ritualism, retreatism, or rebellion.

According to Merton, the response chosen in particular situations depends upon cultural patterns and individual personality systems, including the relative extent of emphasis on cultural goals and the institutional means of achieving them. For example, some of the activities of retreatists—"psychotics, psychoneurotics, chronic autists, pariahs, outcasts, vagrants, vagabonds, tramps, chronic drunkards and drug addicts" (Merton 1938, 677) and, we might add, suicidal persons—are seen as occurring when "both the cultural goals and institutionalized procedures have been thoroughly assimilated by the individual and imbued with high positive value, but where those institutionalized procedures which promise a measure of successful attainment of the goals are not available to the individual" (Merton 1938, 677). In essence, Merton's theory tries to do what Gabriel Tarde (1886b; see chapter 2) said couldn't be done. It seeks to incorporate a variety of forms of nonconforming behavior into a single middle-range theory as alternative responses to similar underlying structural conditions (that is, anomie).

In Palmer's (1972; Palmer and Linsky 1972) work, homicide is seen as arising in social settings where unreciprocity in role relationships is great and social integration is minimal. "The homicidal individual is one who, because of that unreciprocity and because of other reasons . . . experiences great frustration in early life and in later life as well. . . . Suicide tends to be a consequence of either high reciprocity or an absence of unreciprocity and often of high social integration as well" (Palmer 1972, 143).

Stuart Palmer and Arnold S. Linsky (1972) identify homicide and suicide as adaptations to the disjuncture between goals and means that Robert Merton (1938) suggested as an occurrence in anomic situations. The rebellious deviant adapts by striking out against social structures and their participants (by killing them, perhaps) while the retreatist deviant withdraws from, or seeks to isolate himself or herself from, the so-cial structure and its participants (the most extreme as well as perma-nent form of isolation is suicide). Since Merton stated that frustration is the first consequence of anomie, Palmer and Linsky's (1972) extension is plausible.

As an explanatory variable for homicide and suicide, however, anomie has attracted comparatively little attention. In one study, John Humphrey and Harriet Kupferer (1977) examined county homicide data from North Carolina, a state on the regional dividing line between the North, where suicide rates are higher, and the South, where homicide rates are higher. They conclude that socioeconomic strain provides an external target for blame, leading to higher homicide rates, while the ab-sence of such strain increases attachment of blame to the self, leading to higher levels of suicide. Their attempt to link social structural position to the locus of control orientation is consistent with Henry and Short, but unfortunately it has received little attention from other investigators.

A second and more critical attempt to extend Henry and Short's theory is presented by Ken Levi (1982). Building on Emile Durkheim's work, Levi views segregation, or social isolation (the opposite, or ab-sence, of social integration), as a major source of both homicide and sui-cide. Following Hugh Whitt, Charles Gordon, and John Hofley (1972) and Roger Lane (1979), he views the social changes accompanying in-dustrialization as channeling aggression toward the self, thus leading to higher suicide and lower homicide rates.

At the social-psychological level, Levi's views are influenced by both frustration-aggression and locus of control concepts. Homicide and suicide are viewed as alternate means of conflict resolution, with the definition of conflict, an "undesirable divergence from what one expects," (105) closely paralleling the definition for frustration pro-posed by John Dollard and his associates (1939). Both homicide and sui-cide, therefore, flow from similar motives, with homicide involving a focused other-fixation on a particular person and suicide a focused other-fixation on a generalized other, or society at large. Why Levi does not see suicide as involving a focused self-fixation is unclear. He con-tends that three factors influence the person toward suicide: the physi-cal unavailability of the other, ambivalence toward killing the other, and self-blame for failure. Thus, Levi follows in the tradition of Sig-mund Freud and Dollard and his collaborators by viewing suicide as displaced homicide.

While Levi's conceptualization of lethal violence as conflict reso-lution is an interesting idea, his theory is essentially a restatement of the basic frustration-aggression hypothesis. The primary contribution of his approach is to elaborate factors that may effect a shift in the target of aggression. Overall, his theoretical ideas are consistent with Henry and Short as well as with the model that is presented in chapter 6.

RESEARCH WITH NATIONS AS UNITS OF ANALYSIS

Consistent with most past inquiries, Robert Winslow (1970) and Levi (1982) report inverse relationships between per capita homicide and suicide levels within nations during the 1960s and 1970s, respectively. Reminiscent of the moral statisticians and Whitt, Gordon, and Hofley (1972), their studies also support the hypothesis that industrialization alters the balance between self- and other-directed violence at the national level, a position echoed by Chesnais (1992). Specifically, Winslow reports that industrialization is negatively related to homicide ($r = -.40$) but positively related to suicide ($r = .48$); a pattern of findings that is also replicated by Levi.

By far the most prolific author in this area of research, Lester (1987, 1989a, 1990a) has examined the relationships between a large number of social variables, including several quality-of-life indicators, and homicide and suicide rates in nation-states. Surprisingly, Lester (1990a) reports a strong, positive correlation between quality of life, measured by health, welfare, and education variables, and homicide rates in forty-three nations. Although quality of life was also positively correlated with suicide rates, the magnitude of the relationship was weaker than for homicide. These findings should be viewed cautiously until replicated by other researchers. Indicators of a national population's health and welfare are positively related to the level of industrialization, a variable that is widely reported to be related in opposite directions to homicide and suicide rates; and Lester's finding that both types of lethal violence move in the same direction with quality-of-life measures is suspect. Lester has also reported a direct relationship between GNP, a measure of industrialization, and homicide levels, a finding that is contradicted by the extant literature (Braithwaite and Braithwaite 1980; Conklin and Simpson 1985; Krahn, Hartnagel, and Gartrell 1986; for an exception, see Ortega et al. 1992).

In a study of religion and lethal violence, Lester (1987) reports that the number of religious books published, a measure of religiosity, does not affect homicide or suicide rates in eighteen industrialized nations. This finding conflicts with Stack (1983), who shows that religious book production influences suicide rates. Lester's sample is smaller than Stack's, however, and he analyzes lethal violence rates for men and women together, while the relationship reported by Stack held primarily for women. It is likely that the discrepancies between the two studies may reflect differences in samples and methods. Nonetheless, Lester interprets his results as refuting Durkheim, although he recognizes a need for better indicators of the strength of religious beliefs. It may be prudent to postpone drawing strong implications for Durkheim's views on the effect of religion on homicide and suicide until more precise measures of religiosity are developed for cross-national research.

Using the same sample of eighteen industrialized nations, Lester (1991b) tests Durkheim's proposition that overregulation leads to fatalistic suicide. Contrary to expectations, the level of government sanctions was positively related to homicide rates only. As noted by Lester, this finding is consistent with Henry and Short, who propose that external control increases the odds that aggression will be directed outward.

In other research continuing the homicide-suicide tradition, Matti Virkkunen (1974) found that, over a fifteen-year period, the rate of suicide linked directly to homicide remained stable in all areas of Finland. A similar conclusion was reached in two separate studies of the United States. Using time-series data, R. H. Franke, E. W. Thomas and A. J. Queenen (1977) find that homicide and suicide have common sources and a stable relationship. Without positing any necessary linkage between the two measures, A. John Klebba (1981) examined rates for homicide and suicide in the United States between 1900 and 1976. He finds that both types of lethal violence have increased in times of national distress and decreased during "periods of national prosperity and humaneness," (147)—that is, the rates have paralleled each other over most of the twentieth century. The issue of why the more common inverse relationship over time between homicide and suicide rates was not found in these studies deserves further investigation. The implications of these findings for the validity of the stream analogy and an integrated model of homicide and suicide will be addressed in chapter 6.

In 1992, N. Prabha Unnithan and Hugh P. Whitt published an article explicitly based on the stream analogy in the *International Journal of Comparative Sociology*. They used data on lethal violence from thirty-one nations aggregated for the period 1950 to 1970. Investigating the effects of inequality and development on the lethal violence rate (LVR) and the suicide-homicide ratio, they report that inequality but not development affects the LVR in nations, although the relationship is curvilinear. Furthermore, inequality increases the proportion of lethal violence in a nation that is expressed as homicide (that is, it is negatively related to the SHR), while the opposite relationship exists for development. An extension of Unnithan and Whitt's research, using a larger sample of nations, is presented in chapter 7.

RESEARCH IN THE UNITED STATES

Racial Differences in Lethal Violence

Generally, the effect of race/ethnicity on lethal violence in the United States has been consistent across different studies and time periods, with minorities exhibiting higher homicide rates and lower suicide rates than dominant groups. This pattern is reaffirmed by Ezra Griffith and Carl Bell (1989), who propose that suicide and homicide should be viewed as public health problems that result in proportionately more deaths among blacks than whites in the United States. From 1950 to 1986, the highest rates of suicide were reported for white men, followed in order by black men, white women, and black women. After examining a variety of theories, Griffith and Bell decided that there is no viable explanation for the observed pattern of suicide. For homicide, the highest rates are found among black men, followed in order by white men, black women, and white women. To explain these findings, Griffith and Bell turn to sociological arguments stressing the effects of poverty, overcrowding, mass media, and the subculture of violence. In summary, they conclude that none of the theories explain why there are such vast differences in rates of suicide and homicide between men and women of the same race.

An important development in research on race/ethnicity and lethal violence is an expanded focus beyond traditional comparisons between blacks and whites. Early studies of lethal violence among Native Americans reported high levels of *both* homicide and suicide, with acculturative pressures, poverty, alcohol consumption, and blocked assimilation offered as explanations (Levey 1965; Stewart 1964). Harriet Kupferer and John Humphrey (1975; Humphrey and Kupferer 1982) focus on variations in homicide and suicide rates among the Cherokee and Lumbee tribes, or nations, in North Carolina. Traditionally, the Cherokee had low rates of lethal violence, a pattern that Kupferer and Humphrey attribute to cultural mechanisms for defusing disputes. When an interpersonal conflict occurred, the antagonists would call on a third party as a mediator. This tradition defused a high percentage of arguments that might otherwise have led to physical altercations. Furthermore, among the Cherokee there was a strong cultural disbelief that anyone would take his or her own life. For Cherokee following the traditional ways, therefore, homicide or suicide was usually associated with heavy alcohol use or having lived away from the reservation for a lengthy period of time. Younger Cherokee were less likely to refer arguments to a mediator, and Humphrey and Kupferer predicted that the eventual demise of this mechanism of conflict resolution would lead to higher rates of homicide.

The traditional cultural pattern among the Lumbee, in contrast to the Cherokee, encouraged both men and women to be aggressive and independent. Physical combat was not avoided, and men were expected to drink heavily. Both factors appeared to influence the high rate of homicide and low rate of suicide found among the Lumbee. As a caveat, we agree that aggressiveness and alcohol consumption are usually correlated with higher rates of homicide, but the attribution literature suggests that groups placing a high value on independence should also have relatively high rates of suicide (see chapter 5).

Humphrey and Kupferer (1982) found, as predicted, that homicide among the Cherokee increased dramatically between 1974 and 1976. Unexpectedly, levels of suicide also rose during this period. Homicide among the Lumbee, however, decreased while suicide rates increased. Once age effects were controlled, Humphrey and Kupferer noted that the elevated homicide rates were concentrated among the younger Cherokee, providing some support for their hypothesis. They offer no reason for the higher suicide and lower homicide rates found among younger Lumbee, although the pattern of findings may be explained by a decline of traditional beliefs, values, and practices for both groups. Humphrey and Kupferer's work is important for several reasons. First, it suggests that cultural differences in beliefs—such as the perceived correlates of masculinity—may mediate the impact of social structure on levels of lethal violence. Second, it offers some support for the proposition that anomie, in this case caused by the breakdown of the traditional cultures of the Cherokee and Lumbee, may be directly related to rates of lethal violence. Last, it demonstrates the utility of research on lethal violence among racial/ethnic groups other than blacks and whites for theory development.

In a national study of lethal violence among Native Americans, Thomas Young (1990) predicted that high levels of poverty should lead to high rates of homicide and low rates of suicide among the twelve Indian Health Service areas in the United States. Contrary to expectations, however, overall poverty was directly related to both homicide and suicide levels. A striking anomaly was that the Navajo, who experienced the highest poverty rate, also had the lowest rates for *both* homicide and suicide. Reinforcing Humphrey and Kupferer, whose work he surprisingly ignores, Young argues in conclusion that cultural as well as structural influences must be considered in future studies.

Perhaps the most ambitious study of Native American homicide and suicide to date is the recent monograph *Death and Violence on the Reservation* by Ronet Bachman (1992). She analyzes lethal violence rates for states and one hundred reservation counties for the years 1980–84. Homicide and suicide are moderately related at the county level (r = .34), and economic deprivation is a source of both types of violent death. Bachman also calculates the suicide-homicide ratio for Native Americans at the national level, reporting that it is higher than that for blacks but lower than that of whites. She does not, however, view homicide and suicide as being linked but instead proposes the existence of separate subcultures conducive to each type of lethal violence: "the American Indian population seems to have elements of both self- and other-directed violent subcultures coexisting within its cultural environment" (Bachman 1992, 26). In contrast, the integrated model connects homicide and suicide through a single theoretical perspective.

Thomas Becker, Jonathan Samet, Charles Wiggins, and Charles Key (1990) compare rates of homicide and suicide among Anglo, Native American, and Hispanic populations in New Mexico between 1958 and 1987. New Mexico was specifically chosen by these researchers because the state is among the nation's leaders in homicide and suicide rates as well as in minority percentage in the population. The authors find that both homicide and suicide rates have increased for all three groups. Results concerning the relationship between homicide and suicide rates were mixed, however. When examined by gender, Native American women exhibited the highest rate of homicide but the lowest rate of suicide for the three groups. Native American men between fifteen and forty-four years of age had the highest rates of both homicide and suicide. Hispanic men consistently had a lower suicide rate than Native Americans or Anglos over the period, while their homicide rates were higher than those for Caucasians but lower than those for Native Americans. Hispanic women's homicide rates were comparable to Anglo women—sometimes a bit higher, sometimes a bit lower. Anglo women, however, committed suicide at a much higher rate than either Native American or Hispanic women. Generally, these reported patterns support the proposition that minority status is related to higher rates of homicide but lower levels of self-destruction. The obvious exception is the high suicide rates among Native American males.

Becker and his colleagues attribute the patterns of homicide and suicide rates shown among the three groups to alcohol abuse and economic status. In New Mexico, alcohol abuse affects a high percentage of Native Americans and Hispanic men (Chavez et al. 1989). "For Native Americans, a higher proportion of violent deaths is estimated to be related to alcohol use (80% of homicides, 75% of suicides), compared to the state's overall statistics for alcohol presence in all victims of suicide and homicide (42% of suicides, 54% of homicides)" (Becker et al. 1990, 332). Thus, among Native Americans in New Mexico, alcohol abuse may be the primary source of high rates of both types of lethal violence.

Becker and his associates also find that with other factors controlled, economic status is inversely related to homicide levels for men among the three groups in New Mexico. Among women, however, homicides are not as clearly affected by economic status. Native American women did exhibit the highest homicide rate, but the levels for Hispanic and Anglo women were nearly equal. On the other hand, economic status provides a more consistent explanation for suicide rates among women than men. Specifically, Native American men exhibited the highest suicide rate but had the lowest economic status. As noted previously, however, alcohol abuse may be responsible for a heightened level of suicide among Native American men. Perhaps the most important implication of the work of Becker and his colleagues is that neither economic deprivation nor minority status is necessarily linked to lethal violence patterns in a specific direction. It is likely that other factors mediate the relationships for specific groups. One intervening variable that may be of special relevance to the United States is cultural differences linked to region.

Regional Differences in Lethal Violence

Since the ground-breaking study by H. V. Redfield (1880), researchers have focused attention on the Southern states' peculiar pattern of lethal violence. Overall, Southerners have traditionally had higher homicide and lower suicide rates than their counterparts in the North and the West (Porterfield 1949; Hackney 1969). Expanding this line of research, R. Page Hudson, John Humphrey, and Harriet Kupferer (1980) examine lethal violence rates in four regions of North Carolina and conclude that the North-South gradient dividing areas of high homicide and high suicide can be detected within as well as across states. Richard Block (1979) shows that region affects migrants as well as natives to an area. Homicide rates increase for persons moving south, while suicide rates increase for those moving north.

Consistent with previous investigations, Lester (1990–91) reports that whites have higher suicide rates than blacks in the South, while

Northern blacks have a higher suicide rate than their Southern counterparts but lower than that for Northern whites. Homicide rates were also higher in the South for both races. Using factor analysis, Lester concludes that the greater a state's social disintegration, as measured by the divorce rate, interstate migration, church attendance, and alcohol consumption, the higher the suicide rate for whites. This relationship confirms parts of Durkheim's theory, and Lester suggests that white "suicide in the United States may be egotistic in nature" (Lester 1990–91, 225). But he claims that this explanation only applies to whites, as black suicide rates do not show significant associations with these measures. Rather than examining the differing historical and contemporary experiences of blacks and whites as recommended by Charles Prudhomme (1938) or noting the potential influence of higher levels of education or income among Northern blacks, Lester argues that black suicide rates are higher in the North because "deviant behavior will be more common in regions where the cultural or social group is less common" (Lester 1990–91, 225). This interpretation directly contradicts other works in sociology, including Claude Fischer's 1975 theory of urbanism and deviance. Opposing the stream analogy, Lester concludes that homicide stems from different sources than suicide, and he relies on the notion of a regional culture of violence to explain high rates of lethal interpersonal violence in the South for both blacks and whites. (For an opposing view, see Gastil 1971; Hackney 1969; Huff-Corzine, Corzine, and Moore 1986.)

Economic Influences on Homicide and Suicide

Researchers continue to examine the relationship between economic measurements, often chosen as indicators of social or status integration (see Gibbs and Martin 1964), and rates of homicide and suicide. For example, Steven Stack (1978) proposes that status integration within a society is inversely related to the level of women's labor force participation. He found that the percentage of women working outside the home was a significant positive predictor of the suicide rate for the total population.

Bijou Yang and David Lester (1988) extend Stack's research in two ways. First, they examine the effect of women's labor force participation upon men and women separately. And second, following Henry and Short (1954), they argue that suicide and homicide rates should be studied in unison because they are opposite forms of aggression linked to the same social forces. Using states as units of analysis and stepwise regression to identify significant variables from a variety of potential causes (such as the divorce rate, interstate migration, percentage of the population that is white, urbanization), Yang and Lester report that there is a direct relationship between the percentage of women working outside the home and the female suicide rate. The argument that women working outside the home will have a negative effect on men's sense of self-worth and, therefore, increase their suicide rate is, however, not supported. In fact, the higher the percentage of married women in the labor force, the lower the male suicide rate. Stack (1987), on the other hand, does report a positive relationship between female labor force participation and the male suicide rate.

The percentage of *all women* working outside the home tended to decrease the homicide rate among men but had no significant effect on women's rate of homicide in the Yang and Lester study. The effect of the percentage of *married women* in the labor force, however, was more complicated. There was a positive relationship between married women working outside the home *full time* and the male homicide rate. But there was a negative relationship between married women working outside the home *part time* and the rate of homicide for both men and women. Thus, it is possible that married women entering the labor market part time improve the economic well-being of the family and conflict in the home increases only when they are unable to complete traditional household duties because of full-time employment. Caution needs to be taken in reading too much into these findings, however, as data that would allow suicide and homicide rates to be disaggregated by marital status are unavailable.

Most important to the present work is Yang and Lester's finding that as women improve their status by working outside the home, their suicide rate increases. It is questionable if men's rates should be affected because their level of status integration is more stable, a point overlooked by Yang and Lester (1988) and Stack (1978), who link women's labor force participation with societal-level status integration.

Examining the influence of unemployment on lethal violence in the United States, Scott J. South (1984) reports that both high and increasing levels of unemployment are directly related to suicide rates. High levels of unemployment decrease homicide levels, but increasing rates of unemployment increase the per capita level of homicide. Thus, the absolute level of unemployment tips the balance of lethal violence in favor of suicide, but increasing rates of unemployment augment both types of lethal violence.

Following Henry and Short, Lester (1988b) proposes that when people go on strike, they have an external source of blame for their problems and that this orientation extends into other areas of their lives.

Findings supported the hypothesis, as the yearly number of strikes was positively related to homicide rates and negatively related to suicide rates in the United States.

DEVELOPMENTS IN BIOLOGY AND MEDICINE

Since Durkheim's day, most of what has been written about the stream analogy has been from a sociological or social-psychological perspective. Nonetheless, a number of recent clinically and biologically oriented researchers have, in essence, revived Enrico Ferri's idea that the forces of production underlying both suicide and homicide are biological.

Two different, though sometimes overlapping, biological approaches may be identified. The first, derived from evolutionary biology and sometimes called evolutionary psychology, sociobiology, or selection thinking (Charnov 1982), examines homicide and, to a lesser degree, suicide, in the context of natural selection and the concept of inclusive fitness (Hamilton 1964). A second biologically based approach, more clinical than evolutionary biology, is based on the premise that suicidal and aggressive behavior both result from such psychiatric conditions as depression, borderline personality disorders, schizophrenia, and antisocial personality disorders.

Evolutionary Biology

Evolutionary biologists have devoted greater attention to homicide than to suicide. Nevertheless, Jonathan M. Himmelhoch, a medical researcher exploring the question of why, in the face of chronic pain and suffering, so few people take their own lives, suggests that built-in evolutionary mechanisms "reside in us all against the completion of self-destruction" (Himmelhoch 1988, 46).

Selection thinking in some ways parallels functionalism in sociology. The similarities are not accidental because sociological functionalism conceptualizes society in terms of an organic analogy (Davis 1949) in which those sociocultural elements that contribute to the survival of the society tend to persist over time while dysfunctional elements disappear or at best continue on as *survivals* (the sociocultural equivalents of the appendix in biological systems). Sociological functionalism seeks the latent *eufunctions* (Merton 1957) of such seemingly dysfunctional but persistent forms of social behavior as conflict (Coser 1956), organized crime (Bell 1962), and prostitution (Davis 1961; for general discussions of the positive functions of crime, see Durkheim 1894; Pfohl 1985).

From the standpoint of evolutionary biology, violence, including homicide, can have positive functions for the survival of the individual and the group. Robert Plutchik and Herman M. van Praag (1990) approach violence from an ethological perspective (that is, one that makes inferences about human behavior based on the behavior of other species). Aggression, they argue, is universal in animal species. This in itself suggests that violence has survival value. It increases the individual animal's access to resources, deals with conflicts between individuals, and promotes success in passing on genes to future generations. Even intraspecies predation and cannibalism (which Plutchik and van Praag claim occur in sixty human societies and one-thousand three-hundred animal species) serve to regulate population size in relationship to available food supplies. Suicide may serve a similar adaptive function because, according to Plutchik and van Praag (1990), both violence against others and suicide increase in overcrowded human populations.

Similarly, Himmelhoch (1988; cf. Plutchik and van Praag 1990; van Praag and Plutchik 1986) suggests that suicide attempts with low-lethality weapons (such as slashing one's wrists), self-treatment with alcohol and drugs, and even psychosis itself in the form of mania or pathological levels of elation can contribute to the struggle for survival by reducing the helplessness and hopelessness that impel the individual toward actual suicide.

Plutchik and van Praag (1990) use both clinical and ethological evidence to develop a theory of suicide and violence that has strong though apparently unrecognized affinities with the nineteenth-century perspective of Enrico Ferri (1925; Tarde 1883; Zimmern 1896), who also used animal behavior as a basis for theorizing about human violence. Plutchik and van Praag (1990), much like Ferri, distinguish between factors that trigger aggressive impulses (Ferri's forces of production), while Ferri's forces of direction correspond to "a separate set of variables [that] determines whether the goal of aggressive actions will be other people or oneself" (Plutchik and van Praag 1990, 60).

Plutchik and van Praag argue that the triggers that set off aggressive impulses are similar across animal species, including humans. These include threats and challenges by other members of the same or another species, changes in hierarchical status arrangements such as pecking orders, and "various losses" (Plutchik and van Praag 1990, 59). In humans, they argue, the effects of these triggers on overt acts of violence against self or others are amplified by such factors as the availability of weapons, a tolerant attitude toward the expression of violence, and "pervasive feelings of distrust" (1990, 59). On the other hand, the effects of the triggers are attenuated by close family ties, a timid personality style, and appeasement on the part of others.

The countervailing forces identified by Plutchik and van Praag affect the goal or target of aggression. Aggression will be directed toward the self in the presence of depression; work, medical, or family problems; feelings of hopelessness; and recent psychiatric symptoms; but it will be directed toward others in the presence of impulsivity, recent legal problems, menstrual problems in women, or "recent life stresses" (1990, 61).

Suicide is also included in other sociobiological theories of homicide, as exemplified by the work of Martin Daly and Margo Wilson (1988). Daly and Wilson begin with the question of why, as many studies (for example, Wilbanks 1984; Wolfgang 1958b) have found, family members are the most common class of victims of violence, including murder. Intrafamilial homicide constitutes something of a paradox for evolutionary theory, because it flies in the face of expectations based on the concept of inclusive fitness. From this point of view, psychological mechanisms have evolved through natural and sexual selection that favor behaviors contributing to both one's own reproductive success and to the promotion of the reproductive success of others (such as siblings and offspring) who carry copies of one's genetic material. Indeed, according to Daly and Wilson (1988), all adaptive action involves either *resource accrual* or *nepotism*, a tendency to expend effort and other resources creating blood relatives and doing those things that will promote their fitness. "So," Daly and Wilson ask, "if the motivational mechanisms of all creatures have evolved to generate behavior which is effectively nepotistic, . . . what on earth are we doing killing relatives?" (1988, 18).

Daly and Wilson attempt to resolve this paradox by asking which relatives we kill and in what situations. Killing one's spouse or in-laws is more common than murdering relatives who share one's genes; and among blood relatives, the greater the proportion of genes held in common, the lower the homicide rate. Those killings of consanguinal relatives that do occur, Daly and Wilson argue, are often explainable in terms of resource accrual. Fratricide, for example, frequently results from disputes over resources such as inherited land or titles. Similarly, infanticides can be interpreted in terms of "discriminative parental solicitude." As the result of a cost-benefit analysis, newborn children may be killed if their paternity is in doubt, if they are deformed or sickly and unlikely to reproduce, or if they are likely to consume limited resources needed for other children, born or unborn, who might be expected to produce greater fitness benefits for their parents (Daly and Wilson 1988, 42–44). Parents murder their step-children, who do not share their genes, at a higher rate than they do their biological offspring.

Daly and Wilson incorporate suicide into their evolutionary theory of homicide by identifying it with despair, depression, and their own evolutionary-based definition of mental incompetence. Suicide, they found, is far less common among parents who commit infanticide than among those who kill their older children, in whom they have greater investments. Noting that parental homicides of older children are often conceived by parents as acts of love committed by those who despair for their children as well as themselves, Daly and Wilson suggest that such behavior by either sex is viewed by police as symptomatic of mental disorder because it runs counter to self-interest:

> Here as elsewhere, it seems that the sorts of cases that are simultaneously rare and seemingly contrary to the actor's interests—in both the Darwinian and the commonsense meaning of interest—also happen to be the sorts of cases most likely to be attributed to some sort of mental incompetence. The validity of such attributions is of course questionable, and one may reasonably wonder whether the label "insane" tells us more about the labeler than the labeled. But either way, the state that is called "insanity" invites an evolutionary theoretical interpretation: We identify as mad those people who lack a species-typical nepotistic perception of their interests or who no longer care to pursue them (Daly and Wilson 1988, 80).

In general, Daly and Wilson argue, the more a homicide opposes evolutionary interests, the more likely it is to be followed by suicide or a verdict of not guilty by reason of insanity:

> This evolutionary psychological view of the disordered mind can be used to predict the sorts of cases in which the killer is especially likely to commit suicide or to be found insane. Whichever category of homicides is most clearly contrary to the killer's fitness interests is the madder act; it should be unlikely to occur at all, and when it *does* occur, it should be relatively likely to be followed by suicide or an insanity verdict. The obvious example is killing kinfolks: To kill one's relative is madder than to kill one's nonrelative, and is . . . both relatively rare . . .

and relatively likely to be followed by suicide or an insanity verdict. . . . Other comparisons reveal the same pattern (Daly and Wilson 1988, 267).

Thus, evolutionary biology specifies the conditions under which homicide and suicide tend to be found together and links these cases to attributions of mental incompetence. A similar linkage between suicide, aggression, and mental illness may be found in studies guided by the medical model.

SUICIDE, AGGRESSION, AND MENTAL DISORDER

From the standpoint of psychiatric medicine, "most people who kill themselves are mentally ill at the time" (Goodwin and Runck 1992, 2). Black and Winokur (1990), for example, conclude that over 90 percent of suicide victims are mentally ill. Indeed, they contend that "major psychiatric illness is, for practical purposes, necessary for . . . suicide" (Black and Winokur 1990, 136).

While it may be that such statements tell us "more about the labeler than the labeled" (Daly and Wilson 1988, 80; quoted previously), the medical model is a highly legitimated and, indeed, officially sanctioned paradigm (Cockerham 1981; Freidson 1970). This paradigm regards the diagnostic categories outlined in the third edition of the *Diagnostic and Statistical Manual of Mental Disorders* (*DSM-III*) (American Psychiatric Association 1980) as objectively real disease states that (1) produce pain, discomfort, and suffering, and (2) are amenable to treatment by medical means (Cockerham 1981).[1]

The *DSM-III* diagnostic categories most often linked to suicide seem to be major depression, alcoholism, and schizophrenia (Goodwin and Runck 1992), though borderline personality disorder (Jacobs 1992), panic disorder (Goldblatt and Schatzberg 1992; Weissman, Klerman, and Markowitz 1989), and the post-manic phase of bipolar affective disorder (Goodwin and Jamison 1990) have also been implicated. Comorbidity—that is, the simultaneous presence of two or more mental disorders, as, for example, in schizophrenia with secondary depression—apparently increases suicidal risk interactively (Goodwin and Runck 1992; Murphy and Wetzel 1990; Weiden and Roy 1992). According to Stanley and Stanley (1990) the risk of suicide increases in a variety of psychiatric disorders, with roughly comparable suicide rates across diagnoses. Goodwin and Runck suggest that "it is not the illness itself—that is, the underlying pathopsychological or pathophysiologic process specific to the illness—that conveys the risk of suicide" and that "an underlying suicide risk factor (or factors) may cut across all diagnostic classes" (Goodwin and Runck 192, 14).

Psychiatric researchers have identified a long list of potential candidates for status as underlying risk factors, but they remain unable to identify the single generalized hazard underlying suicide regardless of psychiatric diagnosis. Serotonin deficiency in the central nervous system, one of the major contenders, is especially relevant to the stream analogy because it suggests the existence of a common biological source of both suicide and homicide.

The Biochemistry of Cerebrospinal Fluid

There has been considerable research by behavioral neurologists (Pincus and Tucker 1978) relating suicidal and aggressive behavior, including homicide, to central nervous system biochemistry. Some studies (such as Goldblatt and Schatzberg 1992) are primarily concerned with finding an effective psychopharmacological treatment for suicidal ideation, poor impulse control, and aggressiveness, which tend to occur together in such psychiatric conditions as antisocial personality disorder (Weiss and Stephens 1992).

Several medications have been suggested as potential "magic bullets." Lithium carbonate, in particular, is frequently recommended for both depression and the angry and irritable affect sometimes associated with mania and bipolar disorders (Goldblatt and Schatzberg 1992). The faith in lithium as a pharmacological panacea exhibited by some researchers seems to know no bounds. As an admittedly extreme example, Gerhard N. Schrauzer and Krishna P. Shrestha (1990) conducted a study of the relationship of crime and suicide rates to levels of naturally occurring lithium in the communal water systems of twenty-seven Texas counties. Rates of homicide, suicide, rape, robbery, possession of hard drugs, and total crime were significantly higher in low-lithium than in high-lithium counties after controlling for population density by eliminating the counties containing the state's four largest cities from the sample. The relationships between lithium level and possession of marijuana, theft, motor vehicle theft, driving under the influence, drunkenness, and assault were either inconsistent or statistically insignificant. Incredibly (to us), after noting that lithium levels in human hair differentiate violent offenders from nonviolent controls, Schrauzer and Shrestha draw policy implications from their findings that evoke thoughts of a monolithic therapeutic state:

> Low-dose lithium supplementation could become an effective method of violence reduction in institutionalized subjects. In

the general population, the lithiation of the communal water supplies could provide a simple, safe, and economical means of reducing the incidences of violent crimes, suicides, and the use of narcotics (Schrauzer and Shrestha 1990, 112).

Lithium apparently reduces aggressive and self-destructive behavior and symptoms of depression and mania through its effects on phosphoinositide-mediated neurotransmission (Worley et al. 1988). Fluoxetine (Prozac) and tryptophan, two other medications that have been widely used in the treatment of depression and may soothe impulsive aggressive outbursts as well, work by improving serotonin functioning in the central nervous system (Goodwin and Runck 1992; Goldblatt and Schatzberg 1992; S. N. Young 1990). Fluoxene is a serotonin reuptake inhibitor (Goldblatt and Schatzberg 1992), while naturally occurring dietary tryptophan is the primary precursor of serotonin (Brown, Bleich, and van Praag 1991). At least one cross-national study (Mawson and Jacobs 1978) suggests that nations with corn-based diets, which are deficient in tryptophan, have higher homicide rates than those whose diets are based on rice or wheat.

Both drugs have proved controversial, and no one has argued for adding them to communal water supplies. Tryptophan (or an impurity in the brands of tryptophan sold in the United States) has been implicated in eosinophilia-myalgia syndrome, a painful and sometimes fatal muscle and joint disease (S. N. Young 1990); and fluoxetine *may* have the paradoxical effect in some patients of promoting preoccupation with suicide (Teichner, Glod, and Cole 1990; cf. Ahmad 1991). Nonetheless, the use of fluoxetine and l-tryptophan, a synthetic isomer of dietary tryptophan (S. N. Young 1990), follows theoretically from studies of the neurological correlates of aggression (including homicide) and suicide. The focus of these studies, many of which are collected in Mann and Stanley (1986; see especially the articles by Gerald L. Brown and Frederick K. Goodwin and by Richard A. Depue and Michele R. Sproont), is on metabolites of serotonin and the neurotransmitters gamma-aminobutyric acid, norepinephrine, and dopamine. In a series of studies beginning with the work of Marie Åsberg and her associates in 1976, 5-HIAA (5-hydroxyindoleacetic acid), a major metabolite of 5-HT (serotonin), has been found to be depressed in the cerebrospinal fluid of violent suicide attempters (those who used methods other than the ingesting of chemicals or slashing the wrists). HVA (homovanillic acid), a dopamine metabolite, is apparently unrelated to aggression; and research on the effects of MPHG (3-methoxy-4-hydroxyphenylglycol), a metabolite of norepinephrine, has yielded mixed results.

The results linking 5-HIAA to suicide have been mirrored by those for murderers, for whom 5-HIAA seems to be depleted only among those who have murdered sexual partners (as contrasted to nonemotional and nonviolent murderers)(Lidberg et al. 1985). Brown and van Praag conclude that "5-HT dysfunction may be related to suicidality in depression, to suicidality in general, and, finally, to dysregulation of aggression, possibly as a result of impulse control disorder, rather than to depression itself as a single diagnostic or nosological entity" (Brown and van Praag 1991, 5; cf. Brown and Goodwin 1986, 181).

We have reviewed these clinically based studies because they seem to us to point to parallels and areas of potential rapprochement between sociological and medical paradigms. When viewed in the context of the stream analogy, these studies suggest that forces of production may operate at levels of analysis ranging from the social structural and cultural to the genetic and biochemical. Specifically, both lithium depletion and depressed levels of 5-HIAA in cerebrospinal fluid are apparently associated with both suicidal and homicidal tendencies, and there are theoretical reasons for suggesting that tryptophan and lithium function in a roughly similar manner.

It is beyond either our expertise or the scope of this book to suggest detailed linkages across levels of analysis. Nonetheless, we strongly suspect that structural, cultural, and situational factors act as triggers that affect biological states. Thus, we would expect frustrating experiences to reduce levels of serotonin metabolites in cerebrospinal fluid independently of dietary deficiencies in tryptophan and lithium. Indeed, biochemists Keith Wood and Alec Coppen (1980) interpret some studies of serotonin metabolism as suggesting that stress reduces the amount of tryptophan (and presumably serotonin) that depressed patients can maintain in their bodies.

HOMICIDE, SUICIDE, AND ACCIDENTS

Along with homicide and suicide, accidents are the third external cause of deaths that together are the leading cause of mortality for over one-half of the normal life span in industrialized nations, including the United States (Holinger 1980; Rockett and Smith 1989). Like homicide and suicide, accidents claim the lives of more men than women (Greenberg, Carey, and Popper 1987). Accidents resemble suicide more than homicide, however, by producing higher mortality rates among the elderly (Kivela 1985). While the bulk of attention has been on building theoretical and empirical links between homicide and suicide, a small but increasing number of investigators argue that accidents share important characteristics with other forms of violent, or externally caused, deaths (Porterfield 1960; Weiss 1976).

One of the more important empirical studies examining similarities and differences between homicide, suicide, and accidental deaths is Roger Lane's 1979 *Violent Death in the City*, an investigation of deaths from external causes in nineteenth-century Philadelphia. From 1839 to 1901, the mortality rates from homicide in Philadelphia varied directly with those from accidents and inversely with those from suicide. Furthermore, significant changes in all three indices occurred during the 1870s, with fatalities from suicide sharply increasing and those from homicide and accidents falling. Expanding on Henry and Short's framework, Lane argues that the propensity to engage in homicidal behavior is rooted in the same personality characteristics that lead to accidents:

> The personal habits that may lead to manslaughter are essentially the same as those that lead to fatal accident: alcoholic recklessness, thoughtless reflex action, a challenge fiercely accepted. . . . On the other hand, persons who attempt suicide are more likely to be introverted and exhibit a high level of self-control, traits that are opposite those linked to homicide and accidents (Lane 1979, 118).

Consistent with Whitt and his colleagues (1972), Lane attributes the historical shift in the causes of external fatalities (from homicide and accidents to suicide in the 1870s) to societal changes that arrived with the industrial revolution. In brief, Lane's view is that the supervision by foremen, the demands of a precise work schedule, and the coordination of large numbers of workers in factories left little room for the spontaneity and recklessness that often lead to accidents and killings. This transformation shaped an individual who was able to exist, and in some cases to thrive, in the bureaucratic world of the plant and the office. Incidentally, this new individual was also more likely to direct violence inward toward the self instead of outward toward others.

Although Lane's study is historical, he believes that it offers insight into the low SHRs for blacks in the United States. Limited evidence suggests that the SHR for Philadelphia blacks was similar to that for many white ethnic groups, such as the Irish, prior to 1870. With industrialization, however, the SHRs for white groups uniformly increased, indicating a greater propensity for suicide over homicide, while that for the city's black population remained unchanged. The stability in the black SHR is consistent with Lane's thesis of the effect of industrialization because blacks in Philadelphia were systematically excluded from factory jobs until the 1900s.

An important advocate of merging research on accidents with that focused on homicide and suicide is Paul C. Holinger. His theoretical viewpoint, derived from psychoanalytic theory, however, departs significantly from that of Lane. Following Marvin Wolfgang (1959), who asserts that a significant number of homicides are victim-precipitated, Holinger (1979) argues that self-destructive tendencies are an important source of homicide and accidents as well as suicide. For Holinger, then, many accidents and homicides are disguised suicides: "Clinical data repeatedly demonstrate that homicides (people who are killed, not the killers) and accidental death as well as suicides result to some extent from various conscious and unconscious self-destructive motives in the victim" (Holinger 1987, 202).

This view is, of course, opposite that of frustration-aggression models, which assume that suicides are displaced homicides. The stated purpose of Holinger's 1987 book, *Violent Deaths in the United States* is to investigate the role of self-destructiveness in externally caused fatalities. He does not see self-destructiveness as the sole cause of violent death, deny the role of violent aggression in homicide, or excuse perpetrators from responsibility for their acts. Yet he emphasizes that the part played by the eventual victim in homicides and accidents has received too little attention from social scientists.

Summarizing trends in violent deaths, Holinger notes that since 1900 homicide rates have gradually increased, with a peak occurring during the Great Depression of the 1930s. Following World War II, homicide rates decreased through the 1950s, but a steady upswing beginning in the 1960s has produced rates that are currently among the highest recorded for many age and sex groups. Holinger points to similar trends for suicide rates, which were especially high during the 1930s. Accidents present a more complicated pattern, with motor vehicle fatalities, not surprisingly, increasing since 1900. The trend data for motor vehicle fatalities are suspect, however, because Holinger fails to adjust rates for the number of motor vehicles, miles of paved roads, or miles driven, factors that can be expected to affect the death rates from motor vehicle accidents. Mortality rates from other types of accidents have fallen, perhaps because improvements in emergency medical care have increased the survival rate among victims.

Of course, homicide rates are higher for men than women at a ratio of about four to one, and the peak rates for both men and women are found between the ages of twenty and thirty-four. Suicide rates are higher for men than women, but the margin is closer than for homicide.

Reflecting the gender differences found for both homicide and suicide rates, accidental deaths are approximately five times higher among men. Mortality from accidents is also higher among non-whites than whites and resembles homicide more than suicide in that the rates are twice as high for younger than for older persons.

In examining the patterns of violent deaths, Holinger emphasizes that some demographic segments of the population, notably men, are at greater risk of meeting death from each of the three external causes. Although exceptions are recognized, he argues that homicide, suicide, and accident death rates fluctuate together, thereby contradicting the law of inversion. Although Holinger reviews Durkheim's and Henry and Short's works for possible insights into the presumed covariation between externally caused deaths, he eventually settles on Marvin Wolfgang's 1959 notion of *victim precipitation*, viewed as a behavioral expression of an internal urge toward self-destruction, as offering the best explanation. In an interesting twist for public policy designed to reduce violent deaths, Holinger believes that potential victims can be taught how to recognize and control unconscious suicidal tendencies.

Although Holinger's work produces several interesting hypotheses about changes in sources of violent deaths over time, it has serious methodological limitations (Stack 1988). There are no attempts at multivariate analyses, and his presentation of data consists of page after page of time series plots of violent death rates for various population categories. Furthermore, there is no attempt to test the presupposition that the urge to self-destructiveness is an important factor in levels of homicide and accidental deaths as well as suicide. His data do, however, challenge the assumption that homicide and suicide vary inversely, showing that the two measures have risen and fallen in tandem for much of the twentieth century in the United States. This pattern does not present a serious challenge to the theoretical perspective developed in this monograph because we do not assume the law of inversion to be invariant (a fact that was recognized by the moral statisticians). The integrated model in chapter 6 can accommodate positive or negative relationships between homicide and suicide, either in time-series or cross-sectional data.

Although Lane and Holinger have offered the most extensive analyses of the relationships between homicide, suicide, and accidental deaths, there are several other contributions to this line of research. Michael R. Greenberg, George W. Carey, and Frank J. Popper (1987) examine statewide rates of homicide, suicide, and accidents among white youth (fifteen to twenty-four years of age) in the United States from 1939 through 1979. When all three types of violent deaths are combined,

Western states have the highest and Northeastern states the lowest death rates. The authors' explanations for these findings are based on Durkheim's theory of suicide, which focuses on the level of social integration. Divorce rates, unemployment rates, and the migration rate—measures of a lack of social integration—were all directly correlated with higher rates of violent deaths. Because all three types of violent deaths may be alternative victim-precipitated responses to stress, the authors argue that they must be investigated together. In a study that reaches a different conclusion, however, Ira Wasserman (1984b) finds that presidential elections, national events that are presumed to enhance social integration, have no effect on homicide, suicide, or accidental death rates once other factors are controlled.

There has been a smaller number of cross-national studies that investigate the relationships between accidents, homicides, and suicides. Lincoln Day (1984) examined all deaths from external causes in forty-one countries from 1951 through 1977 and found that there was a high level of consistency for both the overall level and pattern of deaths, especially among men. Women's rates of auto accident deaths increased substantially during the period under study, most likely because women drove more during the later than the earlier years. Day does not favor a single explanation for the patterns of violent death but believes that the availability of means, changes in gender roles, social disorganization, and the culture of violence are important factors.

Following Holinger's perspective, S. L. Kivela (1985) examines the role of self-destructive tendencies in homicide, suicide, and accidents for persons age sixty-five and over in Finland between 1951 and 1979. As expected, most of the fluctuation in mortality statistics occurred for accidents, with a decrease in deaths due to falls and other causes and an increase in auto accidents through the 1960s. Suicide rates increased slightly over time, with a peak in 1964, and homicide rates held relatively constant. Contrary to Holinger's thesis, a strong positive correlation between mortality rates was noted only for suicide and motor vehicle accidents among men. Thus, Kivela concludes that although some support was found for self-destructive tendencies among males, his results should be accepted with caution.

Finally, Ian R. H. Rockett and Gordon S. Smith (1989) examine mortality rates from homicide, suicide, motor vehicle accidents, and falls in the United States, France, Japan, West Germany, and the United Kingdom. Accidents accounted for two-thirds to four-fifths of all deaths from external causes in the countries studied. Suicide rates varied greatly among these countries, while homicide was a major cause of death only in the United States. Rockett and Smith contend that handgun ownership is a major factor for the production of higher homicide rates in the United States. They overlook the fact, however, that the rate of gun ownership may also have a similar effect on suicide rates (Lester 1990b).

Have the proponents of extending investigations of lethal violence to include accidental deaths established the validity of their position? The idea that accidental deaths are a purposeful, although perhaps unconscious, mode of self-destruction is intuitively appealing in some cases; and there are correlations between the level of accident fatalities and other types of externally caused mortality within certain demographic categories. This perspective is also finding widespread acceptance in the public health field, both in the United States and abroad. Deaths and injuries from homicide, suicide, and accidents are the focus of the National Center for Injury Prevention and Control, a component of the Centers for Disease Control, and the location of the Second World Conference on Injury Control in Atlanta, Georgia, marks the importance attached to this area of research by public health professionals in the United States.

After substantial thought and several discussions, we have concluded that at this time the theoretical foundation and empirical findings from this growing body of research—that is, injury control—are insufficient to warrant merging investigations of the rate of accidental deaths with studies on homicide and suicide. Currently, research on accidental deaths suffers from a problem of data quality that is more severe than those involved with research on homicide and suicide. Deaths categorized as homicide or suicide are far from homogeneous events, but the variation in the circumstances surrounding incidents of accidental deaths is enormous. Most deaths from motor vehicle and airplane crashes, boating mishaps, falls, electrocutions in the bathtub and elsewhere, mining disasters, drownings, and train derailments may be defined as accidents. It is unlikely that involvement in such a diverse array of fatal occurrences can be attributed to an underlying urge toward self-destruction, as suggested by Holinger. Furthermore, the covariation between different forms of external causes of death may be explainable by factors other than suicidal tendencies. For example, age is directly related to suicide rates and accidental deaths from some causes, such as falls, among males. The elderly may or may not be more likely to fall than younger persons, but their greater physical frailty increases the chances that a fall will prove fatal. Younger males have the highest rates of death from homicide and motor vehicle accidents, but this convergence may reflect a higher willingness to take risks (Wilson and Daly 1985), perhaps based on the common belief among the young that they are invincible.

Theoretically, we see little to be gained from suggesting that young men are particularly susceptible to unconscious suicidal tendencies.

Other methodological problems hamper efforts to understand the etiology of accidental deaths (Lane 1979). For suicides, the perpetrator and victim of the fatal act are, of course, the same individual. For criminal homicide there is a strong consensus that the social characteristics of offenders and victims are similar, except that a majority of women victims are killed by men. With accidents, however, there is little assurance that the deceased is the person responsible for the fatal incident (a fact that can be easily discerned from the frequent prosecution of the living for motor vehicle homicide) or that the perpetrator has much in common with the victim. This lack of information on responsible parties in mortality data is a major problem for calculating valid rates of accidental deaths for different age, race, and sex groups in the population.

An additional reason for our decision to limit the scope of the model outlined in chapter 6 to homicide and suicide derives from our primary purpose in writing this book. Our intent is to revive interest in an important but neglected paradigm for studying homicide and suicide. To expand the model to include accidental deaths is likely to detract from this goal. We have not firmly closed the door on the idea that all deaths due to external causes should be investigated from a single model. Notably, Lane's suggestion that particular personality traits may be common sources of homicide (and perhaps suicide) and some types of accidents deserves further attention. Such an undertaking, however, lies outside the focus of the current work.

Although studies of lethal violence in the 1970s and 1980s lacked a common theoretical perspective (many lacked *any* theoretical perspective) and focused on a broad number of research questions, the literature did produce some consistent empirical findings, many of which reinforce those of early investigators. First, although there are exceptions to the law of inversion (a fact well recognized by Durkheim and other early scholars), a negative correlation between homicide and suicide rates is more common. Furthermore, this inverse relationship has been reported for units of analysis ranging from nation-states to ethnic and other groups within a single society. Second, there is substantial evidence that social change associated with the industrialization process influences the direction of lethal violence so that suicides become proportionately more numerous as people leave agricultural occupations. Third, the comparative status ranks of groups within a society affects their pattern of violence. Specifically, minority groups generally have higher homicide and lower suicide rates than dominant groups. Also, there is limited evidence that the total volume of lethal violence is higher for minority groups. Existing findings on lethal violence for minorities should be viewed with caution at this time, however, because very few studies have been conducted outside the United States.

Unfortunately, there has been scant evidence of cumulative progress in developing an understanding of the sources of lethal violence or the factors that influence its direction during the past two decades. In part, this theoretical stagnation reflects the diversity of disciplinary backgrounds held by researchers with an interest in questions pertaining to lethal violence. Sociologists, anthropologists, psychologists, psychiatrists, historians, and medical and public health professionals have made notable contributions to the empirical literature in this field. We believe that an interdisciplinary effort is important to augmenting our understanding of lethal violence. But a unifying theoretical perspective, a set of commonly accepted concepts, and attention to related developments outside one's own discipline have been lacking. Investigations sometimes appear to have been planned in a vacuum, with researchers ignoring important studies in the same area, such as T. J. Young's 1990 study of homicide and suicide rates among Native Americans. All too often, investigators reinvent the wheel by emphasizing "newly discovered" facts that were accepted by the moral statisticians of the nineteenth century—for example, that the law of inversion is not invariant.

We believe that the pace of cumulative advances in research on lethal violence will be quickened by the establishment of an integrated theoretical perspective, or model, providing linkages between studies that appear in separate disciplines. Furthermore, the acceptance of a model with these characteristics is likely to augment both the proportion and number of empirical studies that view suicide and homicide as related phenomena.

In our view, there is no need to develop an integrated model of suicide and homicide from scratch. We contend that Henry and Short's work, if properly understood from the perspective of the stream analogy and updated to reflect developments in other areas (such as attribution processes), provides a model for investigating the social sources of lethal violence at the individual and aggregate levels. It can also provide some theoretical order for the empirical findings reviewed in this chapter and the previous one. The next chapter discusses recent developments in social psychology that are relevant to the model presented in chapter 6. In chapters 7 and 8, we attempt to demonstrate its utility for resolving long-standing debates in the field.

5

Social-Psychological Underpinnings of the Integrated Model

The devil made me do it.
    —Flip Wilson, c. 1973

In chapter 3, we suggested that Hugh P. Whitt's early statement (1968) of what we today call the integrated model was flawed by its use of locus of control (Rotter 1966) to predict the choice between suicide and homicide. At that time, Whitt (1968; cf. Whitt 1966; Whitt, Gordon, and Hofley 1972) maintained that internal control should be associated with the choice of suicide over homicide, but a series of empirical studies has since shown precisely the opposite. In both cross-national studies of suicide rates (Boor 1976) and investigations of suicidal ideation and behavior at the individual level (Lester 1991a; Melges and Weisz 1971), suicide seems paradoxically to be associated with external locus of control as measured by Julian Rotter's 1966 IE scale. Indeed, as we noted in chapter 3, David Lester (1989b, 1991a) uses such findings to forge a depression paradox theory of suicide that explicitly ties self-destruction to external locus of control.

The depression paradox noted by Lester (1989b, 1991a) was perhaps first noticed by John Lamont (1972a, 1972b), whose discussion of the problem is in the context of the apparent contradiction between D. A. Schwartz's 1964 theory of the paranoid-depressive existential continuum and research reported by S. I. Abramowitz (1969). Schwartz suggests that depressive persons should feel responsibility for what happens to them, but Abramowitz (1969; cf. Calhoun, Cheney, and Dawes 1974; Janoff-Bulman 1979; Miller and Seligman 1973) finds an empirical link between depression and external locus of control as measured by the Rotter (1966) IE scale. Lamont (1972a, 1972b) suggests that the problem lies with Rotter's scale. The *I* items, which measure internal control, are worded optimistically and the *E* items pessimistically. Thus, depressed subjects should chooose the *E* items because of their pessimism rather than because of any feelings of external control. In short, Lamont suggests that the IE scale is invalid; it measures pessimism rather than self-blame.

Lamont's resolution to the paradox is attractive because it suggests a way out of the dilemma posed by studies linking external locus of control to depression and suicide. Nonetheless, it seems to us more apparent than real. Pessimism, after all, implies the expectation that bad things are likely to happen in the future regardless of what one does. Thus, pessimism may be merely an expression of some aspects of external locus of control.

Recent convergences between attribution theory and psychiatry seem to point another way around the paradox. The beginnings of a resolution were identified in 1977 by Lyn Y. Abramson and Harold A. Sackheim, who coined the term *depression paradox*. Later, beginning in the late 1980s, Abramson and other attribution theorists began forging a synthesis between three independently derived theories of the relationships between hopelessness, depression, and suicide. Both the emerging synthesis and its parent theories focus on the implications of the meanings people attach to bad events. Its resolution of the depression paradox constitutes the social-psychological basis for the integrated model as we understand it today.

Abramson and Sackheim (1977) note that two seemingly contradictory characterizations of depression have coexisted since at least the second century A.D. One cluster of defining symptoms centers on such themes as hopelessness, helplessness, powerlessness, pessimism, and the sense of futility. The other stresses guilt, self-blame, self-deprecation, self-reproach, a sense of worthlessness, and the desire for self-punishment. According to Abramson and Sackheim, "the two perspectives of the symptoms of depression, as well as the theories they have generated, appear incompatible. . . . When these two perspectives are joined, a paradoxical view of depression emerges" (1977, 839).

Taken together, the two perspectives seem to be saying that depressives blame themselves for bad events that they believe they neither cause nor control. Abramson and Sackheim argue that "attributing personal responsibility for an outcome believed to be uncontrollable is illogical" (1977, 843). Nonetheless, they cite a number of studies in both experimental and clinical settings (such as Abramowitz 1969; Hiroto and Seligman 1975), which suggest that self-blame and feelings of uncontrollability are empirically linked in depressive subjects, and perhaps in normal individuals as well.

Given that the paradoxical pattern exists empirically, Abramson and Sackheim suggest a number of ways in which it might be resolved. The paradox might result from (1) semantic confusion on the part of theorists; (2) the falsity of one of the theories; (3) the existence of two separate groups of depressives, one characterized by self-blame and the other by feelings of uncontrollability; (4) the use by depressives of self-blame or uncontrollability to generate secondary gains (such as blaming themselves for getting into uncontrollable situations); or (5) the failure of depressives to grasp the illogic of their belief that they are both impotent and omnipotent at the same time.

Abramson and Sackheim's 1977 work alerted researchers to the existence of the depression paradox, but it did not arrive at a definitive resolution. While they suggest that some of the possible resolutions are more likely than others, they leave the final resolution to future research.

More than a decade later, the depression paradox undoubtedly still crying out for attention from the recesses of her unconscious mind, Abramson and several of her colleagues (Lauren B. Alloy, Gerald I. Metalsky, and others) found a solution in the conceptual distinction between helplessness and hopelessness. Abramson had been involved since its inception in a research program led by Martin E. P. Seligman designed to test the attributional reformulation of the learned helplessness theory of depression (Abramson, Seligman, and Teasdale 1978).

Helplessness implies a feeling of uncontrollability. Indeed, early statements of learned helplessness theory (such as Overmier and Seligman 1967; Seligman and Maier 1967) grew out of studies of the debilitating effects in dogs, cats, fish, and other animals of exposure to uncontrollable events. When the theory was extended to humans (Hiroto and Seligman 1975) and reformulated in attributional terms (Abramson, Seligman, and Teasdale 1978), it retained this earlier emphasis on uncontrollability, but it added the hypothesis that some of the symptoms of depression in humans (such as lowered self-esteem) result from the attribution to the self of responsibility for bad events. Thus, learned helplessness theory incorporates the depression paradox within itself.

In the late 1980s, Abramson, Alloy, Metalsky, and others began forging a second reformulation that retains much of the earlier theory and incorporates the perspectives of others working independently along similar lines (such as Aaron T. Beck, George W. Brown, and Tirril Harris). The new synthesis drops uncontrollability from consideration, replacing helplessness with hopelessness as the chief proximal cause of what it calls *hopelessness depression*. Helplessness and hopelessness are not the same thing. As Abramson, Metalsky and Alloy explain the distinction, hopelessness includes "(a) negative expectations about the occurrence of highly valued outcomes . . . , and (b) expectations of helplessness about changing the likelihood of occurrence of these outcomes (a helplessness expectancy). . . . Thus, . . . hopelessness is a subset of helplessness" (1989, 359).

The emerging synthesis is known as the cognitive stress-diathesis model, helplessness/hopelessness theory, or simply the hopelessness theory of depression (Abramson, Alloy, and Metalsky 1988; Abramson, Metalsky, and Alloy 1988, 1989; Alloy, Abramson, Metalsky, and Hartlage 1988; Alloy, Kelly, Mineka, and Clements 1990; DeVellis and Blalock 1992). Its central hypothesis is that there exists a causally defined subtype of clinical depression known as hopelessness depression. This type of depression results when stressful life events are interpreted through the lens of a depressogenic attributional style. Significantly, suicidal tendencies are among the symptoms posited as defining hopelessness depression.

As noted previously, the stress-diathesis model builds on earlier theories (Bebbington 1985), including Aaron T. Beck's (such as, Beck, Kovacs, and Weissman 1975; Beck 1986; Beck et al. 1990; see also Dulit and Michaels 1992; Weiden and Roy 1992) psychiatric model of the relationship between hopelessness, depression, and suicide and George W. Brown and Tirril Harris's (1978) more sociological approach to hopelessness and depression, as well as the reformulated attributional theory of learned helplessness (Abramson, Seligman, and Teasdale 1978). In Beck's work, hopelessness is conceptualized as a cognitive distortion in which the individual "systematically misconstrues his experiences in a negative way and, without objective basis, anticipates a negative outcome to any attempts to obtain his major objectives or goals" (Beck, Kovacs, and Weissman 1975, p. 1147). It is associated with affective states or moods that involve "despair," "pervasive negative expectations," "desire to escape from an apparently insoluble problem," or "a stable schema incorporating negative expectancies" (Beck 1986, 92–93). Although often associated with depression, Beck's hopelessness can exist independently of depression, and Beck has claimed that it "accounts for the relationship between depression and suicidal intent" (Beck, Kovacs, and Weissman 1975, p. 1148). Although he appears to have softened his position in recent years, he still maintains that hopelessness does a better job than comorbid depression in predicting suicide across all psychiatric diagnoses (Beck 1986; Beck et al. 1990; Weiden and Roy 1992).

The chief difference between Beck's approach and the attributional reformulation of Seligman's learned helplessness model in addition to the distinction between helplessness and hopelessness seems to be that learned helplessness theory interprets the attribution of helplessness as sometimes correct given the objective situation while Beck views hopelessness as a cognitive distortion, largely ignoring the question of why people should feel hopeless in the first place. When the learned helplessness perspective was extended during the late 1960s and 1970s to the examination of the effects of uncontrollable events on humans, researchers (such as Hiroto 1974; Miller and Seligman 1973; Seligman, Maier, and Geer 1968) began emphasizing the similarity between the concept of helplessness and Rotter's (1966) concept of external locus of control. Helplessness seemed to be a good predictor of most aspects of depression in humans (Seligman 1972, 1974, 1975), but it could not account for the loss of self-esteem that generally accompanies depressive states (Abramson and Sackheim 1977).

The inability of helplessness or uncontrollability to account for the loss of self-esteem was among the difficulties that led Abramson, Seligman, and Teasdale (1978) to reformulate the theory of learned helplessness under the umbrella of attribution theory (Heider 1958; Kelley 1967; Weiner 1972, 1974). In both the reformulated version of learned helplessness theory and the new synthesis, persons experiencing bad outcomes are seen as asking themselves *why* they are helpless (or hopeless); and the causal attributions they make influence their self-esteem as well as such other aspects of depression as retarded motivation to initiate voluntary responses, learning deficits, and lowered levels of emotional affect. Beck's earlier work had already suggested a link between attributions and lowered self-esteem in depressed patients by noting that "another symptom, self-blame, expresses the patient's notion of causality. He is prone to hold himself responsible for any difficulties or problems that he encounters" (Beck 1967, 21). Rotter (1966) regarded internal and external loci of control as generalized expectancies. His IE scale combines positive and negative outcomes in a wide variety of situational contexts. Learned helplessness theory and the emerging synthesis make finer distinctions. Crandall, Katkovsky, and Crandall (1965) had suggested earlier that locus of control for success and for failure may differ within the same individual. Their research (see also Antobrus 1973; DuCette, Wolk, and Soucar 1972; Gregory 1978; Mischel, Zeiss, and Zeiss 1974) suggests that perceived control over positive and negative outcomes may be largely independent of one another and that the two aspects of control may have different behavioral outcomes. Indeed, Whitt (1968) had speculated that suicidal persons would blame themselves for negative past outcomes but feel powerless to influence future positive outcomes.

Following the reformulated version of learned helplessness theory, the stress-diathesis model, like attribution theory in general, draws explicit distinctions between the causal attributions given to good and bad events and between events in the past or present (explanations, attributions, or locus of causality) and those in the future (expectancies) (Abramson, Seligman, and Teasdale 1978; Hill and Larson 1992; Peterson and Seligman 1984; Weiner 1985). A massive literature in the attribution theory tradition has documented the existence of hedonic bias or self-serving attributional bias (Heider 1958; Kelley 1967; Miller and Porter 1988; Weiner 1985), a tendency for most people to locate causality for success within the self while blaming failures on external causes. Taking credit for successes and denying blame for negative events should, theoretically, enhance self-esteem (Harvey and Weary 1981; Miller and Porter 1988). Both learned helplessness theory and the stress-diathesis model build on findings linking depression and lowered self-esteem to a pattern opposite to hedonic bias, one in which persons blame themselves for failure but attribute success to external causes (Miller and Porter 1988).

Attribution theorists have subdivided both internal and external locus of causality into categories based on finer distinctions. Internal attributions, for example, may emphasize the causal influence of either effort or ability (Heider 1958; Weiner 1985). Effort attributions link the outcome to some specific action of the individual (such as "I failed the test because I didn't study"), while ability attributions have more general implications for the nature of the entire self (such as "I failed the test because I'm stupid"). The effort versus ability distinction parallels the broader contrast between behavioral and characterological self-blame (Janoff-Bulman 1979).

Similarly, external causes may be impersonal forces such as luck, chance, or fate (Rotter 1966); specific other persons (Weiner 1974); situational factors such as task difficulty (Heider 1958); or impersonal institutions such as savings banks or governments (Peterson and Seligman 1984). More generally, Heider (1958) divides them into factors within persons and factors within the environment.

Researchers have argued that the structure of perceived causality contains several additional attributional dimensions, which operate in concert with locus of causality to influence both emotional and behavioral outcomes. Weiner (1985), for example, distinguishes between stable and unstable causes, between those that involve intent and those that do not, and between causes that are perceived as controllable and those that are perceived to be beyond volitional control. Abramson, Seligman, and Teasdale (1978) distinguish between causal attributions that are situation-specific and and those involving global causes that generalize across situations.

According to early statements of the attributional reformulation of the learned helplessness theory of depression, three dimensions of causal explanations are relevant:

> First, the cause may be something about the person (internal explanation) or something about the situation or circumstances (external explanation). Second, the cause may be a factor that persists across time (stable explanation) or it may be transient (unstable explanation). Third, the cause may affect a variety of outcomes (global explanation), or it may be limited just to the event of concern (specific explanation) (Peterson and Seligman 1984, 348).

Until the stress-diathesis model replaced the learned helplessness theory in the late 1980s, each of these three characteristics of explanations was seen as playing a role in generating symptoms of depression. Internal explanations of bad events, which imply self-blame, were hypothesized to contribute to the loss of self-esteem. The belief that the cause of the bad event is stable (in the sense that it is interpreted as likely to persist) and global (in the sense that it cuts across events) was seen as leading to the perception of future uncontrollability and to the symptoms of helpnessness that accompany depression. Thus, psychological depression results when people feel helpless—that is, when the stress associated with bad events is accompanied by internal, stable, and global explanations coupled with the expectation that future events will be uncontrollable.

Learned helplessness theory links internal, stable, and global causal attributions to cognitive or attributional styles. An attributional style is "a tendency or bias to make particular kinds of causal inferences, rather than others, across different situations and over time" (Alloy et al. 1988, 16). According to this perspective, persons who characteristically view bad events as stable, global, and internally caused should be more vulnerable than others to the onset of depression.

According to the stress-diathesis model, negative life events result in generalized hopelessness and the onset of hopelessness depression if the events are perceived to be important and they are attributed to stable and global causes. If the causal attribution is internal as well as stable and global, it will also produce the reductions in self-esteem that sometimes accompany hopelessness depression (Abramson, Metalsky, and Alloy 1989).

Up to this point, the differences between the stress-diathesis model and the earlier learned helplessness formulation are relatively minor. The chief differences so far are that the hopelessness theory de-emphasizes the uncontrollability dimension and suggests that the onset of depression does not require internal causal attributions. These differences do, however, resolve the depression paradox. There is no illogic in feeling that one is responsible for bad events in the past and simultaneously believing that the future looks bleak.

The two formulations also differ slightly in their conceptualizations of the relationships between stress (negative life events), attributional styles, and depression. The newer formulation argues that neither stress nor a depressogenic attributional style can, by itself, trigger the onset of hopelessness depression. Both stress *and* a cognitive diathesis (that is, predisposition to depression resulting from a depressogenic attributional style) are required. According to Abramson, Metalsky, and Alloy,

> Individuals who exhibit the . . . depressogenic attributional style should be more likely than individuals who do not to attribute any particular event to a stable, global cause and view the event as very important, thereby incrementing the likelihood of becoming hopeless and . . . developing . . . hopelessness depression. However, in the presence of positive life events or the absence of negative life events, [they] should be no more likely to develop . . . hopelessness depression . . . than people who do not exhibit this attributional style. . . . The . . . diathesis . . . operates in the presence, but not the absence, of negative life events (the stress) (Abramson, Metalsky, and Alloy 1989, 362).

Stated differently, the stress-diathesis model posits a statistical interaction between the stress and the diathesis as the source of hopelessness and hopelessness depression, one of the symptoms of which is suicidal ideation and behavior. If Whitt's early statement (1968) of the integrated model of suicide and homicide is reinterpreted along attributional lines, replacing his internal locus of control interpretation with one based on internal locus of causality (cf. Huff-Corzine, Corzine, and Moore 1991), the fit between the integrated model and the stress-diathesis theory is remarkable. Indeed, our current formulation of the integrated model (see chapter 6) and the stress-diathesis model may be regarded as two aspects of a single underlying theory of suicide, one dealing with the causes of suicide at the individual level while the other relates stress (frustration) and cultural and structural sources of attributional styles to the suicide rates of populations.

There is no similar close parallel in attribution theory to the prediction in the integrated model that homicide rates should be an interactive function of frustration and attributions of causality to external sources. Nevertheless, recent efforts to interpret such affective states as guilt, shame, pity, pride, and, especially, anger in attributional terms (such as Tangney, Wagner, and Gramzow 1992; Weiner 1985, 1986, 1988) suggest that emotional reactions in part reflect causal attributions. They are also related to what Weiner calls "outcome dependent-attribution independent" responses to the attainment or non-attainment of desired goals (Weiner 1985, 560). The primitive emotions of happiness, sadness, and frustration are based on perceived success or failure, while attribution-dependent emotions such as guilt, shame, or anger depend on characteristics of the perceived cause. Guilt is distinguished from shame in that, while both involve an internal locus of causality, guilt focuses on one's specific actions as a source of failure (behavioral self-blame) while shame involves characterological self-blame (internal, global, and stable attributions for negative events) (Janoff-Bulman 1979; Tangney, Wagner, and Granzow 1992). Extensions of the stress-diathesis model (Tangney, Wagner, and Granzow 1992) suggest that shame is linked more closely than guilt to depression because characterological self-blame redefines the entire self as bad.

Attributional studies (Averill 1982, 1983; Weiner 1985; Weiner, Graham, and Chandler 1982; cf. Pastore 1952) not surprisingly find that anger results from blaming others for one's misfortunes. Several dimensions of other-blame, including causality, responsibility, and blameworthiness (Tennen and Affleck 1990) have been identified. External locus of causality by itself is insufficient to produce anger. In addition, the external agent must be a person rather than some impersonal environmental force (cf. Heider 1958), and the other's role in causing the bad event must be seen as unjustified (Averill 1983). Intentional acts and accidents the other could have avoided carry the implication of blame (Averill 1983), while unintentional acts and acts attributed to lack of ability do not (Heider 1958). According to Heider, "personal responsibility then varies with the relative contribution of environmental factors to the action outcome; in general, the more they are felt to influence the action, the less the person is held responsible" (Heider 1958, 113). Thus, some intentional acts are not blameworthy if they carry with them a mitigating situational excuse or justification.[1] Weiner (1985; cf. Weiner,

Graham, and Chandler 1982) summarizes these findings by suggesting that anger results when negative outcomes are causally attributed to factors controllable by others.[2]

We know of no stress-diathesis theory of homicide and interpersonal violence, but we can suggest in broad strokes what one would look like. Anger would occupy a place comparable to that of self-blame in the stress-diathesis theory of depression, acting as the immediate cause of a subset of violent or aggressive behaviors. To the extent that aggression follows from anger (Averill 1983), negative life events should interact with an attributional style that incorporates other-blame (a diathesis or vulnerability factor for violence) to produce homicidal ideation and behavior. As in the hopelessness theory, neither bad events nor an other-blaming attributional style alone should be sufficient to produce homicide. Interpersonal violence should require both.

Attribution theory is largely silent about antecedents of particular explanatory styles. The attribution literature does offer a few suggestions, however, and a number of studies outside the attribution theory tradition permit inferences about some of the social sources of internal and external attributions, and perhaps about helplessness, hopelessness, and anger as well. The stress-diathesis model of hopelessness depression follows Brown and Harris (1978) by pointing to the importance of interpersonal factors, such as lack of social support, and developmental factors, such as the death of one's mother during early childhood, as vulnerability factors for hopelessness. They suggest that biological and genetic influences may play a part as well (Abramson, Metalsky, and Alloy 1989).

Fritz Heider (1958), in his early landmark statement of attribution theory, argued that both intention and the sense of "can," the latter of which affects the power to influence outcomes, are associated with the attribution of personal causality to self or others (as opposed to the impersonal causality of environmental influences). For Heider, hostile others can both harm the individual and want to do so. Since "can" implies power, it is attributed to those with high status in the group, whether the higher-status person is self or other.

Neither Heider nor the stress-diathesis model directly addresses the sources of self- and other-blame, though the implication can be drawn from Heider that self-blame should be a characteristic attributional style of high-status persons, while blaming others is more common among low-status individuals. Howard Tennen and Glenn Affleck (1990), in support of this view, list the authority, knowledge, and ability of the other as one of several situational factors contributing to other-blame. Others, they argue, are also likely to be blamed if the bad event is especially severe, if the other is physically present at the discrete starting point of the event, and if the other is neither well known nor well liked by the victim.

Tennen and Affleck's 1990 hypothesis that other-blame is more likely when the other is not well known is inconsistent with Averill's 1983 empirical finding that anger is most often felt toward friends and family members and least often toward strangers. Because the pattern identified by Averill closely resembles that found for homicides (Wolfgang 1958b; Riedel and Zahn 1985),[3] we suspect that Tennen and Affleck's hypothesis applies only when, as in their study, an external causal agent is readily identifiable and closely tied to a discrete negative event (such as rape, the death of a child under medical care, or an industrial accident).

Harold H. Kelley (1967), another of the founders of attribution theory, suggests that attributions of causality are made, in part, on the basis of perceived covariation. For example, conditions that are gradually getting better because of environmental changes outside one's control can "create a strong impression of self-control over events that are really externally controlled" (Kelley 1967, 219–20). This is, he argues, especially true if persons are rewarded for and consequently continue actions they just happen to have taken early in the trend. If things begin going badly, however, people try a series of different solutions, none of which is effective. In the absence of covariation of outcomes with their actions, they tend to make external causal attributions.

Outside the attributional tradition, a number of researchers ranging from Sigmund Freud (1915, 1917, 1923) to Harry Stack Sullivan (1956) have implicated self- and other-blame and the attendant emotions of guilt, anger, and rage in a variety of mental disorders. According to Leslie Phillips, "those who feel they have not met their obligations and who feel they are responsible for their actions turn against themselves in symptom manifestation; those who . . . feel others are to blame for the vicissitudes of their existence . . . tend either to turn against others, or avoid others who threaten them" (Phillips 1968, 146).

In the psychiatric literature, self-blame is most often associated with depression (see previous discussion) and other-blame with paranoia and paranoid states. Indeed, as already noted, D. A. Schwartz (1964) posits a paranoid-depressive existential continuum based on the attribution of responsibility to others or to self.

Sullivan (1956) comes close to defining his concept of paranoid dynamism in terms of other-blame. According to Sullivan,

It is by means of refined cognitive processes that the self-system develops the group of processes that make up the paranoid dynamism; and . . . the paranoid dynamism . . . comes with all the trappings of a great insight and illumination. In many cases . . . the person will report, "And then I saw it all!" . . . And the great thing is that finally a happy hypothesis has been received into awareness: It is not that *I* have something wrong with me, but that *he* does something to me. One is the victim, not of his own defects, but of a devilish environment. One is not to blame; the environment is to blame. Thus we can say that the essence of the paranoid dynamism is the transference of blame (Sullivan 1956, 146; his emphasis).

Sullivan links the beginnings of paranoid dynamism to differences in family cultures. "The products of one family," he points out, "will have great ingenuity in discovering how other people are to blame for their sins of omission and commission; and the products of another will be less clever at discovering scapegoats" (Sullivan 1956, 342).

A number of researchers from a variety of scholarly traditions have touched on the question of the relationship between culture, social structure, and the attribution of responsibility for bad outcomes. Edwin Lemert's classic 1962 study of paranoia and the dynamics of exclusion, for example, suggests that a paranoid world view may reflect quite real conspiracies by others to isolate and exclude someone whom they regard as a difficult person. Similarly, Hazel M. Hitson and Daniel H. Funkenstein (1959) suggest that a nonthreatening childhood environment produces a tendency for the child to view the world as something to be manipulated to one's own ends. If, on the other hand, the world is seen as a threatening place whose potentially harmful properties cannot be controlled, the flow of influence is from the environment toward the child, who comes to see himself or herself as an object acted upon by others. The former tendency, Hitson and Funkenstein argue, is manifested both in depressive disorders and in suicide, while the latter is expressed in paranoid disorders and in homicide. Boston (internal) and Burma (now Myanmar) (external) serve as their type cases.

Although Hitson and Funkenstein's 1959 approach, like that of attribution theory, is couched in psychological terms, the paranoid view of the world which they see as responsible for Myanmar's very high homicide rate closely resembles Walter B. Miller's 1958 characterization of lower-class focal concerns, Edward C. Banfield's 1958 treatment of the world views of southern Italian peasant farmers, and, indeed, Marvin E. Wolfgang and Franco Ferracuti's 1967 interpretation of the high homicide rates found in subcultures of violence existing in regional pockets in many societies.

Miller (1958) suggests that lower-class juvenile delinquency is a reflection of a cultural pattern, transmitted from generation to generation in the inner city, that emphasizes values and perceptions that predispose inner-city youth to engage in delinquent activity. One of the central elements of this culture is the belief in fate—the perception that one's outcomes are externally determined by people and forces beyond one's control. Miller links the development of these cultural patterns to the absence of father figures in the home for many lower-class males, who as a result emphasize toughness, smartness, and excitement during adolescence as a means of establishing their masculinity. It may be possible, as Miller suggests, to identify family structure or child-rearing practices as an explanation for the widespread tendency in certain social settings to attribute frustration to external causes and to express aggression extrapunitively. It seems more likely, however, that objective conditions in Myanmar or the realities of existence in inner-city areas of the United States give rise to cultural perceptions and values whose intergenerational transmission does not require some particular pattern of child-rearing practices or family structure to survive.

Banfield (1958) links the development of the expectation for uncontrollability among southern Italian peasants to their very real powerlessness: "A peasant cannot count on achieving anything by his own effort and enterprise. The conditions and means of success are all beyond his control. He may struggle to get ahead, but in the end he will probably be crushed by the insane fury of events" (Banfield 1958, 107). Banfield suggests that the perception of external locus of causality among the southern Italians is not only a reflection of the unpredictable and uncontrollable realities of their situation, but also a factor preventing the area from experiencing any appreciable economic development.

> The idea that one's welfare depends crucially upon conditions beyond one's control—upon luck or the caprice of a saint— and that one can at best only improve upon good fortune, not create it—this idea must certainly be a check on initiative. Its influence on economic life is obvious: one who lives in so capricious a world is not likely to save and invest in the expectation of ultimate gain. In politics, too, it must have an effect. Where everything depends upon luck or divine intervention, there is no point in community action. The community, like the individual, may hope or pray, but it is unlikely to take its destiny into its own hands (Banfield 1958, 109).

Banfield might have added that southern Italy has high homicide rates, at least by European standards, and low rates of suicide.

Marvin E. Wolfgang and Franco Ferracuti's 1967 work on subcultures of violence cites the stream analogy, Henry and Short's 1954 theory, and the inverse relationship between suicide and homicide, but finds frustration-aggression approaches of limited utility for studying violent subcultures and other large groups because of the difficulty in measuring frustration in populations. The subcultures of violence that they identify in such settings as Colombia and Sardinia legitimize the externalized expression of aggression and in some cases go so far as to require that wrongs be righted by violent means. Nonetheless, the recurring theme of external attributions of causality in such diverse settings as Myanmar, southern Italy, and inner-city areas suggests that alienation as powerlessness, hopelessness, learned helplessness, and external attributions of blame may be common features of subcultures of violence. Indeed, Hackney (1969) speculates that the low SHR of the American South reflects cultural patterns embodied in a style of life that he links to fundamentalist religion, structural conditions—such as poverty and subservience—and the historical experience of the region beginning in the late antebellum period. According to Hackney,

> in the search for a valid explanation of southern violence the most fruitful avenue will probably be one that seeks to identify and trace the development of a southern world view that defines the social, political, and physical environment as hostile and casts the white southerner in the role of the passive victim of malevolent forces. . . . Being southern, then, inevitably involves a feeling of persecution at times and a sense of being a passive, insignificant agent of alien or impersonal forces. . . . Historical experience has fostered a world view that supports the denial of responsibility and locates threats to the region outside the region and threats to the person outside the self (Hackney 1969, 924–25).

Both Hackney (1969) and Whitt (1968) add cultural factors to Henry and Short's (1954) rather limited inventory of the sources of variation in the choice between suicide and homicide. They argue for the existence of a causal link between social structure and culture, similar to that identified by Banfield (1958), not limited to childhood experiences. Following Max Weber's 1906 "Protestant Ethic" thesis, Whitt (1968; see also Whitt, Gordon, and Hofley 1972) argues that Protestant religious traditions lead to greater self-blame for frustration than is found in Catholicism and non-Western religions. Thus, the SHR should be (and is) generally higher in Protestant nations. Whitt also argues that economic development and industrialization serve to tame the environment and bring it under control, producing a tendency for persons to view their outcomes as coming from internal rather than external sources. Whitt (1968), Whitt, Gordon, and Hofley (1972), and Hackney (1969) find that in cross-national data the SHR varies directly with a variety of measures of development, industrialization, and modernization.

This chapter has outlined developments in attribution theory that we regard as the social-psychological underpinnings of the integrated model of suicide and homicide. Drawing on the stress-diathesis model of hopelessness depression; attributional studies of self- and other-blame, and of guilt, shame, and anger; we suggest that, at the individual level, both forms of lethal violence result from a combination of negative life events (frustrations, stress) with attributional styles that locate blame either in the self (suicide) or in others (homicide). In this sense, suicide parallels clinical depression while homicide has elements in common with paranoia. Indeed, we suggest that individuals who kill themselves and those who murder others should make causal attributions at opposite ends of the paranoid-depressive existential continuum, but both should find themselves in the grip of pervasive pessimism (that is, hopelessness) about their prospects for the future.

We then suggest some of the situational, cultural, and structural sources of the attribution of blame, including social class, social isolation, economic development, and religion. As Hackney's 1969 discussion of the American South suggests, historical factors may also play a part, and we should probably not exclude child-rearing practices from our inventory. This list is admittedly brief and only loosely documented. We suspect that such factors as gender differences in socialization and gender roles affect causal attributions and that marital status is implicated because those involved in family social networks can, more easily than the single, widowed, or divorced, find someone other than themselves to blame for their frustrations.

Thus, while this chapter has focused on individual psychology, it spells out some of the linkages between levels of analysis. Attribution theory, and in particular the stress-diathesis model of hopelessness depression, closely parallels the macrosociological theory of lethal violence to be presented in chapter 6.

6

The Integrated Model

What do you think our corpses are?
  —Agatha Christie, 1935

A corpse is a corpse.
  —Enrico Morselli, 1879

INTRODUCTION

In preparation for the two empirical studies to be presented in chapters 7 and 8, this chapter presents a formal specification of what we call the integrated model of lethal violence. Although a slightly different form of the model was initially proposed in the 1960s (Whitt 1966, 1968; see also Hackney 1969), it first became widely available to sociological researchers twenty years ago (Whitt, Gordon, and Hofley 1972).

Since that time, the integrated model has been subjected to periodic methodological criticisms (Schuessler 1974) and occasional misinterpretations (Stack 1982), which we attempt to answer by showing what the model can and cannot do. As a part of this response to the model's critics, we also address the theoretical and methodological issues raised by Jack Douglas (1967; see also Hendin 1964, 1969a, 1969b) against *all* theoretical approaches to suicide that rely on the statistical analysis of official data. These authors assume that it is impossible to develop and test generalizations about suicide that apply across cultures and subcultures. Finally, we turn to an examination of our strategy for testing the integrated model by applying it to cross-national variations in the currents of lethal violence and to regional differences in homicide and suicide rates in the United States.

MODELING THE CURRENTS OF LETHAL VIOLENCE

The analyses of data reported in this book make use of the integrated model of lethal violence, which grew out of the long history of suicide and homicide research reviewed in chapters 2 through 4. This model, a modified and extended version of Henry and Short's theory of suicide and homicide articulated by such researchers as Gold (1958), Whitt (1968), Hackney (1969), Unnithan (1983), Huff-Corzine, Corzine, and Moore (1991), and Unnithan and Whitt (1992), conceptualizes suicide and homicide as two alternative channels in a single stream of lethal violence. As Morselli (1879a, 1879b) and Ferri (1883–84) first suggested, the integrated model distinguishes two different sets of causal factors that operate together to generate variations in suicide and homicide rates. While one group of factors, called forces of production by Ferri (1895), is responsible for variations in the total volume of lethal violence, the second, Ferri's forces of direction, is responsible for the diversion of the currents of lethal violence into either the suicidal or the homicidal channel in the stream—the choice between suicide and homicide.

The total volume of "water" in the stream is represented in the integrated model by the lethal violence rate, or LVR, defined as the sum of the suicide rate and the homicide rate. Symbolically,

$$LVR = S + H, \tag{6.1}$$

where S = the number of suicides per one-hundred thousand people, and H = the number of homicides per one-hundred thousand people. The choice between suicide and homicide is represented by the suicide-homicide ratio, or SHR, obtained by dividing the suicide rate by the sum of the suicide rate and the homicide rate (that is, the LVR). Thus,

$$SHR = S/(S + H). \tag{6.2}$$

The task for research based on the integrated model is to identify the two sets of variables that act, respectively, as forces of production and forces of direction. Following the frustration-aggression approach, which dominated suicide-homicide research from 1949 through 1972, the forces of production are typically sought in socially patterned sources of frustration, stress, or negative life events such as structurally based economic inequality and anomie, which are perhaps best summarized by Feierabend and Feierabend's 1966 term *systemic frustration*.

The integrated model identifies forces of direction as structural conditions and cultural patterns that affect the attribution of responsibility for frustration. Unlike earlier statements of the perspective (Whitt 1966, 1968; Unnithan 1983; Huff-Corzine, Corzine, and Moore 1991; Unnithan and Whitt 1992), which relied on Rotter's 1966 concept of internal versus external locus of control, we now specifically link the choice between suicide and homicide to the concept of attributional (explanatory) styles developed in the literature on learned helplessness and the stress-diathesis (hopelessness) model of depression (such as Abramson, Seligman, and Teasdale 1978; Alloy, Lipman, and Abramson 1992; Hill and Larson 1992; Peterson and Seligman 1984). This places the integrated model's predictions for the choice between suicide and homicide firmly in the camp of attribution theory. More specifically, it regards the SHR as a product of situational and cultural factors that contribute to the development of explanatory styles which include causal explanations of bad events (frustrations) that are (1) internal, (2) stable, and (3) global. Bad events interpreted in this way are likely to generate self-blame cutting across negative experiences that are perceived as likely to be uncontrollable in the future (see chapter 5). The resulting learned helplessness (Peterson and Seligman 1984) and hopelessness (Beck 1986; Alloy, Lipman, and Abramson 1992; see chapter 5) may be expected to contribute to both depressed affect and a tendency toward suicide as opposed to homicide.

Designating forces of production (that is, patterned sources of frustration) as P and the forces of direction (that is, structural and cultural sources of variation in causal attributions) as D, the integrated model predicts that

$$LVR = a + bP + e_1 \qquad\qquad (6.3)$$

and

$$SHR = c - dD + e_2 \qquad\qquad (6.4)$$

where a, b, c, and d are constants, and e_1 and e_2 are errors in predicting the LVR and SHR.

Equations 6.3 and 6.4 represent the two general hypotheses upon which tests of the integrated model depend. In practice, P and D are unmeasured variables, each of which is affected by a set of measured variables tapping the extent to which populations are frustrated (P) or the characteristic ways in which their members tend to impute responsibility to self or others (D). The two sets of variables are not mutually exclusive. For example, social and economic inequality may both increase frustration for the depressed segments of a population *and* provide them with a readily identifiable external source of frustration. Our strategy in testing the integrated model in chapters 7 and 8 is to identify some of the variables in each subset rather than to attempt to create an exhaustive catalog. In essence, this book proposes a paradigm shift, leaving to future research the normal science task of fitting additional pieces into the puzzle and fleshing out details.

SOME IMPLICATIONS OF THE INTEGRATED MODEL

Although the integrated model traces one side of its ancestry to psychological theories such as psychoanalytic perspectives and attribution theory, it is not a theory of either suicide or homicide as an individual act;[1] nor, for that matter, is it, strictly speaking, a theory of suicide and homicide rates. Instead, it is a theory of the relationships of cultural and structural factors to the amount and type of lethal violence in human populations, as measured by a pair of composite variables (Schuessler 1974) that correspond to theoretical concepts derived from the stream analogy. These variables are constructed from and contain the same information content as suicide and homicide rates, but combining them into composite variables produces a shift in gestalt. Instead of generating hypotheses about suicide and homicide rates, the integrated model seeks to discover the sources of variation in the size of the stream of lethal violence and the sociocultural factors that divide its flow into two separate, suicidal and homicidal, channels.

There are nonetheless several implications for the study of suicide and homicide rates that follow from viewing lethal violence in terms of the integrated model and the stream analogy that underlies it. First, if variables in the set contributing to the production of lethal violence drop to such low levels that the stream dries up, there will be no suicide and no homicide, regardless of the magnitude of those variables that affect attributions of blame and are thereby responsible for the division of water into the two channels. Second, even if the stream has an ample supply of water due to the operation of forces of production, there will be no suicide if all the water is diverted into one channel, and no homicide if it is all directed into the other. While neither of these hypothetical situations is even remotely approached in large, real-world populations, they illustrate the point that both suicide and homicide rates depend upon both forces of production and those of direction.

Unlike alternative conceptualizations such as social disorganization theory, which focus only on forces of production, and theories in the Freudian tradition that stress only the impact of forces of direction upon the choice between suicide and homicide, the integrated model can deal with both positive and negative relationships between suicide and homicide. If forces of production remain constant while those of direction change, the relationship between homicide and suicide will be negative because the increased flow of water into one channel is diverted from the other. On the other hand, if forces of direction are held constant and, consequently, the relative sizes of the two channels remain unchanged, both channels will increase or decrease proportionately with any change in the total volume of water in the stream; and the relationship between suicide and homicide will be positive.

The concept of statistical interaction provides another way of understanding how the integrated model ties together the forces of production and direction and their respective impacts on suicide and homicide rates. It follows from equations 6.1 and 6.2 that the suicide rate of a population is the product of the SHR and the LVR. Similarly, the homicide rate is the product of the LVR and 1 minus the SHR, the proportion of the population that chooses homicide over suicide. Symbolically,

$$S = (SHR)\,(LVR) \tag{6.5}$$

and

$$H = (1 - SHR)\,(LVR). \tag{6.6}$$

It follows from equations 6.3 through 6.6 that both suicide and homicide rates are multiplicative functions of forces of production and forces of direction. Ignoring error terms (e_1 and e_2) and multiplying equation 6.3 by equation 6.4, we obtain

$$S = ac - adD + bcP - bdPD. \tag{6.7}$$

Similarly, multiplying equation 6.3 by 1 minus equation 6.4 yields

$$H = a(1 - c) + adD + b(1 - c)P + bdPD. \tag{6.8}$$

A note of caution should be inserted at this point. It is tempting to conclude from equations 6.3 through 6.6 and from the fact that all the informational content of the LVR and the SHR is also contained in the suicide and homicide rates themselves that one could simply do regression analyses of the relationships of such variables as social class or inequality to the LVR and the SHR and then multiply these equations together to obtain the regression equation predicting the suicide rate. It seems logical and easy, but it won't work unless the residuals in the equations predicting the LVR and the SHR are uncorrelated with one another. It can be shown that, even though equations 6.3 and 6.4 are least-squares solutions, equations 6.7 and 6.8 are not because of the behavior of the omitted error terms e_1 and e_2 (Whitt 1968, app. A).[2] Nonetheless, equations 6.7 and 6.8 express the integrated model's conceptualization of the relationship of suicide and homicide rates to forces of production and direction. In words, equations 6.7 and 6.8 say that the main effect on both the suicide rate and the homicide rate of the set of variables that act as structured sources of frustration (P) is positive while that of the set of sociocultural variables affecting the attribution of blame to sources outside the self (D) is negative for the suicide rate and positive for the homicide rate. A multiplicative interaction between frustration and the external attribution of blame also enters into the prediction of both suicide and homicide rates, as indicated by the crossproduct term bd in equations 6.7 and 6.8.

Statistical interaction is a situation in which the effect of one variable depends upon the value of another. Multiplicative functions are a special case of statistical interaction in which the joint effect of two independent variables is proportional to their product. This way of looking at the integrated model leads to a number of nonobvious conclusions that suggest that studies of either suicide or homicide rates in isolation from one another may overlook important factors that can affect their results. For example, the integrated model predicts that the attribution of blame for bad events has a greater effect on both suicide and homicide rates in settings characterized by high levels of frustration than it does in less frustrating environments. Similarly, frustration should have a greater effect on suicide rates than on homicide rates under conditions in which persons are culturally predisposed to take responsibility for their own bad outcomes. Conversely, frustration should be more closely related to homicide than to suicide rates under structural and cultural conditions encouraging external attributions of blame.

An additional implication, which is not only nonobvious but counterintuitive as well, is that if the integrated model is correct, it is possible for either suicide rates *or* homicide rates, but not both, to vary inversely with frustration. It is also possible for suicide rates to vary directly with *external* attributions of blame or for homicide rates to vary directly with *internal* explanatory styles. These relationships, of course, are precisely the opposite of what we would expect on the basis of most theories of suicide and homicide, including Henry and Short's 1954 theory.

In the context of the integrated model, an inverse relationship between frustration and the homicide rate can occur if an increase in frustration is accompanied by a shift toward the attribution of responsibility to the self rather than others (that is, internal explanatory styles). Although the LVR increases, the corresponding increase in the SHR may be larger—large enough, indeed, to produce a decrease in the absolute size of the homicide channel. The positive correlation between the business cycle and the homicide rate of black Americans reported by Henry and Short (1954) provides a possible example. As we noted in chapter 3, Henry and Short use variations in the business cycle as their only empirical indicator of frustration. When they find that the correlation between homicide and the business cycle is positive for blacks, they invoke the explanation that blacks are less deprived relative to whites during economic slowdowns than when economic times are good. In other words, decreasing economic inequality between groups during business recessions reduces the homicide rate of economically disadvantaged minorities by making them less deprived in *relative* terms. While we can accept the idea that minorities may suffer less severe losses than the white middle class during recessions, the logical implication of Henry and Short's argument is that blacks actually feel better off when the economy languishes than when it flourishes. This strikes us as stretching a point at best. The integrated model provides an alternative explanation that preserves at least part of Henry and Short's argument. It may be that economic recessions increase the LVRs of both races, but that for blacks recession also increases the SHR by reducing inequality and the externalization of blame as the gap between their incomes and those of whites shrinks. We are not arguing for this interpretation but instead offer it as a possible scenario in which the integrated model would be able to deal with an inverse relationship between sociocultural sources of frustration and homicide rates.

Similarly, Boor's 1976 data indicating a positive relationship between national suicide rates and scores on external locus of control obtained in national surveys does not necessarily contradict the integrated model. His locus of control data consist of results of administrations of the IE scale to college student samples from ten highly industrialized nations—Australia, Japan, New Zealand, Sweden, the United States, Canada, France, Israel, Italy, and West Germany (McGinnies et al. 1974; Parsons and Schneider 1974). We argued in chapter 5 that findings such as Boor's could be accommodated within the integrated model by replacing external locus of control with external attribution of causality for bad events. Let us for the moment, however, leave aside both this distinction and potential arguments based on the ecological fallacy (Robinson 1950). Boor's findings could have been generated by a situation in which (1) cross-national variability in frustration is greater than variability in locus of control and (2) frustration and external locus of control are positively correlated.[3] According to this scenario, as frustration increases across nations, the suicide rate also increases but less rapidly than the homicide rate. Despite the increase in the suicide rate with external locus of control, the SHR drops as the integrated model predicts it should.[4]

The integrated model also alerts us to look for curvilinear relationships of suicide and homicide rates to many of the variables (such as social class and inequality) used in previous studies of suicide or homicide. Although some theories of suicide, including Durkheim's (1897; see also Powell 1958),[5] include predictions or interpretations of curvilinear relationships, the integrated model makes explicit why such relationships are expected to exist. A curvilinear relationship is a statistical interaction of an independent variable with itself—that is, the effect of the variable changes in magnitude or direction across its range.

Because the two sets of variables posited by the integrated model are not mutually exclusive, some variables are seen as indicators of both frustration and locus of causality. For example, studies of the relationship between social class and locus of control (such as Battle and Rotter 1963) suggest that the tendency to attribute responsibility for outcomes to the self varies directly with position in the status hierarchy. Similarly, Walter B. Miller (1958) suggests that fate—that is, an external causal attribution—is a core element of lower-class culture. There is also ample reason to believe that lower-status persons experience both economic and symbolic frustrations as a result of their position in the hierarchy. Indeed, Albert K. Cohen (1955) suggests that the status frustrations of lower-class youth are translated into a Freudian reaction formation that leads them to reject middle-class values. Gresham Sykes and David Matza (1957) include denial of responsibility among the techniques used by lower-class delinquent youth to neutralize their guilt.

Given these relationships of frustration and locus of causality to social class, the integrated model may be able to reconcile the contradictory and puzzling results of studies linking suicide to status variables. As we noted in chapter 2, ecological studies of Northern cities by Cavan (1928), Schmid (1928, 1933), and Queen and Thomas (1939) invariably found high rates of suicide in "disorganized" inner-city neighborhoods and low rates in "better" areas. Porterfield (1952a) and Whitt (1966), however, found curvilinear relationships in Southern cities, where the highest rates were in neighborhoods at the two ends of the status continuum. Powell (1958) reports a similar U-shaped curve, but Henry and Short's 1954 analysis suggests the existence of a positive relationship. Attempting to resolve contradictory findings such as these, Wendling and Polk (1958) used techniques of social-area analysis to explore the relationship between suicide and social-class indicators in three California metropolitan areas. Their results showed a positive relationship in San Francisco, a negative relationship in the East Bay area, and no relationship at all in San Diego!

The integrated model attempts to resolve this hodgepodge of contradictory findings by predicting that social class should affect suicide and homicide rates via two different routes. The SHR should be positively related and the LVR negatively related to class position. Because social class is conceptualized as both a force of production and one of direction (a member of both sets P and D in equations 6.7 and 6.8), it follows that the relationships of social class to suicide and homicide rates should be curvilinear, taking the form

$$S = a - b_1C_p + b_2C_d - b_3C^2 + e_3 \tag{6.9}$$

and

$$H = a - b_1C_p - b_2C_d + b_3C^2 + e_4 \tag{6.10}$$

where C is some measure of social class whose effect on suicide and homicide has two components, one of which (C_p) results from its negative relationship with frustration and the other (C_d) from its negative relationship with external locus of causality. In words rather than equations, high frustration levels coupled with an external attribution of causality work together to produce a strong but decreasingly negative relationship between social-class and homicide rates. As social class levels increase, there is less and less lethal violence, and what violence there is tends increasingly to be expressed as suicide rather than homicide (cf. Whitt 1968).

In the case of the suicide-social class relationship, frustration and causal attributions work against one another. At low social-class levels, the suicide rate *may* be high if the high LVR more than compensates for the low SHR. High suicide rates *may* also be found at high social-class levels because, even though there is little lethal violence, virtually all of it is expressed as suicide rather than homicide. It is also possible for the relationship between social class and suicide to be either positive or negative throughout its range. On the other hand, if b_1 and b_2 are similar in magnitude and b_3 is low, there may be virtually no relationship between social class and suicide, despite strong relationships of social class in opposite directions to the LVR and the SHR. While this does not tell us what relationship between suicide and social class to expect in a given study, it at least gives us the satisfaction of knowing that all those contradictory results were not really so puzzling. Had the original researchers used the integrated model, we would be willing to bet they would have found no contradiction at all.

This rather lengthy digression on the integrated model's predictions for the relationships of suicide and homicide rates to social class variables has had two purposes. First, the example of social class illustrates the model's power both to make nonobvious predictions about curvilinear relationships and to resolve apparent contradictions in previous research. When the relationships of suicide and homicide to status variables are viewed through the lens of the stream analogy, we are able to see things that are invisible when we examine suicide and homicide in isolation from one another. A second purpose of the social class example is to prepare the reader for our treatment of inequality in the analysis of cross-national patterns of lethal violence in chapter 7. The integrated model treats inequality much as it does status variables, suggesting that it is implicated in both the production of violence and its direction. Thus, we expect similar patterns of curvilinearity in the relationship between inequality and homicide, and we are unable to predict at this point what to expect for its relationship to suicide.

Despite the possibility of making inferences from the stream analogy to some aspects of the behavior of suicide and homicide rates, the integrated model stands or falls on its ability to predict the size of the stream of lethal violence (the LVR) and the proportion of that violence expressed intropunitively as suicide (the SHR). Any inferences that can be made about suicide and homicide rates are strictly a bonus.

The failure to grasp the distinction between the integrated model and theories of suicide rates per se has led at least one critic astray (Stack 1983; see also Whitt 1985; Stack 1985). It may also be responsible for Schuessler's 1974 use of the integrated model as an example of the pitfalls of research using ratio variables.

THE CRITIQUE OF RATIO VARIABLES

Karl Schuessler (1973, 1974), building on earlier work by Karl Pearson (1897) and others, has spelled out the implications for multiple regression and path analysis of certain peculiarities in the behavior of ratio variables. A ratio variable is a compound variable formed by dividing one variable by another. For example, both the suicide rate and the homicide rate are compound variables computed by dividing the number of suicides or homicides by the population at risk, and then multiplying by a constant, usually 100,000. Ignoring the constant, which has no effect on the behavior of the rates, we have

$$S = s/p \text{ and } H = h/p, \tag{6.11}$$

where S is the suicide rate, H is the homicide rate, s is the number of suicides, h is the number of homicides, and p is the population at risk.

When we adapt Schuessler's general discussion of ratio variables to place it into the context of the integrated model, his analysis shows that the correlation between S and H will differ from the correlation between s and h. Similarly, the correlations of S and H to some third variable such as D or P will differ from the corresponding correlations of s and h to these same independent variables because the former but not the latter correlation includes as a component the relationship of population to the independent variable.

Using Pearson's 1897 proofs, Schuessler (1973) shows that the correlation between the rates S and H can be relatively large even if there is no correlation between the number of suicides and the number of homicides. The relationship between the suicide rate and the homicide rate depends on the joint relationships between the number of suicides, the number of homicides, and population size. The proofs, which involve somewhat unfamiliar concepts such as rel-variances, are daunting for the nonspecialist, and using the LVR and the SHR introduces additional complexities. Schuessler (1974) cites the integrated model (Whitt, Gordon, and Hofley 1972) as an example of a complex ratio variable whose peculiarities call for caution in interpretation:

> In their study of lethal aggression, Whitt, Gordon, and Hofley (1972) considered not only the suicide rate, x_1/x_3, and homicide rate, x_2/x_3, separately but also the sums of the rates $(x_1 + x_2)/x_3$, and the sum of the rates divided into the suicide rate, $x_1/(x_1 + x_2)$. The correlations among these variables . . . are of interest, since (except for the correlation between x_1/x_3 and x_2/x_3) they are not free to vary on their range, but rather are restricted by the statistical moments of x_1/x_3 and x_2/x_3. In fact, they are completely determined by the moments of x_1/x_3 and x_2/x_3. Since these correlations (with one exception) express statistical constraints as well as social and cultural circumstances, substantive interpretations should be made with caution. For the same reason, the re-

gressions of $(x_1 + x_2)/x_3$ and $x_1(x_1 + x_3)$ [*sic*] on some independent variable w should be interpreted with caution (Schuessler 1974, 393–94).

Equations 6.12 and 6.13, however, show that the SHR and the LVR are chain relatives (that is, the denominator of one ratio is the numerator of the other; see Neifield 1927):

$$LVR = s/p + h/p = (s + h)/p = v/p, \tag{6.12}$$

where $v = s + h$, and, because the p's cancel out,

$$SHR = s/(s + h) = s/v. \tag{6.13}$$

The status of the LVR and the SHR as chain relatives renders them tractable, given the work of Neifield (1927; see also Schuessler 1974; Kasarda and Nolan 1979), who concludes that such variables are generally negatively related to one another because the weight of the relvariance is negative.

Schuessler's critique (1973, 1974) was not intended to discourage the use of ratio variables but to demonstrate the implications of their definitional dependencies upon their components. He suggests a number of guidelines for using ratio variables in research. Translated for the problem at hand, his first rule holds that the relationship among components such as suicide and homicide rates and their relationships to independent variables cannot be settled on the basis of findings involving the LVR and the SHR nor, for that matter, can inferences be made about the behavior of the LVR and the SHR on the basis of relationships involving suicide and homicide rates. Neither the components nor the ratio variables have theoretical or causal priority over the other. As a result, he advises that "a rudimental procedure is to state in advance whether the hypothesis to be tested pertains to component variables . . . or ratio variables" (Schuessler 1973, 203). As we have already pointed out, the integrated model is not a theory of suicide and homicide rates; it pertains to the LVR and SHR, two synthetic ratio variables corresponding to the total amount of lethal violence and its direction of expression (Whitt 1968; Whitt, Gordon, and Hofley 1972). Any inferences that can be made about suicide and homicide rates, the component variables, are strictly a bonus.

Part of Schuessler's concern about the use of ratio variables is that in sociology, "ratio variables generally carry no theoretical justification (unlike, say, density in physics)" (Schuessler 1973, 203–4). This is not true of the LVR and the SHR, whose theoretical meanings, as we have seen, are drawn from the stream analogy and the distinction between forces of production and those of direction. In this sense, our two synthetic variables have much in common with the physicist's concept of density—that is, a clear-cut theoretical justification exists.

Having stated in advance that we are concerned with relationships involving the synthetic variables rather than their components and having developed a theoretical justification for employing the LVR and the SHR, we believe we have met Schuessler's criteria (1973, 1974) for the use of ratio variables. Indeed, Schuessler explicitly points out that he is not arguing against the use of the LVR and the SHR. "Proper caution," he says, "does not require that synthetic variables such as $(x_1 + x_2)/x_3$ [the LVR] and $x_1/(x_1 + x_2)$ [the SHR] be abandoned, but rather that their statistical makeup be taken into account in interpreting them" (Schuessler 1974, 394).

For some time after Schuessler's work appeared, however, researchers were leery of using rates and other ratio variables in their research. Indeed, the technical literature on the topic was divided during the 1970s and 1980s between the work of researchers who recommended extreme caution (such as Logan 1982; Chilton 1982; Freeman and Kronenfeld 1973; Pendleton 1984; Bollen and Ward 1979; Uslaner 1976, 1977; Przworski and Cortes 1977; Vanderbok 1977) and those who regarded ratio variables as a dead issue (Feinberg and Trotta 1984; see also Kasarda and Nolan 1979; Firebaugh and Gibbs 1985; Long 1979). The inconclusive status of the debate and the highly technical nature of some of the arguments about spuriousness, tautology, definitional dependencies, rel-variances, and the like left substantive researchers groping for reliable guidance they could understand. By 1979, "the notion that common terms, by definition, lead to spuriously positive or negative statistical associations ha[d] found its way into and established itself in the literature" (Kasarda and Nolan 1979, 214). As this debate continued unchecked among methodological specialists, substantive researchers whose theories included hypotheses about the behavior of ratio variables (such as the SHR, the relative size of the administrative component in organizations, and the ratio of punishments to crimes as an indicator of deterrence) became distinctly gun-shy, and with good reason. Writing at the time, John D. Kasarda and Patrick D. Nolan lamented that the ratio variables debate was getting out of hand:

> Some critics have been careful to point out that the correlations between ratio variables containing common terms are valid if a theoretical interest lies in the ratio constructs (Schuessler

[1973], [1974]). But many readers have overlooked or ignored such qualifications. Indeed, there is mounting evidence that those articles criticizing ratio correlation may be creating more of a problem for social research than their authors anticipated. Numerous studies that appropriately used ratio correlations have been called into question; . . . journal referees are rejecting or calling for major revisions in research submitted for publication primarily because the statistical analysis contains correlations between ratio variables with common terms; and many theoretically interesting relationships tapped by ratio measurement are not being investigated by researchers for fear of generating empirical tautologies.

What makes the situation all the more disturbing is that as knowledge of possible problems of ratio correlation spreads through the professional audience, the use of ratios and proportions is increasingly criticized by people who are aware of the literature dealing with the issue, but who are unfamiliar with the details of the arguments and the important qualifications being made. As a result, ratio and other compound measures are being rejected out of hand, only to be replaced by other measures that are sometimes conceptually and statistically inferior (Kasarda and Nolan 1979, 213).

Kasarda and Nolan's work, along with that of Logan (1982) and Firebaugh and Gibbs (1985), has gone a long way toward demystifying ratio variables. Many of the alleged difficulties cited in the early literature disappear when the focus shifts from correlation to regression, thus making it clear that coefficients based upon components and those based on ratio variables test completely different models (Firebaugh and Gibbs 1985). Indeed, the newer literature suggests that the use of ratio variables may produce fewer problems (such as heteroskedasticity and multicollinearity) than the more cumbersome residualization procedures the earlier literature suggested as alternatives (Kasarda and Nolan 1979).

The debate over ratio variables and Jack Douglas's 1967 critique of the use of official statistics in studies of suicide are in many ways parallel. Substantive researchers in both cases dropped for a time otherwise interesting theoretical ideas because of the spread of a generalized belief that methodological biases were unavoidable in studies of suicide rates. One major difference, however, was that while Schuessler and the other early critics of ratio variables were probably surprised by the overreaction to their work, Douglas's stated intent (1967) was to replace all existing theories of suicide with his own.

THE HENDIN-DOUGLAS CRITIQUE

At about the time the integrated model was beginning to fall into place in the late 1960s, Herbert Hendin (1964, 1969a) was arguing forcefully against sociological theories of suicide and homicide on the basis of his psychoanalytic case studies of suicidal patients in Scandinavia and the black ghetto in New York.

These efforts, from Halbwachs to Henry and Short, seem to aim at finding propositions about suicide that will be true of all cultures at all times. . . . Most of these theories are based on efforts to relate data about suicide and other variables—namely age, sex, marital and social status, alcoholism, and homicide—in a framework that will explain all of the data with a few central theories. Somehow, the idea that suicide, homicide, or even age, sex, and social status can have different meaning and significance in different cultures never seems to enter such work (Hendin 1969a, 133–34).

Hendin's conclusions are based on intensive psychiatric tests and interviews of a relatively small number of suicidal patients—twenty-five each in Denmark, Norway, Sweden, and the New York ghetto—supplemented by interviews of subjects' relatives, nonpatients, and nonsuicidal patients. He found differences in the sources of suicide across the three Scandinavian countries and between black and white Americans. Performance suicides, based on self-hatred derived from the failure to meet rigid standards of performance, predominated in Sweden. Danes were more likely to kill themselves because of dependency loss, while Norwegians engaged primarily in moral suicides associated with guilt feelings surrounding the violation of strict puritanical conduct rules (Hendin 1964).

Similarly, suicide by urban blacks in the United States results from sources that differ from those leading white Americans to kill themselves. Their "murderous rage and self hatred . . . are an integral part of their racial experience and form part of the burden of being black in America" (Hendin 1969a, 138). Among younger blacks, rage is mixed with a combination of guilt, self-hatred and loathing for all the characteristics of blackness, which may equally well be expressed through either suicide, homicide, crime, or drugs. Their elders more often kill themselves when previously successful adaptive strategies fail (Hendin 1969a). White Americans, Hendin argues, (1964, 1969a) are more likely to commit performance suicides.

As a result of such cultural and subcultural variations in the meaning and significance of suicide, Hendin concludes that explanations of suicide that apply cross-culturally are "so general as to be meaningless."

> Studies that take statistical data based on status or social integration and formulate theories that cover all cultures and subcultures reflect a rigidity and a sterility that unfortunately characterize much of contemporary sociology.... Much of the time society is viewed by sociology as a collection of age groups, sex ratios, and social statistics. Somehow the influence of each society's institutions in determining what kind of human being is shaped by the particular society is lost in the process. The search for theories that will explain Eskimo suicide in the same terms as United States suicide is a search for fool's gold—if you find it you have nothing of value (Hendin 1969a, 134–35).

At about the same time that Hendin was leveling his attack on sociological theories of suicide (and homicide), Jack Douglas (1967) was taking the even more extreme position that suicide researchers, and indeed all sociologists, should abandon macrolevel analyses in favor of case studies focusing on how actual participants construct the social meanings of the situations in which they find themselves. The case study method has a long and honorable history in the study of suicide. Psychiatrically oriented researchers, in particular, have used it as the method of choice. Douglas's approach to case study materials, however, differs markedly from the psychiatric approach, including Hendin's (1964, 1969a, 1969b), which seeks to discover theoretically significant subconscious or unconscious motivations unrecognized by the subject or patient. Douglas might look at the same suicide note as a psychiatric researcher; but instead of the workings of repressed wishes to die or be killed, for which the psychiatrist has been alerted by psychiatric theory, he would find microcultural themes such as the belief that suicide represents an attempt to hasten a meeting with God or deceased loved ones, get revenge, or gain pity. These meanings, he argues, need to be understood on their own terms rather than being forced into categories imposed by some deductive theory of suicide.

Douglas views meanings as being constructed by everyone directly or indirectly concerned with suicidal actions—the victim, friends, relatives, psychiatrists, sociologists, and public officials responsible for classifying causes of death. His approach is concerned with uncovering the commonsense understandings used in particular social contexts. These situated meanings are problematic in the sense that they may differ from the general cultural meanings attached to suicide in the abstract.[6]

The meanings imputed to suicide independent of concrete situations in which the communicator is involved are different from the meanings imputed to concrete situations in which the communicator is involved. In general terms this means that the *situated meanings* are different from the *abstract meanings*. This finding has two fundamental meanings for all investigations and analyses of social meanings and, therefore, for all of sociology. First, it is not possible to predict or explain specific types of social events, such as suicide, in terms of abstract social meanings. . . . Second, it is not possible to study situated social meanings (e.g., of suicide), which are most important in the causation of social actions, by any means (such as questionnaires or laboratory experiments) that involve abstracting the communicators from concrete instances of the social action (e.g., suicide) in which they are involved. Both of these implications would seem to demand a fundamental revision of the methods and theories of sociology (Douglas 1967, 339 emphasis in original).

Douglas notes that what little is known about the situated meanings of suicide is drawn from case study reports, and even this source may be biased by the assumptions guiding the writer of the report. From Douglas's perspective, any kind of theoretical generalization will remain impossible until a great deal of descriptive research using case studies has been accomplished. Studies intended to test theories based on cultural and subcultural variations in abstract cultural meanings (Hendin's, for example) are doomed to fail because the situated meanings rather than the abstract meanings are the proximate causes of suicide.

Moreover, Douglas (1967) maintains, the data on which statistical studies of cultural and subcultural variations in suicide depend are based on official statistics that are inherently biased to the point of uselessness in testing general theories of suicide.[7] Official suicide rates, he argues, reflect not only the number of suicides committed but also how suicide is socially constructed by public officials responsible for classifying deaths. Whether suicide will be imputed as the cause of death depends on the objective criteria employed by officials and the search procedures used to evaluate whether those criteria apply in the particular concrete situation the officials are evaluating. Coroners and medical examiners, as individuals, bring their own interpretations of the meanings of suicide with them into the work settings where they make specific decisions about the causes of death. These ideas include socially shared notions about what internal states and external conditions cause suicide. In the Western world, evidence of internal states such as unhappiness, melancholy, or depression are seen by officials as clues that the death was a suicide. These internal states are linked in the minds of both the general public and the officials responsible for categorizing deaths to such social situations as self-imposed isolation, the loss of love objects, and status loss. An economic recession, for example, increases unemployment and bankruptcies. According to Douglas, "the officials trying to categorize the official causes of death will, therefore, be presented with a higher rate of presumptive external causes of internal motives for suicide. This would give the officials a higher rate of situations that *mean* 'suicide' " (Douglas 1967, 222; his emphasis).

If the errors made in classification as a result of individual differences in official practice were random, no bias would be introduced, and official rates would be usable as tests of general theory. Douglas, however, suggests that such variation is far from random. Changes over time in procedures, population bases, and indeed the social and moral meanings of suicide invalidate time-series analyses. Cross-sectional analyses, even within particular societies, suffer because of differential rates of both the attempt to conceal suicide and success of those attempts. Attempts to hide suicide, he argues, will be most widespread in those subcultural groups that most severely condemn suicide and, holding the degree of condemnation constant, in those groups that are most socially integrated. Thus, Douglas maintains, Catholics and middle-class persons, though for different reasons, should be especially likely to attempt to conceal the suicide of a loved one. The success rate of attempted concealment is, he argues, a function of the ability and willingness to control the communication process. The higher the social status and the more integrated the deceased was into the local community, the more likely such attempts will be successful.

Douglas argues that differences in rates of attempted and successful concealment of suicide can account for the observed ecological distribution of suicides within urban areas and for patterns of variation in official suicide rates by social class, sex, and rural-urban residence. Thus, there is "a fundamental bias in the testing of almost all sociological theories tested with official statistics, a bias which would result in the acceptance of most of these theories regardless of the state of real-world events" (Douglas 1967, 216).

Douglas is clearly correct that official statistics on suicide, like those on crime, are socially constructed by public officials who may be influenced by countless unofficial criteria in generating rates (cf. Kitsuse and Cicourel 1963; Cicourel 1968; Jenkins 1988). The crucial question is not whether official statistics on suicide and crime are biased (they are),[8] but whether the bias in suicide and homicide statistics is of sufficient magnitude and direction to preclude their use in testing theories such as the integrated model.

Douglas argues that such researchers as Gibbs (1961; cf. Gibbs 1968) simply assert that the level of bias is acceptable. He fails to note that he himself merely asserts that it is not. This is an empirical question that cannot be settled by mere assertion, but the immediate reaction to Douglas's 1967 monograph was quite similar to the response by sociologists to Schuessler's (1973, 1974) critique of ratio variables. As Douglas's ideas began taking hold among sociologists in the late 1960s and early 1970s, reviewers began rejecting manuscripts solely on the basis that they used official rates, which "everyone knows, or ought to if they have read Jack Douglas, are hopelessly biased."[9] The instinct for professional self-preservation led some researchers to abandon the study of suicide in favor of topics more likely to result in publication, while others began a concerted effort to evaluate Douglas's assertions. It was not until the 1980s that researchers could once again comfortably use official statistics on suicide in their research.

As Norman Kreitman (1988) remarked twenty years later, on receiving the Dublin Award from the American Association of Suicidology and the International Association for Suicide Prevention, Douglas's 1967 critique

> created a stir that I judge is now subsiding—largely, I suspect, because it is slowly being realized that to identify a question as involving social meanings is not the same as removing the matter from the realms of empirical research. . . . Most (if not quite all) of the issues raised by the constructionist critique not only can be, but long have been, widely researched by students of suicide. The upshot of this work is, I think, rather impressively in favor of the continued usefulness of suicide data, though of course they must be sensibly treated, and we have gained useful understanding of their limitations.

The empirical literature since 1967 on bias in suicide statistics is extensive. A thorough review by Patrick W. O'Carroll (1989) concludes that it is clear that suicides are undercounted, and that the extent of undercounting varies from time to time and place to place. According to O'Carroll, the handling of ambiguous cases, which might be classified as either suicides, accidents, or deaths from undetermined circum-

stances is especially important for assessing the validity of reported suicide rates. Because only 2 to 5 percent of all deaths fall into the undetermined category (Murphy 1979), however, and because combining
suicides with accidents or deaths from undetermined causes does not
appreciably alter research findings in diverse cultural settings (McClure
1984; Sainsbury and Jenkins 1982), "the potential impact of such certifi-
cation errors is limited. . . . There simply are not that many equivocal
cases" (O'Carroll 1989, 6, 14).

Similarly, Stack (1987) explored the question of what would happen if possible disguised suicides—deaths from single-vehicle motor
vehicle accidents, accidental falls, accidental drug poisonings, and
deaths from undetermined causes were included in the suicide rate. In
the unlikely event that *all* such deaths were actually suicides, the suicide rate of the United States would be approximately double its reported rate. Stack concludes that "the official data, then, may be more
accurate than the critics claim" (Stack 1987, 137).

By far the most sophisticated assessment of whether the social
construction of suicide rates by public officials invalidates the use of official data to test theories of suicide rates was conducted by Bernice A.
Pescosolido and Robert Mendelsohn (1986). Instead of focusing on the
extent of the misreporting of suicide rates, Pescosolido and Mendelsohn
directly address the question of whether misreporting does or does not
distort the findings of tests of theories of variation in suicide rates. Using a variety of multivariate techniques, they explore the effects of social construction and social causation factors on official suicide data on
404 county groups (aggregations of relatively homogeneous contiguous
counties) in the United States.

Pescosolido and Mendelsohn find that suicides are indeed systematically misreported and that the pattern of misreporting is related
to how agencies are legally and organizationally constituted. Suicides
are systematically hidden in other causes of death, including but not
limited to automobile accidents. Nonetheless, they find that social-
causation variables used in sociological theories of suicide also have an
impact on official rates even after corrections are made for the effects of
social construction variables. Indeed, they conclude that

> misreporting has little effect on the relationship between suicide
> rates and indicators of concepts in sociological theories of suicide.
> Whether or not misreporting is taken into account, the coefficients
> of social causation factors have the same sign and the same ap-
> proximate magnitude. . . . Misreporting, in fact, rather than ex-

plaining all variations in official rates from one area to another, actually masks the true variation. The importance of social factors may have been *underestimated* by the use of official rates in empirical research. Rather than dampening attempts to uncover the social causation of suicide, our results underscore the importance of pursuing these sociological investigations. (Pescosolido and Mendelsohn 1986, 94–95; our emphasis)

The findings of Pescosolido and Mendelsohn (1986), Stack (1987), and O'Carroll (1989) took some of the wind out of the social constructionists' sails. By the end of the 1980s it had become clear that, if used cautiously, official statistics, like ratio variables, could be used in studies of suicide. These methodological developments suggested that *both* social constructionist approaches and studies of the social causes of suicide are legitimate ways of studying suicide rates. Instead of being mutually exclusive alternatives, the two approaches are complementary.

Pescosolido and Mendelsohn's 1986 findings are limited to the United States. No comparable analysis exists for cross-national data, and the suicide rate of the United States is highly atypical of industrial nations (Stack 1987). Moreover, social constructionists have also challenged the reliability and validity of official homicide data. Phillip Jenkins (1988), in particular, has suggested that Justice Department data on motiveless homicides and serial murders grossly inflate true rates. The presence of a corpse no more guarantees the correct classification of a homicide than it does a suicide; some homicides are undoubtedly misclassified as accidents, suicides, or even the result of illness. Nonetheless, the dark figure for homicides is probably lower than for any other crime (Archer and Gartner 1976; Ferdinand 1967; Hindelang 1974), and the percentage of ambiguous cases is likely to be no greater than the 2 to 5 percent estimated by Murphy (1979) for deaths under undetermined circumstances.

The homicide rate of the United States is as atypical as its suicide rate. When the United States is included in tests of the integrated model, both its high LVR and its relatively low SHR stand out from those of other industrial nations (Whitt, Gordon, and Hofley 1972; Unnithan and Whitt 1992). While we feel relatively confident in using ratio variables and official data on suicide and homicide in testing the integratated model, we have employed a strategy that combines cross-national analysis with intensive investigation of the United States, which some researchers have found to be an outlier on both the LVR and the SHR (Unnithan and Whitt 1992).

RESEARCH STRATEGY

Data on suicide and homicide rates that might be used in testing the integrated model are available for nations, states, county groups, counties, metropolitan areas, cities, and census tracts. It is even possible to generate crude approximations of rates for tribal societies by searching ethnographic materials or using the Human Relations Area Files (cf. Palmer 1965). The strategy we have chosen combines cross-national analysis with the intensive examination of state-level data for the United States. This strategy allows us to explore the utility of the integrated model in answering questions and resolving issues arising from the two separate and distinct research traditions associated with studies of suicide and homicide. In addition, it combines variable-oriented and case-oriented research as urged by macrosociologists (Ness 1985; Ragin 1987).

Our research strategy follows a somewhat modified version of the approach recommended by Gayl D. Ness (1985), who suggests supplementing cross-national analyses with case studies of statistical outliers. Cross-national studies, including our own, are plagued by awkward sample sizes. There are currently over 150 nation-states that could potentially be used as data sources if only they submitted data to central data collection agencies such as INTERPOL or the United Nations. But many of these nations, for political or other reasons, fail to submit suicide or homicide data. The emerging nations of Africa and the nations of Southeast Asia are conspicuously among the missing. When one adds the necessity of gathering data on independent variables, the number of cases can fall to under fifty—too few for an effective statistical analysis to stand on its own and too many for detailed individual scrutiny.

Ness (1985) suggests that theoretical models can be tested using multiple regression techniques with as few as twenty cases *if* both influential cases (that is, those with a disproportionate impact on estimates of parameters in the regression model) and deviant cases (that is, statistical outliers) are then identified for more detailed analysis. We know in advance that the homicide rate of the United States, and consequently its SHR, are atypical of industrial nations, though the cross-national analysis in chapter 7 does not reveal it as a statistical outlier. Thus, in chapter 8, we supplement the cross-national analysis with a detailed look at lethal violence in the United States.

N. PRABHA UNNITHAN
LIN HUFF-CORZINE
HUGH P. WHITT

7

Cross-National Patterns of Lethal Violence

Something is rotten in the state of
   Denmark.
          —*William Shakespeare c. 1610*

One of the major issues in the macrosociological study of violence concerns the impacts of social inequality and economic development on lethal violence (Braithwaite 1979; Braithwaite and Braithwaite 1980; Durkheim 1897; Hackney 1969; Hansmann and Quigley 1982; Krohn 1976; Masaryk 1881; McDonald 1976; Messner 1980; Stack 1983; Unnithan and Whitt 1992; Whitt, Gordon, and Hofley 1972). Much of this research has been at the cross-national level, focusing on how structural and cultural features of nation-states are affected by development and inequality. The impact of these two societal features, however, has not been extensively examined from the perspective of the stream analogy. The cross-national analysis presented in this chapter is an attempt in this direction. We seek to show the utility of the stream analogy in answering persistent questions about the impact of economic development and social inequality on violence and its expression as homicide or suicide.

   We begin by assessing what is known about the relationships of inequality and development to suicide and homicide, and then sketch out the expected impact on the lethal violence rate (LVR) and the suicide-homicide ratio (SHR). The derived hypotheses are then tested using multivariate analyses of a data set for eighty-eight nations.

INEQUALITY AS A PREDICTOR OF VIOLENCE

There is general agreement in cross-national analyses of violence that inequality increases homicide rates. Nevertheless, recent studies of cities and Standard Metropolitan Statistical Areas in the United States have called the relationship between inequality and homicide into question. Empirically, Judith R. Blau and Peter M. Blau's 1982 findings emphasize the importance of inequality in augmenting homicide levels, while Steven F. Messner (1982b), William Bailey (1984), Kirk R. Williams (1984), Colin Loftin and Robert Nash Parker (1985), and Steven Messner and Kenneth Tardiff (1986) find absolute poverty to be more important. Theoretically, the debate is over the importance of relative and absolute deprivation as measured by income inequality and the size of the population living below the poverty line, respectively.

In the cross-national literature, inequality continues to be the deprivation variable of choice. This is due, perhaps, to the large differences among nations in defining what constitutes poverty and, consequently, the size of the population living below the poverty line. One theoretical justification for using inequality in cross-national analyses is that "judgments of economic well-being involve not local (neighborhood or citywide) norms but national norms" (Messner and Tardiff 1986, 311). Questions remain, however, about the specific nature of the relationship and the extent to which cross-national findings are confounded by an apparent link between inequality and the level of economic development.

Lynn McDonald (1976) reports that intersectoral income inequality is directly related to homicide rates. Furthermore, John Braithwaite and Valerie Braithwaite (1980) show that the association survives controls for protein consumption, political freedom, and ethnic fractionalization. On the other hand, several studies find that inequality is closely related to economic development in an inverted U-curve function (Adelman and Morris 1973; Ahluwalia 1976; Bollen and Jackman 1985; Chenery and Syrquin 1975; Crenshaw 1992; Fields 1980; Kuznets 1963; Lenski 1966; Lydall 1977; Muller 1988; Paukert 1973; Weede 1980, 1989). In the early stages of development, inequality increases and then reaches a peak, after which it drops at high levels of industrialization.

Attempts to determine whether inequality affects homicide independently of economic development have led to inconsistent results. Most studies (such as Krohn 1976; Messner 1980, 1982a; Krahn, Hartnagel, and Gartrell 1986; Unnithan and Whitt 1992) find that inequality remains an important predictor of homicide after controlling for economic development, although Braithwaite (1979) reports that the relationship disappears when nations are categorized by gross national product (most often used as an indicator of economic development).

A second unresolved issue is the nature of the inequality-homicide relationship: is it linear or nonlinear? Messner (1980), Unnithan and Whitt (1992), and Braithwaite and Braithwaite (1980) note curvilinear patterns, but the Braithwaites opt for the parsimony and simplicity of a linear solution. These findings, as well as theoretical considerations to be discussed later in the chapter, alert us to check for nonlinear relationships in our analyses.

Given that a relationship exists between inequality and homicide, what would the integrated model lead us to expect with respect to the LVR and the SHR? Hansmann and Quigley (1982) argue that inequality contributes to the homicide rate by producing both absolute and relative poverty. Under conditions of high inequality, the poor are not only economically frustrated by their meager resources, but also are relatively deprived in comparison to the few very wealthy persons in their societies. Hansmann and Quigley's argument may be extended to suggest that inequality tends to polarize a society, with the poor blaming the rich for their plight. The externalization of blame is common among the disadvantaged in many societies (Banfield 1958; Miller 1958; Wolfgang and Ferracuti 1967). Thus, the extent of the gap between the rich and the poor can be seen as a contributing factor in this widespread cultural pattern.

Based on the foregoing, inequality and homicide appear to be connected by two separate causal paths, and the relationship between the two variables would be expected on theoretical grounds alone to be curvilinear. First, inequality raises the level of systemic frustration for a substantial proportion of the population, thereby increasing the size of the stream of total violence, the LVR. Second, it diverts blame from the self and consequently increases the proportion of violence expressed as homicide rather than suicide—that is, it reduces the SHR (cf. Unnithan and Whitt 1992).

Our hypothesis that the relationship between inequality and the homicide rate should be curvilinear also follows from the definitional relationships between the homicide rate, the SHR, and the LVR. A reasonable assumption can be made that both of the synthetic variables are linear functions of inequality. If this were the case, it would follow from equation 6.6 in chapter 6,

$$H = LVR\,(1 - SHR)\,LVR$$

that both the total amount of violence and the proportion expressed as homicide should increase linearly with inequality, resulting in an accelerating upward slope in the relationship between homicide and inequality, as Braithwaite and Braithwaite (1980), Messner (1980), and Unnithan and Whitt (1992) report. This approach also suggests that the relationship between inequality and suicide should be curvilinear because equation 6.5 in chapter 6 states

$$S = (SHR)\ (LVR).$$

The form of the curve would depend on the relative strengths of the relationships of inequality to the SHR and LVR.

ECONOMIC DEVELOPMENT AS A PREDICTOR OF VIOLENCE

It has been known for more than a century that suicide increases and homicide decreases with economic development (see Ellner 1977; Grollman 1971; Labovitz and Brinkerhoff 1977; Lester 1972; Levi 1982; Masaryk 1881; Morselli 1879a, 1879b; Stack 1978, 1982, 1983; Unnithan and Whitt 1992; Whitt, Gordon, and Hofley 1972). Although there is little consensus as to the theoretical basis of the relationship, Levi (1982) speculates that development increases suicide rates by weakening social support systems and decreases homicide rates by tightening governmental control over life. Whitt, Gordon, and Hofley (1972) maintain that development increases control over the environment, fostering the sense that people are responsible for their own fate. These same researchers also report a strong positive relationship between nonagricultural employment and the SHR. Messner suggests that "the more developed societies do not exhibit especially high levels of homicide because the greater equality in the distribution of income accompanying development serves to deflate the homicide rate" (Messner 1982a, 240).

Although theoretically based hypotheses relating economic development to the LVR and SHR are difficult to formulate, past empirical research suggests that inequality and economic development stand in differing causal relationships to the currents of lethal violence. Inequality should both increase the LVR and lower the SHR. On the other hand, the major impact of development should be on the SHR. Both prior research (such as Hackney 1969) and the theoretical positions espoused by Whitt and his colleagues (1972), Lane (1979), and others suggest that economic development acts to channel blame for frustration inward, with lethal violence increasingly expressed as suicide. As the industrial process brings the forces of nature under human control, personal blame for perceived failure is more likely to be placed on the self.

The diffusion of values stressing individual responsibility and self-reliance may also be involved in the shift from homicide to suicide, as the self is likely to be blamed for failure when others are seen to be succeeding. Empirically, Hackney (1969) reports that the SHR increases with virtually every available measurement of economic development. Whitt and his colleagues (1972) found a positive relationship between the SHR and nonagricultural employment, and Unnithan and Whitt (1992) report similar findings using GNP/capita.

The relationship between economic development and the LVR is more problematic. Research showing that suicide increases and homicide decreases with development has been noted earlier. Thus, the two rates may be expected to cancel each other out, producing a fairly constant amount of total violence, all else being equal. In the absence of compelling theoretical reasoning in favor of either a positive or negative relationship, we offer no prediction for the relationship between economic development and the LVR.

DATA AND METHODS

Comparative or cross-national approaches to the study of violence are relatively uncommon. Differences among countries in legal definitions of violence, their changing cross-temporal interpretations (for example, during periods of civil strife, military rule, or colonialism), varying legal processes, and the lack of uniformity in reporting information all impede research efforts. Cross-national studies of lethal violence, however, allow us to examine the impact of one of the most influential features of modern life, the structural features of the nation-state, on what may appear to be essentially personal decisions (suicides) and interpersonal transactions (homicides). In this context, using the currents of lethal violence rather than homicide or suicide rates can be advantageous. Whether a death is labeled as a suicide or a homicide by a nation's legal system becomes relevant only in its contribution to the direction of lethal violence. It nonetheless remains a part of the data on overall lethal violence.

The analyses presented in this chapter will describe our findings on the impact of inequality and economic development on the LVR and the SHR as well as on the separate homicide and suicide rates. This is done because we wish to demonstrate the theoretical relevance of the integrated model and the stream analogy in macrosociological analyses, while at the same time maintaining a degree of continuity with literature that examines these rates separately. The discussion of our findings will also be in terms of both traditions but will indicate why we prefer the stream analogy.

In cross-national research, the necessary transition from theoretical construct to operational measure is complicated by inaccuracy, incomparability, non-representativeness, and misspecification (Merrit and Rokkan 1966). In particular, there is considerable case attrition when data on a number of indicators are needed from each nation under investigation (cf. Messner 1980). An earlier study by two of us (Unnithan and Whitt 1992) found complete data on suicide, homicide, inequality, and economic development for the period 1950–70 to be available for only thirty-one nations.

The analysis of data from the early 1970s through 1990 reported here increases the number of cases to eighty-eight by employing a method of handling missing data first proposed by Jacob Cohen and Patricia Cohen (1975). The procedure recommended by the Cohens allows us to use all nations for which we have data on lethal violence and at least one of our independent variables. This technique will be discussed in some detail in a later section.

One of the major problems posed by missing data in cross-national studies is that it tends to be nonrandom. Little or nothing other than noting limitations of coverage can be done when data on lethal violence is missing; but, in the case of missing independent variables, the absence of data is itself a datum that the Cohen and Cohen procedure allows us to include in the analysis.

The nonrandom pattern of missing data on suicide and homicide, and, consequently, on the LVR and SHR, is such that our sample overrepresents highly developed Western nations, though some less-industrialized Eastern European and Third World societies are also included. Detailed data on causes of death, including suicide and homicide rates, were available for the vast majority of industrialized nations, for most of Latin America, for parts of the former Soviet bloc (the USSR itself, Poland, Hungary, Czechoslovakia, and Bulgaria), and for a few Middle Eastern and Asian nations (notably China, Kuwait, Egypt, Sri Lanka, Singapore, Turkey, and Hong Kong). Data from sub-Saharan Africa and the rest of Asia are conspicuous by their absence. Indeed, some of the nations of central Africa do not collect data on crime and suicide, and the coverage for some other nations (Brazil, China, and Turkey) is limited to selected portions of their populations. Some nations, including Cuba and Romania, report data on other causes of death to the World Health Organization but treat data on suicide and homicide as classified (cf. Beirne and Messerschmidt 1991). Lethal violence data for China, the former Soviet Union, and some of the latter's republics (Russia, Belarus, and Ukraine) have only recently become available.

Annual rates of homicide and suicide were taken from the United Nations' *Demographic Yearbook* (1971–90) and the World Health Organization's *World Health Statistics Annual* (1971–91), both of which provide statistics on causes of death for various countries. The data are for the most recent year, working backwards from 1990 to 1971. We were able to locate figures for 104 political units, some of which are colonies or overseas administrative units of other nations. Of the 104, five (Gibraltar, Monaco, Montserrat, Niue, and St. Christopher) were eliminated from the analysis because they reported no instances of either suicide or homicide and their SHRs were consequently undefined. An additional eleven political units (Bermuda, the British Virgin Islands, the Cayman Islands, the Channel Islands, Greenland,[1] Guadaloupe, the Isle of Man, Macao, Martinique, Samoa, and St. Helena) were excluded because of the absence of data on both economic development and inequality. Although separate data were available for England and Wales, Scotland, and Northern Ireland, we have used a single set of figures for the United Kingdom. Similarly, we use data for the former USSR as a whole rather than including Russia, Belarus and Ukraine as separate nations.

We have included data based on incomplete population coverage for five nations (Brazil, China, South Africa, Turkey, and Zimbabwe). Brazil, China, and Turkey exclude certain geographical areas. The excluded populations are small in the cases of Turkey and Brazil, where isolated areas and portions of the Amazon Basin are not enumerated. China's data are claimed to be representative of that nation's population, including both urban and rural areas, but only a small fraction of the population is included.

The data from South Africa and Zimbabwe exclude persons of African ancestry. In South Africa, only whites, "coloureds," and "Asiatics" are included, while Zimbabwe's data are restricted to the European population. With considerable trepidation, we included these two nations despite the severe limitations of coverage of their populations. As shown later in the chapter, we would have paid a heavy price for doing so had we not examined scatterplots and tested for the presence of influential cases.

Most industrialized nations report death statistics on an annual basis, but returns from some polities are more sporadic. Tests using time periods of three to five years, however, indicate a very high degree of stability (Heise 1969) in these data, suggesting that the use of a single year's figure to measure national rates of lethal violence is probably representative in the absence of major dislocations such as war and civil strife. As elsewhere, the LVR is the combined rate of suicide and homicide per one-hundred thousand people, while the SHR is the proportion of violent deaths expressed as suicide rather than homicide.

Given data on the LVR and SHR and the suicide and homicide rates from which they are derived, we were able to include a nation in our analysis if we also had information on either inequality or economic development. Most researchers have used income inequality to measure inequality within nations. As Gary S. Fields puts it, "Income is the single best measure of economic condition and . . . change in income is the single best measure of improvement in that position" (Fields 1980, 5).

Nonetheless, as Bollen and Jackman (1985) point out, income inequality per se is probably less theoretically relevant than inequality in the distribution of wealth. Wealth is undoubtedly more unequally distributed than annual income, but cross-national data on the distribution of wealth are not available.

Although we used four different sources for data on income inequality (Muller 1988; Hoover 1989; Simpson 1990; World Bank 1991; see also Crenshaw 1992), these data are not without problems. The base years vary over the quarter of a century from 1965 through 1989. Although many studies (Ahluwalia 1976; Bollen and Jackman 1985; Lacaillon et al. 1984; Paukert 1973) assume that inequality is relatively stable over a period of roughly two decades, Simpson (1990) points out that it can change considerably in a short time. Indeed, Jain (1975) cautions that scores can change as much as 30 percent over ten years in some developing countries. Muller (1988) contends that scores are reasonably comparable over an eleven-year time span, but Menard (1986) cautions against using observations more than five years apart. While we cannot resolve this issue here, an examination of the four data sources we employed suggests that while differences exist, they tend not to be large.

The income inequality measures are based on sample surveys rather than tax records or complete censuses (World Bank 1991). These surveys vary in the extent of population coverage and whether the distribution is for households or for individuals. Menard's analysis suggests that "personal income inequality is a relatively unbiased estimate of household income inequality. Substantively this means that mixing household with personal income inequality should have little effect on the results of an analysis using national income inequality as a variable" (Menard 1986, 780; see also Lecaillon et al. 1984).

The data on inequality used in the following analysis is based primarily on household income, though figures for some nations are for individuals. Data tend to be limited to market and mixed economies;

planned economies are generally excluded. The secondary sources used (Muller 1988; Hoover 1989; Simpson 1990) draw from such primary compilations as Ahluwalia (1976), Ballmer-Cao and Scheidegger (1979), Jain (1975), Lecaillon et al. (1984), Roberti (1974), Sawyer (1976), earlier editions of the World Bank's *World Development Report* (1979–85) and United Nations economic reports.

Earlier studies of income inequality have usually employed either the Gini index (for example, Muller 1988; Simpson 1990) or the Kuznets index (Kuznets 1957; Unnithan and Whitt 1992) as operational measures of income inequality. Both of these measures tap the extent to which the entire income distribution, from top to bottom, departs from equality. Our cross-national analyses use another measure of income inequality, the percentage of total income accruing to the 20 percent of households or individuals with the highest incomes. The income share of the highest quintile was chosen because it is more sensitive than the Gini and Kuznets indices to income concentration in the hands of an economic elite. In those cases in which two or more estimates of income distribution were available, we have used their average value in our analyses.

As in most earlier studies, economic development was measured by gross national product per capita. Data were drawn primarily from the World Bank (1991). A few additional cases were obtained from the *World Almanac and Book of Facts* (1993). In the analyses, all figures are converted into 1989 U.S. dollars and reported in thousands of dollars for convenience.

The data were analyzed using ordinary least-squares (OLS) regression techniques using the mean-plugging procedure recommended by Jacob Cohen and Patricia Cohen (1975). The Cohens' technique divides the effects of independent variables with missing values into two components, each represented by a variable in the analysis. Missing observations are assigned an arbitrary constant, conventionally the mean, and an additional dichotomously coded dummy variable is added to the analysis to represent the presence or absence of missing data. Taken together, the mean-plugged independent variable and the missing-value dichotomy represent all the information in the original distribution. When both the mean-plugged variables and the dichotomous missing-data measures are included in the regression analysis, an analysis over all cases both makes maximum use of non-missing cases and estimates the impact of missing data. After controlling for the missing-data dichotomy, the contribution to explained variance and the standardized and unstandardized regression coefficients attached to the mean-plugged independent variables are identical to those that would have been obtained from OLS regression over only those cases for which inequality or economic development scores are available. The regression coefficients attached to the missing-data dichotomies estimate the extent of systematic, nonrandom, bias that would be introduced by excluding cases with missing data from the analysis (Cohen and Cohen 1975; Whitt 1986).

HOW TO READ THE TABLES

Results are reported first for the suicide and homicide rates themselves and then for the LVR and SHR. In each case, we begin with a summary table that shows eight different regression models relating the dependent variable to GNP/capita, income inequality, and the two dummy variables representing the presence or absence of missing data. Because both prior research (Braithwaite and Braithhwaite 1980; Messner 1980; Unnithan and Whitt 1992) and theoretical considerations (see chapter 6) alert us to the importance of possible curvilinearity, the models in these tables allow us to examine both linear and nonlinear specifications.

Models I and II, respectively, explore the zero-order linear and nonlinear effects of economic development, including the impact of missing GNP/capita data. Models III and IV take a similar approach to the effects of inequality. The remaining models examine various combinations of linear and nonlinear effects when both independent variables are entered as predictors. In model V, the effects of both GNP/capita and income inequality are assumed to be linear, while models VI and VII assume that one variable has linear and the other nonlinear effects. Finally, model VIII allows for nonlinear effects of both independent variables. Nonlinearity is assessed in the four summary tables by adding squared terms (GNP^2 and $INEQ^2$) to the appropriate equations (Jagodzinski and Weede 1981; Stimson, Carmines, and Zeller 1976). The polynomial terms allow for a single bend in the curve.

Even a cursory glance at the tables reveals that in the models including squared terms, the values of some of the standardized regression coefficients exceed ±1.00. These very high values result from the extreme multicollinearity between the independent variables and their squares. Indeed, the correlation between GNP and GNP^2 is +.964 and that between INEQ and $INEQ^2$ is +.995. Under these conditions, standard errors are inflated and the individual regression coefficients can be highly misleading (Cohen and Cohen 1975). Unlike multicollinearity between two separate independent variables, however, a high correlation between a variable and its square is not a cause for concern.

Each polynomial has both a linear element (GNP or INEQ) and a nonlinear component (GNP^2 or INEQ^2). These two parts of the relationship together define the curve relating economic development or income inequality to the dependent variables,[2] but their statistical significance is tested using different models and a hierarchical logic. The summary tables add the squared terms GNP^2 and INEQ^2 after the statistical significance of linear components of relationships have been evaluated. In reading the tables, it is important *not* to pay attention to the reported significance of GNP or INEQ in models that also include the respective nonlinear components GNP^2 and INEQ^2 (cf. Cohen and Cohen 1975).

GNP and INEQ are first entered into the analysis and their significance assessed. For example, the significance of the zero-order effects of GNP and INEQ are taken, respectively, from models I and III. Model V yields the significance levels of these variables when the effects of both GNP and INEQ are assumed to be linear. Model VI gives the statistical significance of the linear effect of inequality when the effect of GNP/capita is treated as nonlinear, while model VII tests the significance of the linear component of economic development (GNP) assuming that income inequality has a nonlinear effect. Models II, IV, and VIII, which include the independent variables only when accompanied by their squared terms, are not involved in assessing linear relationships, and the significance levels associated with GNP and INEQ in these models are meaningless. One may, however, read the significance levels attached to GNP^2 and INEQ^2 directly from the summary table (Cohen and Cohen 1975).[3]

As Cook and Weisberg (1982) have pointed out, regressions based on small samples such as ours may be dominated by a few cases, while much of the data is ignored in fitting the parameters. Thus, it is possible that some or all of the equations in the summary tables would change radically if even a single case were deleted. To explore this possibility, we examined the residuals and various case statistics for the various models. Primary emphasis was placed on Cook's D, a statistic that estimates the overall impact of each case (nation) on the parameters of the model (Cook 1977; Cook and Weisberg 1982). If the value of D is large, the case may be unduly influential. Cook and Weisberg hedge on identifying the magnitude of D that should be considered large but do suggest that a value exceeding 1.00 "usually provides a basis for comparison" (Cook and Weisberg 1982, 345).

No instances of excessive influence were found in the equations using the 1.00 criterion for identifying an influential case. There were, however, several equations in which Cook's D was too large for complete comfort. The last two rows of the summary tables show the values of Cook's D for the most influential case and the identity of the nation making the greatest contribution to parameter estimates. As a precautionary measure, all thirty-two equations were rerun after eliminating the most influential case. In no instance does the reanalysis (not shown) change the conclusions presented in the tables and text.

FINDINGS

Table 7.1 shows the means and standard deviations of all variables in the analysis and the zero-order correlations among them. Despite the presence of missing data, this table includes all eighty-eight nations in the sample. While table 7.1 contains some items of interest, it is presented primarily to allow other researchers to reproduce our analysis and examine alternative models.

Table 7.1 shows a weak and statistically insignificant inverse relationship between suicide and homicide rates ($r = -.102$). There is little if any correlation between the LVR and the SHR ($r = -.010$) in this data set. Technically, table 7.1 should not be used to assess relationships involving GNP, INEQ, and their squares because the Cohen and Cohen (1975) procedure that makes this large sample possible affects the magnitudes of variances, covariances, and correlations. Zero-order relationships between independent and dependent variables should instead be taken from the summary tables presented later in the chapter.

To explore the relationship between economic development and inequality, INEQ was regressed on GNP, GNP^2, and MDGNP, the dummy variable for missing data, across the fifty-two cases for which we have data on income inequality. The results are shown in table 7.2. Perhaps not surprisingly, the relationship takes the form of a U-curve rather than the inverted U-curve widely reported in the literature. This is not the place to become involved in the current debate over the causes of what has come to be known as "the great U-turn" (Harrison and Bluestone 1988), but income inequality has mushroomed in the United States since about 1973, reversing a long-term downward trend (Braun 1991a, 1991b; Jirovec 1984). At least one theorist (Amos 1988) suggests that other industrial nations should experience similar reversals. From his perspective, once the inverted U-curve is completed, income inequality once again increases in highly developed nations.

If Amos (1988) is correct, the addition of the cube of GNP to the equation predicting INEQ should capture the relationship between income inequality and economic development by specifying two bends in the curve. This would allow inequality to rise, then fall, then rise

TABLE 7.1 Bivariate Correlations, Means, and Standard Deviations for Cross-national Analyses of Lethal Violence Rates and Suicide Homicide Ratios, N=88

Variable	Mean	S.D.	1	2	3	4	5	6	7	8	9	10
1 Suicide	9.92	8.41	—									
2 Homicide	5.41	9.48	-.102	—								
3 LVR	15.33	12.02	.620[c]	.718[c]	—							
4 SHR	.65	.32	.611[c]	-.556[c]	-.010	—						
5 GNP	7.55	7.97	.452[c]	-.247[a]	.123	.486[c]	—					
6 GNP^2	119.69	118.31	.456[c]	-.208	.155	.423[c]	.964[c]	—				
7 MDGNP	.01	.11	.209	-.054	.104	.111	.000	-.037	—			
8 INEQ	47.73	7.00	-.499[c]	.447[c]	.004	-.601[c]	-.465[c]	-.382[c]	-.265[a]	—		
9 INEQ^2	2374.98	933.30	-.481[c]	.434[c]	.006	-.589[c]	-.469[c]	-.387[c]	-.220[a]	.994[c]	—	
10 MDINEQ	.41	.49	-.179	-.207	-.288[b]	.072	-.130	-.116	-.089	.000	.000	—

[a] $p < .05$
[b] $p < .01$
[c] $p < .0001$

TABLE 7.2   Regression of Income Inequality on GNP/Capita (Unstandardized Regression Coefficients, $N = 52$)

	b	b	b
Constant	53.752	56.469	57.797
GNP	−0.656****	−1.781****	−2.658**
GNP^2		0.048***	0.131
GNP^3			−0.002
MDGNP	−18.351*	−15.398*	−13.951*
R^2	0.425****	0.511****	0.521****

*$p < .05$
**$p < .01$
***$p < .001$
****$p < .0001$

once again as he suggests. The effect of GNP^3 is not significant, however, and the signs attached to the parameter estimates for all three components, GNP, GNP^2, and GNP^3, are the reverse of what Amos would predict.[4] Nonetheless, we strongly suspect that the pattern in our data, in which income inequality first decreases and then increases with GNP/capita, can be accounted for by Amos's 1988 hypothesis. Our sample largely excludes nations in which inequality is expected to rise during the very early stages of development, and we see only the decrease in inequality at intermediate levels and the recent increase in highly developed nations.

Although the relationship between development and inequality is interesting in its own right, our primary concern is with the association of these two variables with patterns of lethal violence. We turn now to their relationships to national suicide rates.

Suicide Rates

Results for cross-national variations in suicide rates are shown in table 7.3. In the linear models, suicide rates increase with development and decrease with income inequality. This is true for both zero-order relationships (models I and III, respectively) and when both GNP and INEQ are entered into the regression equation (model V). Inequality, with standardized regression coefficients (betas) of −.504 ($p < .0001$) in model III and −.347 ($p < .01$) after controlling for GNP/capita in model V, does a somewhat better job than economic development ($\beta = .454$, $p < .0001$ in model I; $\beta = .274$, $p < .01$ in model V) in predicting suicide rates in these three models.

Nonlinearity is significant in the zero-order relationship between inequality and suicide (model IV), but GNP^2 fails to attain statistical significance in model II. Turning to model VIII, it is clear that *both* relationships have significant nonlinear components after controls. Treating the relationship between development and suicide rates as curvilinear increases R^2 by .034 ($F_{df=1,81} = 4.69; p < .05$) and the comparable increment for INEQ^2 is .032 ($F_{df=1,81} = 4.40; p < .05$). The existence of both curvilinear relationships, but not the forms of the curves, was predicted in advance by the integrated model outlined in chapter 6. Finally, it should be noted in passing that having missing data on GNP/capita is significantly related to the suicide rate in zero-order data but that this relationship all but disappears when inequality is controlled.

The statistical significance of the squared terms in model VIII forms the basis for deciding between linear and nonlinear specifications, but it tells us little about either the strength of the nonlinear relationship or the form of the curve. We are less interested in decomposing the curve estimated by model VIII into linear and nonlinear components than in asking about its shape and how well it predicts suicide rates. Table 7.4 and figures 7.1 and 7.2 assess these questions. Table 7.4 presents the J-W betas (Unnithan 1983; Unnithan and Whitt 1992; Whitt 1986) relating suicide rates to income inequality and GNP/capita under the nonlinear specification in model VIII. J-W betas (after Wolfgang Jagodzinski and Erich Weede [1981], who apparently first suggested their use) combine the linear and nonlinear components of a curvilinear relationship into a single standardized regression coefficient. Technically, they are a special case of the sheaf coefficient (Heise 1971; Whitt 1986). Briefly, the Jagodzinski-Weede procedure involves the creation of composite variables for inequality and economic development separately using the unstandardized regression coefficients (shown in the first column of table 7.4) from model VIII as weights. These new variables, which are of the form

$$X' = b_1 X + b_2 X^{2,}$$

are then regressed together with the two missing data codes against the suicide rate to yield the curvilinear effects of inequality and development. The X' measures represent the linear combinations of the independent variables and their squares that best predict suicide under model VIII.

The second column of table 7.4 shows the J-W betas for GNP' and INEQ'. These standardized regression coefficients provide estimates of the relative importance of inequality and economic development when

TABLE 7.3   GNP/Capita, Income Inequality, and National Suicide Rates (Standardized Regression Coefficients, $N = 88$)

				Model				
	I	II	III	IV	V	VI	VII	VIII
GNP	.454****	.087			.274*	−.458	.262*	−.468
GNP²		.380				.728*		.727*
MDGNP	.210*	.223*			.105	.113	.006	.015
INEQ			−.504****	−2.436**	−.347**	−.408***	−2.345*	−2.400*
INEQ²				1.947**			1.981*	1.977*
MDINEQ			−.189*	−.079	−.141	−.152	−.040	−.052
R^2	.250****	.260****	.286****	.325****	.345****	.379****	.377****	.411****
Maximum Cook's D	.118	.089	.242	.323	.476	.403	.825	.684
Nation	Hungary	Hungary	Hungary	Hungary	Hungary	Hungary	Hungary	Hungary

*$p < .05$
**$p < .01$
***$p < .001$
****$p < .0001$

TABLE 7.4   Nonlinear Relationships of Suicide Rates to GNP/Capita and Income Inequality (Unstandardized Regression Coefficients for Model VIII, $N = 88$)

Variable	b	$Beta_{jw}$
GNP	−0.049	
GNP²	0.032*	
GNP'		.302**
INEQ	−2.890	
INEQ²	0.024*	
INEQ'		.488**
MDGNP	1.192	
MDINEQ	.876	
R^2	.411****	.411****

*$p < .05$
**$p < .01$
***$p < .001$
****$p < .0001$

curvilinear relationships are considered.[5] As in the linear model discussed previously, the suicide rate is more strongly related to income inequality ($\beta_{jw} = .488$, $F_{df=2,81} = 9.66$, $p < .001$) than to GNP/capita ($\beta_{jw} = .302$, $F_{df=2,81} = 5.84$, $p < .01$). J-W betas are always positive (Jagodzinski and Weede 1981); they tell us nothing about the nature of the relationships between suicide and the two independent variables, but their magnitudes can be compared in the same way as other standardized regression coefficients.

The shapes of the curves relating GNP/capita and income inequality to suicide rates are shown in Figures 7.1 and 7.2, which were constructed by plotting the values of GNP' and INEQ' against GNP and INEQ, respectively, with all other variables in the respective equations held constant at their means (Whitt 1986). Figure 7.1 shows that the curvilinear relationship between GNP and the suicide rate is positive through most of its range, with an increasingly positive slope. The relationship is very weak and slightly negative for nations in the first stages of development, but its sign quickly shifts to positive and grows steeper as development progresses. The inflection point, or vortex, where the sign shifts from negative to positive, lies at a GNP/capita of slightly more than $7,600 per year.[6] This value exceeds the mean for our sample of nations by less than $100; the level slightly exceeds the GNP/capita figures for such nations as Bahrain and Guam.

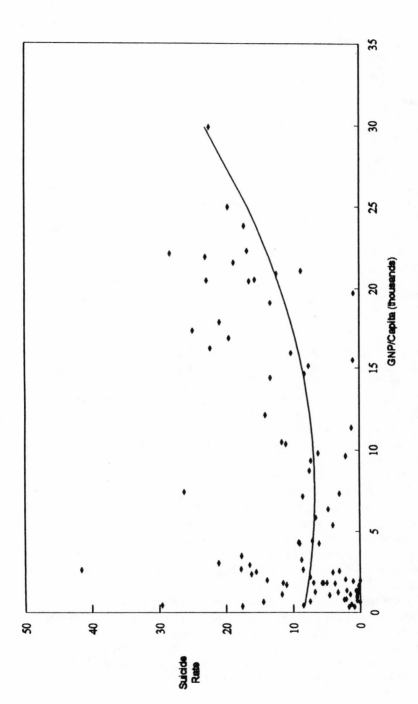

FIlGURE 7.1   Suicide Rates by GNP/Capita, 88 Nations

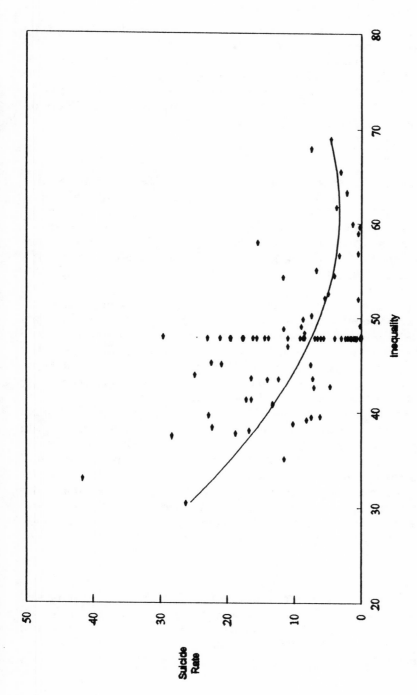

FIGURE 7.2 Suicide Rates by Income Inequality, 88 Nations

Figure 7.2 shows that the relationship between income inequality and the suicide rate is generally negative but shifts to positive for nations in which inequality is very high. At the inflection point, 61.3 percent of the nation's income is monopolized by those in the upper quintile of the income distribution. Only five nations in the sample— Ecuador, Zimbabwe, Brazil, Mexico, and Panama—have levels of income inequality exceeding this level.

Homicide Rates

Table 7.5 shifts our attention from suicide to homicide rates. Homicide has significant zero-order relationships to both GNP/capita ($\beta = -.247; p < .05$ in model I) and INEQ ($\beta = .440; p < .0001$ in model III). These relationships are linear; neither model II nor model IV shows even a hint of nonlinearity. Model III also shows that the homicide rates of nations for which we lack inequality data are significantly lower, on the average, than those of nations whose scores on INEQ were available ($\beta = -.198; p < .05$).

The association between development and homicide virtually disappears in model V, in which GNP, INEQ, and the two missing data codes all enter the equation. The relationship between the homicide rate and inequality remains positive and statistically significant ($\beta = .411; p < .001$) in this equation. Similarly, homicide rates continue to be reduced in nations whose inequality scores are unavailable ($\beta = -.206; p < .05$). Models VI through VIII, which explore the possibility that nonlinearity might emerge after controls as it did for the relationship between development and suicide, add little to our understanding. In contrast to earlier studies (Braithwaite and Braithwaite 1980; Messner 1980; Unnithan and Whitt 1992), there is absolutely no suggestion of nonlinearity in this data set.

In summary, only income inequality and the absence of data on inequality are significant predictors of homicide rates in our cross-national data. Homicide increases with inequality, but rates are lower than average in the thirty-six nations whose levels of inequality are unavailable.

Lethal Violence Rates

Table 7.6 shows our findings for the LVR. Very little can be said about this table, which is largely devoid of significant relationships. Indeed, R^2 attains statistical significance only in models III and IV, and there is no evidence that either inequality or economic development is related to the LVR in this sample.

TABLE 7.5 GNP/Capita, Income Inequality, and National Homicide Rates (Standardized Regression Coefficients, $N = 88$)

				Model				
	I	II	III	IV	V	VI	VII	VIII
GNP	-.247*	.632			-.082	-.168	-.077	-.164
GNP²		.399				.086		.086
MDGNP	-.054	-.040			.037	.038	.078	.079
INEQ			-.440****	.912	.411***	.404***	1.249	1.243
INEQ²				-.476			-.832	-.832
MDINEQ			-.198*	-.244*	-.206*	-.207*	-.248	-.249***
R^2	.064*	.075	.236****	.238****	.243****	.244****	.249***	.249***
Maximum Cook's D	.162	.121	.287	.331	.259	.219	.226	.196
Nation	S. Africa	S. Africa	S. Africa	S. Africa	S. Africa	S. Africa	S. Africa	S. Africa

*$p < .05$
**$p < .01$
***$p < .001$
****$p < .0001$

Suicide-Homicide Ratios

Table 7.7 shows that both GNP and INEQ are significantly related to the suicide-homicide ratio. As development increases, so does the percentage of lethal violence that is expressed as suicide rather than homicide. This pattern, significant in the zero-order equation in model I ($\beta = .484; p < .0001$), persists after inequality is controlled in model V ($\beta = .279; p < .001$). The negative effects of INEQ on the SHR are even stronger ($\beta = -.596; p < .0001$ in model III; $\beta = -.467; p < .0001$ in model V). The relationships of both economic development and income inequality to the SHR appear to be linear. Adding squared terms does not add significantly to R^2. Nonetheless, the R^2 of model V, which includes both independent variables plus their missing data codes, is .419, higher than those for any of the models predicting suicide, homicide, or the LVR.

CONCLUSIONS

Our cross-national analyses have taken two different approaches to studying lethal violence. The first investigates these two forms of individual violence separately, while the other links them together by means of the stream analogy and the integrated model. Our purpose in doing this has been twofold. First, as stated in previous chapters, we resurrect a useful macrosociological research tradition that considers suicide and homicide rates as alternate expressions of lethal violence. Next, we show that the stream analogy does not undercut analyses that have dealt with suicide and homicide rates separately, but rather that it may even clarify and strengthen them. The two approaches are alternative and, somewhat, equivalent ways of conceptualizing reality. Both make use of the same information. Due to their definitional dependencies on suicide and homicide rates, the LVR and SHR contain neither more nor less information than the original rates themselves. The major difference between the two approaches is in terms of conceptualization.

In the stream analogy, two theoretically relevant dimensions—the total amount of lethal violence and the proportion expressed as suicide or as homicide—are posited. The alternative is to view suicide and homicide in isolation from one another and to view each as a response to its own complex of causal factors. In the cross-national analyses, we have used the usual dependent variables, suicide and homicide rates, as well as those derived from the stream analogy, the SHR and LVR. Thus we have explored both of the two alternative, though statistically equiv-

TABLE 7.6 GNP/Capita, Income Inequality and National Lethal Violence Rates (Standardized Regression Coefficients, N = 88)

				Model				
	I	II	III	IV	V	VI	VII	VIII
GNP	.123	−.438			.127	−.453	.122	−.457
GNP²		.582				.578		.577
MDGNP	.104	.125			.102	.109	.066	.073
INEQ			−.120	−.986	.081	.034	−.655	−.669
INEQ²				.988			.731	.727
MDINEQ			−.262**	−.233	−.261*	−.270	−.224	−.233
R²	.026	.082	.083*	.093*	.101	.123	.106	.127
Maximum Cook's D	.131	.100	.345	.271	.208	.183	.187	.168
Nation	S. Africa	S. Africa	S. Africa	S. Africa	S. Africa	S. Africa	S. Africa	S. Africa

*$p < .05$
**$p < .01$
***$p < .001$
****$p < .0001$

TABLE 7.7 GNP/Capita, Income Inequality, and National Suicide-Homicide Ratios (Standardized Regression Coefficients, N = 88)

	Model							
	I	II	III	IV	V	VI	VII	VIII
GNP	.484****	1.051****			.279**	.509	.273**	.504*
GNP²		-.588				-.229		-.230
MDGNP	.112	.091				-.077	-.049	-.052
INEQ			-.596****	-1.216	-.467****	-.488***	-1.372	-1.355
INEQ²				.625			.898	.900
MDINEQ			.055	.090	.093	.097	-.139	.143
R²	.234****	.271	.360****	.364****	.419****	.423****	.426****	.429****
Maximum Cook's D	.027	.076	.137	.202	.048	.098	.117	.100
Nation	Switzerland	Bahamas	Zimbabwe	Zimbabwe	Bahamas	Bahamas	Zimbabwe	Zimbabwe

*p < .05
**p < .01
***p < .001
****p < .0001

alent, realities. Depending upon which reality we choose, somewhat different conclusions arise from the analysis.

If we posit a reality in which suicide and homicide are causally separate phenomena, our analysis has established that (1) suicide rates increase with development independently of inequality, but once inequality is controlled, the inverse relationship between homicide and economic development disappears; (2) suicide rates decrease and homicide rates increase with inequality, independent of economic development; (3) the relationship between development and suicide is curvilinear with a generally increasing curve, independent of inequality; and (4) the relationship between suicide and inequality is curvilinear with a generally decreasing curve, independent of development.

Shifting gears to accommodate the alternative reality of the stream analogy, our findings indicate that (1) the total amount of lethal violence is generally unrelated to either economic development or inequality; (2) as inequality increases, lethal violence is more likely to be directed against external targets than toward oneself; and (3) the greater the economic development, the greater the probability that lethal violence will be turned against the self as suicide.

These results have points of both similarity and difference when compared with earlier studies. Like Unnithan and Whitt (1992), we find little relationship between GNP/capita and the LVR. This is not disturbing because no such relationship was theoretically predicted.[7]

We did predict, however, that the LVR would increase with income inequality, and Unnithan and Whitt (1992) found a generally positive curvilinear relationship that emerged only after controlling for GNP. The divergence in findings between the two studies may result from differences in samples, base years, or measures of inequality. Nonethelesss, the absence of a relationship between inequality and the LVR in our data casts doubt on our hypothesis that inequality acts as a force of production. One possibility is that a widening gap between the rich and the poor reduces the stress experienced by the "haves" at the same time that the "have nots" become more frustrated. If so, the total level of violence might be expected to remain more or less unchanged.

Our results for the SHR are similar to those of Hackney (1969), Whitt, Gordon, and Hofley (1972), and Unnithan and Whitt (1992). All four studies show that the SHR increases with economic development. Hackney (1969) and Whitt and his colleagues (1972) did not include inequality in their analysis, but both the present study and Unnithan and Whitt (1992) find that the SHR decreases with increasing inequality.

The integrated model also makes the nonobvious prediction that the relationships of the suicide and homicide rates to inequality and development should be curvilinear. We found curvilinear patterns in the relationships of suicide but not homicide to both independent variables in our sample, while Unnithan and Whitt (1992; cf. Braithwaite and Braithwaite 1980; Messner 1980) found both independent variables to be curvilinearly related to homicide but not suicide. Taken together, these studies suggest the utility of searching for nonlinear relationships, but support for the integrated model would be greater if curvilinearity could be found for both suicide and homicide in the same study.

Whether one favors the integrated model or the traditional approach, which studies suicide and homicide independently of one another, is a matter of individual taste, vested interests in one or the other of the two approaches, or judgments about the theoretical elegance of one theory over the other. On these grounds and based on our position developed in chapter 6, we prefer interpretations based on the stream analogy. Nonetheless, we also recognize that our findings are relevant to both approaches. Having demonstrated this, we drop separate analyses of homicide and suicide rates in chapter 8.

Several caveats are in order. In using international data based on official reporting of suicides and homicides, we risk the possibility that the figures are biased either because of poor reporting procedures or for reasons of ideological competitiveness. Similarly, data on economic development and inequality have geopolitical overtones. Officials would presumably want their nation to look good, or at least as good as possible, in the international context. Thus, nations may try to minimize rates of inequality, suicide, and homicide and maximize economic development in the information they submit to international organizations. There is little to compel any nation to report, and many nations, in fact, do not do so. Some researchers have, therefore, preferred to use data from a single developed nation such as the United States, organized according to cities, metropolitan areas, or counties. Although deriving from another research tradition, the state-level analysis reported in chapter 8 takes this approach in attempting to explain regional variations in lethal violence in the United States.

Even though our cross-national analysis includes eighty-eight cases, it is admittedly a biased sample. Nonetheless, the use of the Cohen and Cohen (1975) mean-plugging technique has allowed us to analyze data from far more nations than are typically found in studies of suicide and homicide. Quinney's 1965 sample included forty-eight nations, but he did not use the LVR and SHR. In studies using these variables, Hackney (1969) used fifty-six nations, Whitt and his colleagues (1972) used forty-seven, and Unnithan and Whitt (1992) used only thirty-one.

Taken together with these other studies, our findings convince us that differently constituted samples would yield broadly similar conclusions. Overall, studies in the tradition of the integrated model have established the cross-national relevance of the stream analogy in understanding lethal violence by showing that a model based on inequality and economic development can be used to predict whether violence will take the form of suicide or homicide. It is less clear whether these variables affect the total amount of violence in societies. It may be that neither development nor inequality affects the LVR and that some other approach (such as Feierabend and Feierabend 1966, 1972) to assessing systemic frustration cross-nationally will prove more fruitful.

Nonetheless, national economic development and inequality levels have implications beyond their own distributions. They affect many forms of behavior at the individual or interpersonal level, including suicide and homicide. The characteristics of macrosocial units such as nation-states exert an important influence on the social life of individuals and on social interaction at the microlevel (cf. Ragin 1987). We are confident that future research will flesh out the integrated model by incorporating additional cultural and structural sources of systemic frustration and the attribution of blame into the framework of the stream analogy.

JAY CORZINE
LIN HUFF-CORZINE

8

Deadly Connections in the United States

It's just that there are more Southerners
that need killing.
                    —Anonymous

In the cross-national context, the United States stands out as having the highest homicide rate but a below-average suicide rate among the industrialized nations. It has long been recognized, however, that killing is not distributed randomly within the United States, and H. V. Redfield's early report (1880) that homicide rates were highest in the Southern states has proven to be one of the most stable findings in the field of American criminology. In fact, Raymond D. Gastil (1971, 412) asserts that "it is a predisposition to lethal violence in Southern regional culture that accounts for the greater part of the relative height of the American homicide rate."

Although research during the past century has consistently replicated Redfield's finding of a positive relationship between the Southern region and levels of homicide (Brearley 1932; Huff-Corzine, Corzine, and Moore 1986; Messner 1982b, 1983; Nisbett 1993; Shannon 1954),[1] attempts to develop a theoretical explanation for the South's predominance in homicide have been inconclusive. Two distinct approaches, the first emphasizing the importance of high rates of severe poverty (Loftin and Hill 1974) and the second the existence of regional cultural differences (Hackney 1969; Gastil 1971), have appeared in the literature.

In this chapter, we examine the issue of Southern violence from the perspective provided by the model presented in chapter 6. Specifically, we investigate the relationship between homicide, suicide, and region in the United States. This question guided early studies by Austin Porterfield (1949) and Sheldon Hackney (1969), but it is has been absent from the literature on Southern violence for the past twenty-five years. Analyses of statewide lethal violence rates (LVRs) and suicide-homicide ratios (SHRs) for blacks and whites support the usefulness of the model and suggest that both high levels of poverty *and* cultural differences affect the pattern of lethal violence in the South.

EXPLANATIONS OF SOUTHERN VIOLENCE

Southern Homicide

Although early studies by Redfield (1880) and H. C. Brearley (1932) proposed that a combination of both cultural and structural factors contributed to the high level of Southern homicide, articles by Hackney (1969) and Gastil (1971) stimulated a renewed effort to understand the region's predominance in murder. Using multiple regression techniques, both researchers found that measurements of Southernness remain robust predictors of variations in state homicide levels after controlling for several social and demographic characteristics. Hackney argued that the historical experience of white Southerners produced a cultural tradition conducive to interpersonal violence, a position also supported by Gastil. Finally, both investigators agreed that it is primarily Southern *whites* who are bearers of a cultural legacy leading to violence, with high rates of homicide among blacks stemming from other factors.

Colin Loftin and Robert H. Hill (1974), however, forcefully challenged Hackney's 1969 and Gastil's 1971 conclusions on methodological grounds. Specifically, they noted that Hackney's and Gastil's models are biased in favor of a cultural interpretation because the total effect of the regional variable is attributed to cultural distinctiveness. This implies that all structural variables linked to both region and homicide are included in the model, an assumption that is difficult to justify. More importantly, Loftin and Hill argued that lethal violence is influenced more by the proportion of the population living in *severe* poverty, so that the average indicators of economic standing used by Hackney and Gastil are inappropriate. When a structural poverty index (SPI) measuring the percent of the population at the lowest level of economic well-being is substituted for these measures in the regression models, the coefficients for Hackney's and Gastil's measurements of Southernness are reduced to nonsignificance. Loftin and Hill admit shortcomings in their work, concluding that,"our data and those analyzed by Gastil and Hackney are not adequate to delineate precise cultural and non-cultural effects" (Loftin and Hill 1974, 722).

Following Loftin and Hill's 1974 critique, several studies extended the scope of research on Southern homicide by employing alternative units of analysis, including cities (Bailey 1984) and SMSAs (Messner 1983), or by introducing new variables such as refined measures of medical resources (Doerner 1983; Doerner and Speir 1986). Although bringing attention to important methodological questions and introducing new measurements affecting levels of homicide, these investigations left the basic issue of whether a Southern influence contributes to high homicide rates unresolved. Some studies reported that controlling for social and demographic variables explains away the bivariate relationship between region and homicide (Allen and Bankston 1981; Bailey 1984), while others found that measures of the Southern region remain significant predictors of killing (Doerner 1983; Messner 1982b, 1983).

Lin Huff-Corzine, Jay Corzine, and David C. Moore (1986) suggest two avenues for improving empirical research in this area. Concerning the measurement of Southern culture, or Southernness, they argue that the common use of a dummy variable for the South (see Blau and Blau 1982; Messner 1983; Parker 1989; Parker and Smith 1979) is methodologically questionable because it assumes regional factors influencing homicide conveniently end at state lines, a presupposition that is contradicted by R. Page Hudson, John A. Humphrey, and Harriet J. Kupferer (1980). Moreover, Gastil's 1971 Southernness Index (SI) is a more precise indicator, but the formula for its calculation is unpublished. Therefore, it is unclear what the SI measures, and it is impossible to compute scores using more recent data.

Huff-Corzine, Corzine, and Moore (1986) propose that the percent of the population born in the South is a more appropriate indicator of Southernness, a position also adopted by Peter M. Blau and Reid M. Golden (1986). Their second criticism concerns the failure of many researchers to disaggregate homicide totals by race (Baron and Straus 1988; Blau and Blau 1982). Although both Hackney and Gastil specify that it is *white* Southerners who are more likely influenced by a regional culture of violence, most subsequent studies, including Loftin and Hill (1974), have analyzed homicide rates calculated for total populations.

Using the SI and percent born in the South as alternative measures of Southernness in ridge regression analyses of race-specific homicide rates, Huff-Corzine, Corzine, and Moore (1986) show that influences on homicide levels differ for blacks and whites.[2] White homicide rates are directly related to Loftin and Hill's SPI (1974) and both measures of Southernness. For blacks, however, neither the SPI nor the percent of the population living below the poverty level significantly affects homicide rates. Moreover, findings for a regional influence vary with the measure used, with only the SI having a positive relationship to homicide levels among blacks. Given current explanations, these results are theoretically ambiguous for blacks; but they demonstrate the importance of disaggregating total homicide rates by race, the need for further theory development, and the possibility that adequate models for explaining violence will differ by race.

Huff-Corzine, Corzine, and Moore (1986) interpret their results as supporting the existence of a regional effect on homicide rates and assert that cultural as well as structural characteristics influence differences between the South and other sections of the United States. Our primary goal in this chapter is to extend their research beyond the narrow focus on homicide rates by examining cultural and structural influences on the LVR and the SHR for blacks and whites. In so doing, we also hope to advance beyond the theoretical logjam that has produced stagnation in this area of research in recent years.

SUICIDE AND HOMICIDE IN THE SOUTH

Porterfield (1949) first noted that the ratio of homicides to suicides tended to be higher in Southern than in non-Southern cities and states. Twenty years later, Hackney (1969) concluded that the pattern of violence characteristic of the South is marked by both high rates of homicide *and* low rates of suicide or, in other words, by a low SHR. In support of this proposition, he shows that Southernness increases the homicide rate and the LVR but decreases the SHR for whites. A Southern regional measure is also positively related to the homicide rate and LVR among blacks, but it has no significant effect on the SHR. There are weaknesses in Hackney's methodology, however, that make uncritical acceptance of these findings problematic. In addition to the use of questionable measurements for both poverty variables and region, he failed to check for the presence of multicollinearity, a chronic problem in homicide research (Light 1984). Finally, it is important to update Hackney's research with more recent data.

Although the question of a Southern influence on the *direction* of violence, as opposed to the *volume* of homicide, has been neglected since Hackney, examining the conjunction of homicide and suicide rates may advance our understanding of regional violence patterns. While theoretical criminology offers several explanations for a link between economic deprivation and criminal activity, the positive association between poverty and violent crime is usually accounted for by a frustration-aggression model (Balkwell 1990; Blau and Blau 1982; Parker 1989). But chronic poverty may lead to a number of collective reactions, and some of these are not conducive to high rates of violence (Ball 1968). Moreover, as shown in chapter 6, systemic frustration may be expected to lead either to suicide or to homicide dependent on the attributional tendencies within a particular segment of the population. Therefore, it is necessary to identify more closely the social-psychological processes that mediate the relationship between economic frustration and violence. Similarly, Hackney (1969) and Gastil (1971) assume that Southern cultural differences increase interpersonal violence in the region, thereby producing higher homicide rates. It is plausible, however, that Southernness instead alters the mix of lethal violence in favor of homicide over suicide.

Social-psychological research on attributional processes supports the relevance of the attribution of blame for understanding the direction of lethal violence, including the regional variations in suicide and homicide. In attributing causal interpretations to negative life events, individuals who assume that their personal situation is dependent on their own actions operate from an internal locus of causality, while those who see outside forces, including the actions of other persons, as responsible for their condition, display a tendency to blame others (see chapter 5). Importantly, the attribution of blame influences behavior through emotional responses to negative outcomes (that is, frustrations). Attributions of internal causes for failure produce guilt, shame, and lowered self-esteem, but locating the causes of one's problems in external forces leads to anger (Weiner, Russell, and Lerman 1979). There is also evidence that internal and external attributions, with their resultant emotional states, are related to actions (Weiner 1980), including interpersonal aggression (Shields and Hanneke 1983). Persons who characteristically blame themselves for bad events are more likely to channel aggression toward the self, while there is greater likelihood that the violence of those who characteristically attribute causal responsibility to external sources will be directed toward others.

Psychologists have traditionally conceived of attribution as an individual-level process, but the integrated model (see chapter 6) is consistent with recent work showing that attributional tendencies are also influenced by demographic characteristics and cultural patterns (DuCette, Wolk, and Friedman 1972; Guimond, Begin, and Palmer 1989;

Miller 1984). To our knowledge, there are no studies specifically comparing differences in attributions of blame between the residents of different regions of the United States,[3] but there are persistent regional differences in other attitudes and values (Reed 1982; Abrahamson and Carter 1986; Hurlbert 1989). Importantly, Hackney (1969) argues that the South's particular history (that is, defeat in the American Civil War, which Southerners call the "War between the States," and subsequent economic dependency on the North) produced a conception of the external environment as hostile and threatening, so that Southerners tend to locate the causes of personal troubles outside the self (also see Reed 1972).

Studies linking Protestant fundamentalism, more common in the South than in other regions, to preference for retribution in criminal sentencing are indirectly relevant to the proposition that the attribution of blame affects the direction of lethal violence in the Southern states. Michael Lupfer, Patricia J. Hopkinson, and Patricia Kelley (1985) propose that fundamentalists, because they focus on a person's internal traits, are more likely to attribute intentionality to the acts of others. Harold G. Grasmick, Elizabeth Davenport, Mitchell B. Chamlin, and Robert J. Bursik, Jr., (1992) conclude that this tendency to rely on dispositional rather than situational cues may explain why fundamentalists are more likely to favor the retributive doctrine in judging the appropriateness of criminal sentences. Extending this argument, adherence to a fundamentalist doctrine would increase the chances of attributing the causes of one's failures and frustrations to the malevolent acts of others, thus resulting in aggression being directed outward rather than inward. This type of attributional pattern would be consistent with a low SHR at the aggregate level.

Based on the frustration-aggression hypothesis and the research reviewed in earlier chapters, we predict that high rates of severe poverty are positively related to the LVR for both blacks and whites. Thus, economic deprivation is viewed as a force of production increasing both homicide and suicide. If our hypothesis that the attribution of blame is a key cultural element mediating the effect of Southern region on violence is correct, then Southernness is not expected to have a significant effect on the LVR. However, it should have an inverse impact on the SHR, thus increasing the probability that lethal aggression is expressed as homicide rather than suicide for both races. Because there are no direct data on regional patterns of the attribution of blame in the United States, attributional tendencies are treated as an unmeasured, intervening variable.[4]

DATA AND METHODS

To enhance comparability with past studies of Southern violence, the forty-eight contiguous states of the United States were analyzed. Dependent variables for the following analyses are computed
from suicide and homicide totals for blacks and whites reported by
the National Center for Health Statistics (1974a, 1974b, 1974c).[5] Because there is random fluctuation in the annual levels of both types
of lethal violence, a three-year average was calculated for the years
1969 to 1971. As defined earlier, the LVR for each race is the total
of suicides (S) and homicides (H) per one-hundred thousand people
(that is, LVR = 100,000 $(S+ H)$/population). The SHR is the number
of suicides divided by the total of suicides and homicides [SHR =
$S/(S + H)$]. The most complex of the independent variables is the SPI
introduced by Loftin and Hill (1974) and used in several subsequent
studies of homicide (such as Huff-Corzine, Corzine, and Moore 1986;
Parker 1989; Parker and Smith 1979). Loftin and Hill derive SPI scores
from six indicators of low economic standing: (1) infant mortality rate,
(2) percent of people age twenty-five years and over with less than five
years' education, (3) percent illiterate, (4) percent of families with less
than $1,000 annual income, (5) percent of Armed Forces Mental Test
failures, and (6) percent of children under eighteen years of age living
with one parent. Following their procedure, the homicide rate is regressed on these variables, and the resulting unstandardized regression coefficients are used as weights to obtain an index score. Using
data for 1970, our calculation of the SPI differs from that of Loftin and
Hill in two ways. First, following Huff-Corzine, Corzine, and Moore,
the percent of children not living with both parents is substituted for
the percent of children living with one parent as a measure of family
instability. Second, because data for percent illiterate and percent of
Armed Forces Mental Test failures are not available by race, our SPI
scores comprise a four-item index. Faced with the same problem, Huff-
Corzine, Corzine, and Moore report little difference between the
amount of variation in total state homicide rates explained by SPI
scores computed from the six variables used by Loftin and Hill and the
four race-specific variables. This is not surprising given the high correlations among the indicators used to construct the SPI (Loftin and Hill
1974). There is little reason to believe that our inability to exactly repli-
cate Loftin and Hill's procedures has a significant impact on our findings or conclusions. Separate SPI scores are computed for each of the
four models in the following analyses (that is, those explaining the
LVR and SHR for whites and blacks). Data used to construct the SPI in-

dexes are taken from the 1970 census (United States Bureau of the Census 1973).

We follow Blau and Golden (1986) and Huff-Corzine, Corzine, and Moore (1986) by employing the percent of the population born in the census South to measure regional influence. To enhance comparability with past studies, the four control variables used by Loftin and Hill (1974), Parker (1989), and others are included in the regression models. These are percent rural, percent of people age twenty to thirty-four years, hospital beds per one-hundred thousand people, and the Gini index of family income inequality. Data for the first three variables are taken from the U.S. census (1973); scores for the Gini Index are from Grasso and Sharansky (1980). Unfortunately, the suicide and homicide data used to calculate the dependent variables are for non-whites rather than blacks alone. Because the measurements of the independent variables are for blacks only, the percent of a state's non-white population that is not black is entered as an additional control variable for analyses of the black LVR and SHR.

As noted by Stephen C. Light (1984), a major problem plaguing research on homicide is multicollinearity, which occurs when a high percentage of the variance in one or more independent variables is explained by other predictors in the model. As a diagnostic measure, we performed auxiliary regressions, where each predictor is, in turn, regressed on the other independent variables, with $1-R^2$ representing the amount of independent variance for each variable. As expected, the results (not shown) indicate serious multicollinearity problems for each model. In the presence of multicollinearity, regression estimates are unbiased. The parameter estimates are not efficient, however, because their standard errors increase as the degree of multicollinearity increases (Kmenta 1971). The problem faced by investigators is that estimates with low efficiency, even though unbiased, may be less desirable than those that have a small amount of bias if their efficiency is high (Feig 1978).

Joseph C. Fisher and Robert L. Mason (1981) discuss the problems associated with multicollinearity and describe a number of techniques for computing estimates in its presence. Jeffrey W. Bulcock and Wan Fung Lee (1983) and James Fennessey and Ronald J. D'Amico (1980) assess the results obtained by using different estimation procedures and address the issue of whether a particular tool for computing estimates is better than others. They conclude that while it is preferable to handle the problem of multicollinearity at the data collection level, researchers (especially those using secondary data) seldom enjoy that luxury. We follow their recommendation for dealing with multicollinearity at the data analysis level by computing the optimal bias quantity k using normalization ridge regression (NRR) procedures.[6]

SAS programs were used for both OLS and ridge regression analyses. Optimal bias was computed using an iterative BASIC program written for use on the Apple II computer by David C. Moore.

RESULTS

Zero-order Correlations

Bivariate correlations, means, and standard deviations for variables included in the regression analyses are reported in table 8.1. Several zero-order correlations between independent variables have magnitudes of .70 or higher, which is an indicator of the presence of multicollinearity.[7]

From the first table, it is apparent that both volume and type of lethal violence differ significantly by race. The LVR for blacks is more than twice that for whites (38.4 versus 16.9), and the corresponding SHR values of .22 and .76 indicate that suicide is proportionately much higher among whites than blacks. These racial differences are consistent with both prior research on attribution theory and past empirical studies of lethal violence among blacks and whites.

White Lethal Violence Rates

Table 8.2 presents findings from OLS and ridge regressions of state LVRs for whites. Similar to Loftin and Hill's 1974 findings for homicide, the SPI is the strongest predictor of variation in the total volume of lethal violence among whites.

Consistent with past studies (Doerner 1983; Doerner and Speir 1986), the availability of hospital beds, a measure of available health care resources, decreases the LVR, suggesting that access to medical treatment decreases the chances that a life-threatening injury from an assault or suicide attempt will prove fatal. There is also a significant, positive effect of age structure on the white LVR in the ridge regression model. Notably, the percentage of the population born in the South is not significantly related to the white LVR.

Black Lethal Violence Rates

Table 8.3 shows both similarities and differences in the determinants of lethal violence rates for blacks as compared to whites (see table

TABLE 8.1 Bivariate Correlations, Means, and Standard Deviations for White (Upper Triangle) and Non-white (Lower Triangle) Lethal Violence Rates and Suicide-Homicide Ratios

Variable	1	2	3	4	5	6	7	8	9	10	MEAN	S.D.
1 LV		-.43	.68	-.31	.52	.56	-.10	-.54	.23		16.89	4.32
2 SH	-.18		-.34	.74	-.69	-.42	.12	.25	-.53		.76	.09
3 SPI-LV	.29	-.60		-.46	.48	.42	-.05	-.34	.21		20.81	2.94
4 SPI-SHR	-.28	.63	-.96		-.08	-.40	-.08	.16	-.59		-.24	.07
5 % Born South[a]	-.00	-.64	.63	-.63		.54	.16	.60	.73		2.24	1.52
6 % Age 20-34	-.19	.68	-.86	.83	-.75		-.17	-.33	.17		20.21	1.43
7 % Rural	-.24	.04	.17	-.14	.44	-.24		.17	.27		.35	.14
8 Hospital beds	-.27	.09	-.14	.12	-.15	.27	.02		-.20		7.81	1.57
9 Gini index	.11	-.19	.39	-.24	.53	-.46	.53	-.20			.38	.02
10 % Non-black	-.27	.78	-.63	.70	-.05	.70	-.22	-.16	-.25			
Mean	38.42	.22	16.24	-.49	3.51	21.96	.17	7.81	.38	27.96		
S.D.	11.65	.19	3.35	.12	.86	5.11	.17	1.57	.02	30.10		

[a]Natural log transformation.

TABLE 8.2   OLS and Ridge Regression Analyses of White Lethal Violence
Rates, 1969–71, Forty-Eight States

	OLS		NRR	
	b	beta	b	beta
White structural				
poverty index	.638***	.434	.570***	.387
% Born in South[a]	.426	.150	.418	.147
% Age 20–34	.651	.216	.632*	.210
% Rural	.037	.001	−.331	−.011
Hospital beds	−.772**	−.281	−.709**	−.258
Gini index	−10.398	−.059	−5.950	−.034
Intercept	−.599		−.845	
R²	.632			
Estimated ridge k			.135	

[a]Natural log transformation
*p < .05
**p < .01
***p < .001

8.2). The black SPI attains a significant, positive relationship with lethal violence among blacks in the ridge regression model. In view of past work where the SPI did not have a significant influence on black homicide rates (Huff-Corzine, Corzine, and Moore 1986), it is possible that the SPI is related to suicide levels among blacks. In supplementary regression analyses (not shown), however, the SPI is not a significant predictor of black suicide rates. Further analyses of the separate components of the SPI and their specific relationships to the two types of lethal violence are necessary before this finding can be adequately explained. For both races, however, our results are consistent with frustration-aggression explanations of the relationship between poverty and violence.

Consistent with results for whites, the percent of blacks born in the South, our measure of Southernness, has no significant relationship with the LVR in the ridge regression analysis. Thus, for blacks, as well as whites, structural effects have a stronger influence on the LVR than do regional measures. It may be, however, that cultural differences and regional socialization patterns exert an indirect effect on lethal violence rates. If so, behaviors resulting from cultural differences, such as carrying a firearm for protection (Bankston and Thompson 1989), may be significantly related to rates of lethal violence.

TABLE 8.3   OLS and Ridge Regression Analyses of Black Lethal Violence
Rates, 1969–71, Forty-Eight States

	OLS		NRR	
	b	beta	b	beta
Black structural				
poverty index	1.705	.490	.930*	.267
% Born in South[a]	−7.126*	−.529	−3.631*	−.270
% Age 20–34	1.039	.455	.232	.102
% Rural	−19.396	−.285	−17.440*	−.276
Hospital beds	−3.192**	−.430	−1.927*	−.259
Gini index	155.455	.327	88.909	.187
% Non-black	−.234*	−.605	−.102*	−.265
Intercept	−11.369		18.041	
R^2	.373			
Estimated ridge k			.165	

[a]Natural log transformation
*$p < .05$
**$p < .01$

Given the high rates of homicide among blacks in the United
States, it is not surprising that higher proportions of non-blacks are negatively associated with rates of lethal violence. Moreover, negative coefficients for percentage rural and hospital beds indicate, respectively,
that the LVR for blacks is higher in urban areas and where medical resources are limited.

White Suicide-Homicide Ratios

Estimates of OLS and NRR regressions analyzing white SHRs are
contained in table 8.4. Remember that the SHR represents the proportion of lethal violence in a population that is expressed as suicide. Thus,
positive coefficients show that an independent variable increases the
relative likelihood of suicide, while negative signs are related to proportionately higher levels of homicide in a population.

The structural influence of the SPI for whites is highly significant
and positively related to the SHR, indicating that severe poverty
increases the odds that lethal violence will occur as suicide. Because
suicide is an act directed inward, this finding contradicts research
reporting lower-class persons to be more externally oriented than
those from the middle class (Schmidt, Lamm, and Trommsdorff
1978). On the other hand, the significant, negative relationship between

TABLE 8.4   OLS and Ridge Regression Analyses of White Suicide-Homocide
Ratios, 1969–71, Forty-Eight States

	OLS		NRR	
	b	beta	b	beta
White structural				
poverty index	.658***	.489	.556***	.413
% Born in South[a]	−.017	−.282	−.015*	−.247
% Age 20–34	−.001	−.014	−.003	−.054
% Rural	.140**	.217	−.116**	.181
Hospital beds	.001	.024	.002	.029
Gini index	.330	−.089	−.456	−.122
Intercept	1.037		1.112	
R²	.643			
Estimated ridge k			.150	

[a]Natural log transformation
*p < .05
**p < .001

percent born in the South and the SHR shows that white Southerners
are more likely than non-Southerners to express lethal violence as
homicide.

Also, the significant, positive relationship between the SHR
and percentage of the population living in rural areas shows that
lethal violence is more likely to be expressed as suicide among rural
rather than among urban whites. This finding may reflect non-
regional cultural differences that favor the development of an internal
attribution of blame among rural residents in the United States.

Black Suicide-Homicide Ratios

Finally, table 8.5 presents results for analyses of the black SHR for
states. Once again, both similarities and differences are apparent between blacks and whites. The most theoretically important difference is
the SPI's lack of significance for the black SHR. Apparently, structural
poverty affects the volume but not the direction of lethal violence that
occurs among blacks. As with whites, however, suicide-homicide ratios
among blacks are negatively influenced by Southernness. Thus, consistent with hypotheses derived from the model in chapter 6 and research
on the cultural origin of attributional tendencies, region is linked to the
external expression of violence among both races.

TABLE 8.5   OLS and Ridge Regression Analyses of Black Suicide-Homocide Ratios, 1969–71, Forty-Eight States

	OLS		NRR	
	b	beta	b	beta
Black structural poverty index	−.142	−.089	−.068	−.045
% Born in South[a]	−.031	−.145	−.041*	−.190
% Age 20–34	.008	.231	.007*	.196
% Rural	.307**	.282	−.248**	.226
Hospital beds	.014	.117	.008	.063
Gini index	.080	.011	.119	.016
% Non-black	.004***	.658	.003***	.456
Intercept	−.225		.019	
R^2	.727			
Estimated ridge k			.170	

[a]Natural log transformation
*$p < .05$
**$p < .01$
***$p < .001$

Replicating the results for whites, rurality among blacks is directly related to the SHR. Of course, this does not mean that rural blacks or whites are more likely to commit suicide than their urban counterparts, but that a greater proportion of lethal violence among rural residents occurs as suicide. In contrast to findings for whites, however, there is a significant and positive relationship between the percentage twenty to thirty-four and the SHR for blacks. Interestingly, there has been sub-stantial attention to high rates of homicide among young black males, but this finding indicates that compared to older generations of blacks, recent cohorts have experienced a relative increase in the proportion of violent deaths expressed as suicide.[8] If this trend continues, there should be a convergence in the patterns of lethal violence of blacks and whites in the future. Herbert Hendin (1969a), however, reports a higher suicide rate for younger black males than their older counterparts in New York City in the late 1960s. Therefore, it is possible that today's black youth, as they age, will experience a lower risk of suicide similar to older generations. Finally, the positive coefficient for percentage non-black indicates that homicide is relatively more common than sui-cide. While this is certainly a plausible interpretation of the findings, it risks committing the well-known ecological fallacy in the absence of in-dividual-level data.

CONCLUSIONS

Overall, the findings in this chapter reinforce the need to extend the range of theoretical perspectives and empirical questions that have dominated the recent literature on lethal violence, particularly that literature associated with the South. Since Gastil (1971) and Loftin and Hill (1974), the focus of investigators has been on explaining why there is a greater volume of homicides per capita in the South than in other sections of the United States. But Southern violence is more complicated than this approach presumes. Specifically, the present research supports Hackney's 1969 contention that it is the juxtaposition of high homicide and low suicide rates—that is, a low SHR—that defines the South's peculiar pattern of violence for both races. This is the same pattern of lethal violence that makes the United States an anomalous case among industrialized nations.

As measured by percent born in the South, Southernness has no effect on the lethal violence rate for either blacks or whites. A Southern regional influence, however, channels violence toward other persons rather than the self for both races. In situations where individuals perceive violence as an acceptable response to personal failure, external attributions increase the odds that aggression will be directed at others rather than the self. The result is a propensity toward homicide; and if particular segments of the population (such as Southerners) are inclined toward external attributions, this should be reflected in relatively high homicide and low suicide rates.

Our interpretation of the results would be on a firmer foundation if research showed black and white Southerners are more likely to make external attributions than their Northern and Western counterparts. Although such data are currently not available, the underlying theme is consistent with dominant interpretations of Southern history. Hackney (1969) and Reed (1972) have noted that major social changes in the South, from the end of slavery to the demise of legal segregation, have originated outside the region. Furthermore, Rupert B. Vance (1935) argued that the Southern economy remained in a colonial status to the North well into the twentieth century. Hackney's position, already quoted in chapter 5, comes closest to attribution theory by concluding that:

> In the search for a valid explanation of southern violence the most fruitful avenue will probably be one that seeks to identify and trace the development of a southern world view that defines the social, political, and physical environment as hostile and casts

the white southerner in the role of the passive victim of malevolent forces (Hackney 1969, 924–925).

There are, however, important differences between the findings of Hackney and our research. He reported that Southernness increased the LVR for both races and decreased the SHR for whites only. Our findings show no impact on the LVR for blacks or whites, but negative and significant influence on the SHR for both races. Possible explanations for these differences include temporal change (Hackney's data are for 1940), alternative measurements of key variables, and Hackney's failure to test for and deal with multicollinearity.

Several studies have emphasized differences by race in the causes of violence (Gastil 1971; Hackney 1969; Huff-Corzine, Corzine, and Moore 1986), but our findings point to similarities, especially for the role of a regional influence on the SHR. There is some evidence in our analyses, however, for different effects by race of poverty on violence. Contrary to the finding for whites, the SPI for blacks did not have a significant impact on the SHR, a pattern that reflects the lack of effect for poverty on black homicide rates that was first noted by Prudhomme (1938) and has been recently reconfirmed by Huff-Corzine, Corzine, and Moore (1986).

As an important caveat, a limitation of our measurement of Southernness advises caution in interpreting our findings as the results of regional cultural differences. Percentage born in the South is a preferable measure to the use of a dummy variable for the South, but we are assuming that it is an indicator of differences in regional patterns of attitudes, values, and beliefs that are acquired by individuals during early socialization. It is possible, however, that unmeasured variables reflecting either elements of structure or culture are related to both the percent of the population of Southern origin and one or more dependent variables. While this argument has been frequently exhorted by critics of the Southern culture-of-violence thesis (Loftin and Hill 1974; Parker 1989), the underlying problem is not unique to this area of research. It is incumbent upon proponents of the cultural perspective to identify and measure those aspects of Southern culture, including fundamentalist religious beliefs, that affect regional patterns of violence so that more precise tests can be accomplished.

As a final point, proponents of structural explanations for Southern homicide have been correct in asserting that severe poverty is a determinant of lethal violence. They have erred, however, in assuming that other regional differences are unimportant influences on violence once economic and demographic characteristics have been controlled. Although Southernness does not influence the LVR at the state level, it has a substantial impact on the choice of target—the self versus others—of lethal aggression. It is time to end the debate about whether structural *or* cultural perspectives provide better explanations of Southern violence. Both are important and necessary for comprehending the South's pattern of lethal violence. In this chapter, we demonstrate that the gestalt shift accomplished by the integrated model is able to resolve at least one issue that has developed from a focus on homicide apart from suicide. Future research will determine if it will be similarly useful in shedding new light on other debates and questions in the area of lethal violence.

N. PRABHA UNNITHAN
HUGH P. WHITT
LIN HUFF-CORZINE
JAY CORZINE

9

Charting the Currents of Lethal Violence

A research tradition dating back to the formative years of the so-cial sciences conceptualizes suicide and homicide as alternative cur-rents in a stream of lethal violence. In previous chapters, we have traced the history of this idea from its early antecedents in social philosophy through various theoretical manifestations. We have shown its rela-tionship to attribution theory in social psychology and its relevance for unraveling and understanding cross-national and United States regional patterns of lethal violence.

In a sense, it is remarkable that the stream analogy has survived the transformations and withstood the changes that the social sciences have undergone since the first third of the nineteenth century. Of course, the history of the stream analogy reflects theoretical shifts in the social sciences over time. Modern approaches linking suicide and homi-cide have largely discredited the particular sorts of biological and geo-graphical determinants of the choice between suicide and homicide favored by the nineteenth-century criminal anthropologists, but their distinction between the forces of production and forces of direction re-mains intact.

During its long history, the stream analogy has been advanced as an empirical generalization (Andre-Michel Guerry), formulated as a general theory (Morselli, Ferri), debunked (Durkheim, Tarde), aban-doned (Halbwachs, Quinney), reformulated (Freud), resurrected (Porterfield, Henry and Short) formalized (Gold, Whitt), expanded (West, Lane), declared theoretically and methodologically inadequate

(Douglas, Schuessler), and more or less neglected before being reexamined in our work.

The history of the stream analogy lends itself to either of two interpretations. The first suggests that the continued reliance upon nineteenth-century ideas reflects the disarray and lack of progress that have characterized the social sciences. From this perspective, the survival of the stream analogy is symptomatic of the failure of the social sciences to develop empirical research conclusive enough to allow them to move beyond cherished theoretical notions that have outlived their usefulness.

The second interpretation, which we obviously prefer, is that the idea of the stream analogy refuses to die because it corresponds to empirical reality. According to this view, the stream analogy was a good idea in the nineteenth century and continues to be a good one today. Its continued relevance reflects the cumulative nature of studies linking suicide and homicide, and further attention should be devoted to the refinement and extension of the integrated model of suicide and homicide presented in this book.

In line with this implicit research agenda, we briefly summarize conclusions from our empirical tests of the integrated model. We then discuss its theoretical and empirical utility and its strengths and limitations, suggesting avenues for further research in this tradition.

MACROSOCIOLOGY AND LETHAL VIOLENCE

The integrated model using homicide and suicide rates presented in chapter 6 was tested using two sets of data, the first at the cross-national level and the second based on regional variation in suicide and homicide in the United States. Following the strategy advocated by Ness (1985), we subjected the United States, an outlier in an earlier cross-national analysis (Unnithan and Whitt 1992), to intensive investigation requiring "more explicit consideration of historical, cultural and political-economic particularities" (Kohn 1989, 79–80).

When coupled with previous studies, our cross-national analysis suggests that the stream analogy is useful in understanding and explaining the production of overall lethal violence rates as well as the particular form (suicide or homicide) that violence takes in different nations. Although we were unable to predict lethal violence rates in our sample, these studies, taken as a whole, demonstrate that inequality, and to a lesser extent economic development, affect both the level of lethal violence and the direction of its expression. Our interpretation of these cross-national studies suggests that both cultural and structural factors need to be considered in future research.

The homicide rate of the Southern region of the United States is quite high in comparison to other regions and to the norm for industrialized societies, while its suicide rate is relatively low. Chesnais (1992, 218) observes that the homicide rate in the United States is "almost ten times the average of other Western nations." This atypical pattern provides us with an opportunity to examine the impact of cultural and historical factors on the amount and direction of lethal violence. We argue on the basis of our findings for regional variation in the United States that the pattern of lethal violence in the South reflects a culturally and historically based tendency for Southerners to make external attributions of blame more frequently than their Northern counterparts.

One benefit of analyses based on the integrated model is that researchers can use the model to move theory beyond simplistic and misleading dichotomies such as structure versus culture. The debate on Southern violence (homicide) has traditionally been posed in terms of whether the high homicide rate of the region is due to structural factors such as poverty *or* cultural factors such as Southernness. Our analysis using the integrated model suggests that the answer is "both/and" rather than "either/or." By examining the LVR and the SHR rather than focusing exclusively on the homicide rates that have been the staple of studies in the Southern violence debate, we have pointed to a way out of the morass of claims and counterclaims about structure and culture that have characterized this tradition.

This is not to suggest that the study of suicide and homicide in isolation from one another should be abandoned. All the statistical information contained in the LVR and the SHR, the two dependent variables implied by the integrated model, is also contained in the suicide and homicide rates themselves. Nonetheless, using the integrated model accomplishes a gestalt shift that allows us to view suicide and homicide in a different light. As in the classic figure-ground experiments in which one may see either a duck or a rabbit in a single line drawing, it is possible to shift back and forth between the concepts of suicide and homicide and those of the amount and direction of lethal violence.

It is meaningless to ask whether the gestalt psychologists' line drawing *really* depicts a duck or a rabbit. Similarly, one cannot rely upon statistical analysis alone to decide whether reality works the way traditional studies of suicide and homicide suggest or according to the theoretical processes identified by the integrated model. If, however, the use of the integrated model generates useful insights that are hidden when one views reality through the lens of traditional approaches, its theoretical utility may lead to the choice of one of the two pictures over the other. Our own position is that the traditional approach and the integrated model are alternative and complementary approaches to conceptualizing reality.

From the perspective of the integrated model, changes in the size of the stream of violence (the LVR) and its division into suicide and homicide rates (the SHR) occur as the distribution of wealth within societies varies and with the level of economic development. Involved in this transition are changes in social meanings and attributions of blame based on definitions of what is frustrating, what is the source or cause of the frustration, and what one ought to do about it. Implicit and explicit messages about the imputation of blame for frustration are transmitted through the orientational institutions (Eister 1972) of societies, including the family, the schools, and the mass media. They are also carried in the quasi-theories (Hall and Hewitt 1970) conveyed in informal day-to-day social interaction.

To illustrate the importance of meanings for interpreting frustrating situations, consider the following example taken from Roy H.Saigo:

> Vincent Chin and his friends were attacked as they left a bachelor party at a tavern the evening before his wedding. The attackers—a man and his son-in-law—were laid-off auto workers who had observed Chin's group at the tavern. Thinking Chin was Japanese, the men became angry with him for in some way being responsible for their unemployment. They went home, got baseball bats, came back to the tavern, and waited outside for Chin and his friends. They then chased them down, caught Chin, and battered him to death. His friends escaped (Saigo 1989, 8).

This incident took place in Detroit in 1982, and the two auto workers who had been laid off were white Americans. Industry and work are core American values (Williams 1970). American culture is filled with messages extolling the centrality of work in one's life and productivity for the nation's economic well-being. The media constantly emphasize the debilitating effects of unemployment on the individual and society. At the time of the incident, newspapers, radio, and television attributed the problems of the American automobile industry to Japan's success in car manufacturing and marketing. These attributions were no doubt picked up by the auto workers, who probably viewed their homicidal attack on Chin as an acceptable response to their personally frustrating situation. They saw in Chin (ironically, a Chinese American) the personification of Japan and attributed to him responsibility for the loss of their jobs. In addition, one can also see in this incident attributions involving group and cultural superiority and inferiority (Williams 1970).

We wonder whether such an incident would have taken place in a culture or subculture in which self-blame for personal failure and difficulties and the fatalistic acceptance of one's lot were the normatively approved responses. The integrated model suggests that an individual who in one society would commit murder would in another commit suicide when confronted with a similar or identical situation. It is easy to imagine a laid-off Japanese auto worker responding by committing *seppuku* (hara-kiri) rather than face disgrace.

The integrated model predicts that the total amount of lethal violence in human populations varies with structural conditions such as poverty and inequality that generate patterned sources of frustration. Although we suspect that structural conditions have a greater impact than cultural factors on the LVR, cultural definitions of what is frustrating may in some cases mediate the impact of these structural factors. For example, there is some evidence that the relationship between economic development and the total amount of lethal violence varies by religious tradition (Whitt, Gordon, and Hofley 1972), perhaps because of the greater compatibility of Protestant religious traditions with industrial values.

Both structural conditions and cultural factors (such as the content of religious doctrines, socialization practices, and cultural legitimation of violence against external targets) alter the ratio of suicides to homicides. Thus, structurally induced lethal violence is subject to culturally mediated messages that affect its channeling against self or others. These messages derive from culture as "a 'tool kit' of symbols, stories, rituals and world-views, which people may use in varying configurations to solve different kinds of problems" (Swidler 1986, 273). Structural conditions themselves may also affect the choice between suicide and homicide by providing readily identifiable objects of blame. Economically depressed populations, for example, seem very likely to externalize blame, while the more successful generally attribute blame intropunitively.

Nonetheless, we suspect that future research will show that the LVR is affected more by structural conditions than by cultural factors, while the SHR is more closely tied to cultural interpretations of responsibility for frustration. For example, Goldstein (1986) argues that in a cultural context where there is a high degree of acceptance of violence, it would not be unusual for children to learn violent behavior as a result of patterns of child rearing that are considered appropriate and normative. Further, it is possible that groups that share similar locations on the stratification systems of various social structures may share similar propensities toward violence (the LVR). Whether such violence is turned inward or outward (the SHR) is likely to be based on world views consisting of attributions, targets of blame, and imputations of causality that are culturally mediated. Lacking refined measurements or data, however, we can offer only loosely supported conclusions at this point.

STRENGTHS AND LIMITATIONS OF THE INTEGRATED MODEL

One of the major strengths of the integrated model is its ability to deal with overall patterns of lethal violence and account for regularities that cannot be addressed by traditional studies of suicide or homicide in isolation from one another. Given the long history of the stream analogy and its demonstrated utility, it is unfortunate that researchers have ignored this model and conducted their inquiries as though suicide and homicide were causally unrelated. We have emphasized several times in the preceding pages, however, that the integrated model should not be viewed as opposed to perspectives that call for the study of immediate antecedent or precipitating circumstances of suicidal and homicidal events. The integrated model focuses on the structural and cultural background within which individual suicides and homicides take place. Detailed and intensive case studies at the microlevel are complementary to the macrolevel analyses provided in this book. If the integrated model is correct, however, case studies should show that suicidal and homicidal individuals experience similar levels of frustration, which they respond to differently because of differences in the attribution of blame. This, of course, is what the stress-diathesis model suggests for suicide.

There are certain homicidal and suicidal acts to which the integrated model may not be applicable at the microlevel. So-called felony homicides, in which the victim "gets in the way" during the commission of some other crime (such as robbery) belong in this category. It could be argued that the victim in such cases becomes a new source of frustration by offering active resistance or non-cooperation, but the imputation of blame in such cases is momentary and situated rather than a product of culturally based patterns of attribution. Theoretically, also, this stretches the definition of a frustrating situation beyond recognition.

Leonard Berkowitz (1989; see also Berkowitz 1962) draws a distinction between instrumental aggression and angry, expressive, hostile, or emotional aggression. Instrumental aggression is "oriented mainly to the attainment of some other objective," while in expressive aggression "the primary goal is to injure someone" (Berkowitz 1989, 62). The integrated model appears to fit expressive aggression better than it does the type of instrumental aggression found in felony homicides.

In the case of suicide, the integrated model does not appear to apply well at the microlevel to situations in which the victim suffers from extreme pain or incurable terminal diseases—what have recently been described as Kevorkian suicides.[1] It might be possible to interpret such suicides as resulting from self-blame for contracting the disease or engaging in behavior that led to the debilitating condition. This is obviously stretching a point to fit a theory, but it is consistent with the the view that many accidents and certain diseases such as lung cancer and cirrhosis of the liver, which are caused by unhealthy habits (for example, smoking or consuming large amounts of alcoholic beverages), result from unconscious suicidal tendencies.

It is important to note that the heterogeneity of both homicide and suicide events has implications for testing the integrated model. We believe the stream analogy is more applicable to angry or expressive homicides than to killings carried out for instrumental purposes. It is probably also more applicable to suicides committed for some reasons (such as frustration resulting from personal failures) than others (such as a desire to escape chronic pain). Unfortunately, it is difficult or impossible to distinguish between different types of homicide and suicide in the data collected by government agencies. In the United States, data on violent deaths available from the National Center for Health Statistics cannot be disaggregated by type of either homicide or suicide. Information collected through the Supplementary Homicide Reports program of the U.S. Federal Bureau of Investigation since 1976 allow for the calculation of separate rates for felony and nonfelony homicides (a dichotomy that closely parallels the distinction between instrumental and expressive killings). For most nations, only figures for the total number of annual homicides and suicides are available.

The effect of the discontinuity between theory and data on attempts to test the stream analogy is unknown. If the ratio of instrumental to expressive killings differs by region, percentage urban, or other predictor variables included in the regression models in chapters 7 and 8, then national and state level SHRs will systematically differ from those that would be obtained from data more consistent with the underlying theory. The solution to this data problem is the more precise classification of lethal events based on information in primary sources, such as coroners' or medical examiners' records and police reports. The prospects, however, for completing this type of enhanced data collection outside the United States and a few other industrialized nations are not good. Even in the United States, time and financial constraints are likely to limit such a project to a handful of jurisdictions. Further, as reviewed in chapter 4, a variety of forms of violent death are classified as accidental fatalities (such as single-vehicle, single-occupant traffic accidents), for which we are unsure about the applicability of the integrated model despite the persuasive arguments of Lane (1979) and Holinger (1987). The model *may* explain certain accidents, but the heterogeneity of circumstances that surrounds accidental deaths makes it virtually impossible to distinguish between "pure" accidents and those in which the death was consciously or unconsciously intentional. Data problems also occur in the official categorization of certain lethal events as accidents and suicides. For example, Newman observes in describing the high suicide rate in Sweden that "suicide does not as readily incur a stigma there, so that officials are less likely to record such deaths as accidents" (Newman 1979, 82). Obviously, there are many other places where the opposite is true. Finally, it is also difficult to separate out diseases such as lung cancer and cirrhosis of the liver in which there may be subconscious suicidal tendencies and victim-precipitated homicides that may involve the wish to die on the part of the "victim."

EXTENSIONS AND AVENUES FOR FURTHER RESEARCH

Conceptually, the integrated model and the analyses of data presented in this book have been pitched at the macrolevel. We deal with overall national and regional rates in terms of the amount and and direction of lethal violence. At the same time, much of our discussion has employed microlevel concepts such as frustration and the attribution of blame. Some of this discontinuity is due to the crossing of disciplinary boundaries.

Frustration-aggression and attribution theories have been developed primarily by psychologists. At the macrolevel, the concepts of anomie (Merton 1957) and systemic frustration (Feierabend and Feierabend 1966) correspond closely to the individual-level concept of frustration. Indeed, Merton's anomie is a patterned blockage to goal attainment for a segment of the population. Similarly, systemic frustration is "defined as unsatisfied needs, expectations, or aspirations of many people" (Goldstein 1986: 179) in a society. The Feierabends (1966) conceptualize it as a disparity between "want desire" and the satisfaction of that desire. Want desire is measured by literacy because it is assumed that literacy increases a society's material desires. Satisfaction of desire is measured by economic development and the numbers of radios and newspapers available. Despite the idiosyncratic operational definition of systemic frustration, it appears to be conceptually identical to Merton's anomie. Both are the macrolevel conceptual equivalents of individual frustration (cf. Krohn 1978).

It is less clear what macrolevel concepts correspond to the attribution of responsibility or blame. Attempts to measure this concept at the macrolevel have apparently not been made. McClelland's 1961 attempt to measure the related concept of need for achievement by examining cultural themes in children's literature is one promising avenue that might be pursued. Indeed, Peterson and Seligman (1984) suggest the use of written accounts as a source of data on attributions of causality. Clearly, much work remains in the development of valid, general-use, macrolevel measures of frustration and the cultural-based attribution of blame to self or others. Overall, we agree with the argument made by Travis (1990) that in order to explain lethal outcomes, intervening personality variables need to be measured along with structural and cultural ones.

One possible extension of the model and a fruitful avenue for research would be the inclusion of a third stream of lethality pertaining to collective violence. Political assassinations and deaths as a consequence of riots, strikes, insurgencies, and wars would be included in this third channel. Traditionally, depending on their classification by authorities, these deaths may or may not be included in the homicide statistics. The literature on collective violence (such as Gurr 1980; Ball-Rokeach and Short 1985) has been more concerned with explaining the geographical and temporal distribution of these events than with the number of people killed. Consistent with the integrated model, however, Feierabend and Feierabend (1972) found that political violence was positively correlated with systemic frustration in the sixty-two nations that they studied. Suicide and homicide rates both tend to drop during popular wars, suggesting that the hostility directed toward the enemy is diverted from the self and other domestic targets. Furthermore, Archer and Gartner (1976) have shown that postwar homicide rates of former combatants increase as a result of the residual effect of officially sanctioned killing of the enemy on the field of battle.

It is likely that blame will be placed on a whole group of "others" in situations of international tension (such as conflict between Israel and its Arab neighbors or the recently concluded Cold War between East and West). When circumstances lead to clashes between such opposing groups and their respective interests, lethal outcomes often result. A similar tendency undoubtedly characterizes societies and regions deeply divided along racial, ethnic, or religious lines (such as South Africa, the former Yugoslavia, Northern Ireland, or the American South and the inner cities of the United States). In such situations, attributions of blame for bad events and frustrating situations (such as massive unemployment, preferential policies for particular groups, political setbacks to a group's agenda, or symbolic attacks such as those defiling places of worship) will be placed upon an entire group of outsiders. The implication here is that information about the number and salience of international cleavages or internal social divisions would be needed in order to explain collective violence between and within nations using an expanded version of the integrated model. This would have to be combined with knowledge about events and issues perceived by entire groups to be frustrating and the attributions of blame made by such groups.

A model incorporating collective violence would resemble Robert K. Merton's 1938 theory of the various adaptations to anomie, which Stuart Palmer and Arnold S. Linsky (1972) have already applied to suicide and homicide. The major difference would be that the structural sources of patterned frustration would be elaborated and that, unlike Merton's theory, the expanded model would use structural, cultural, historical, and situational factors affecting the attribution of blame to the self, other persons (singly or as entire categories of outsiders), or "the system" as predictors of the choice between retreatism (suicide), innovation (homicide), and rebellion (collective violence). Indeed, such an expanded theory would be a step in the direction of accomplishing what Merton so elegantly attempted and what Gabriel Tarde (1886b) contemplated but said couldn't be done—a single model conceptualizing many forms of deviance as channels in a single stream.

For now, however, we must be content to restrict the integrated model to suicide and homicide. For this more limited purpose, the stream analogy has remained remarkably robust. It has made demonstrable contributions to the understanding of the use of violence against self and others. Much can be gained from studying suicide and homicide in their relationships to one another.

Notes

CHAPTER 2

1. Durkheim also discusses an early attempt by Alexandre Lacassagne to draw a connection between rates of suicide and crimes against property. Durkheim (1897, 338) thoroughly demolishes this argument, and no one takes it seriously today. For a thorough discussion of the role of studies of suicide in French sociology, see Giddens (1965).

2. Surprisingly, an early precursor of Tarde's imitation theory was originally presented by none other than Karl Marx (1853). Marx, writing on 18 February 1853, as the London correspondent of the *New York Daily Tribune*, reported on one of the first empirical studies linking homicide and suicide to the same independent variable. The study, conducted by the *London Daily Advertiser* in response to a pro-capital punishment article in *The Times* of London, covered executions, suicides, and murders over a forty-three-day period in 1849 (Marx 1853; cf. Bowers and Pierce 1980), during which time eight executions were followed by eighteen deaths due to murder or suicide, including a mass murder in Liverpool, two murders of parents by their children, and two murders followed by suicide. *The Times* had noted in its article "Amateur Hanging" on 25 January 1853 that "it has often been remarked that in this country a public execution is generally followed closely by instances of death by hanging, either suicidal or accidental, in consequence of the powerful effect which the execution of a noted criminal produces upon the morbid and unmatured mind" (quoted in Marx 1853, 495). Nonetheless, to Marx's dismay, *The Times* "extolled" capital punishment in its lead article. His commentary evokes thoughts not of typical Marxian perspectives but instead of Tarde's imitation theory, the work of modern researchers on mass-media effects, and the current debate over whether the death penalty contributes to brutalization and the cultural legitimation of violence. According to Marx, the data showed "not only suicides but murders of the most atrocious kind following closely upon the execution of criminals. . . . It would be very difficult, if not altogether impossible, to establish any principle upon which the justice or expediency of capital punishment could be founded, in a society glorying in its civilization" (Marx 1853, 496).

The resurrection of Tarde's theory of imitation was accomplished almost single-handedly by David P. Phillips (1974). In a series of connected studies, Phillips and his associates (Bollen and Phillips 1981, 1982; Phillips 1977, 1978, 1979, 1980, 1983; Phillips and Bollen 1985) have reported that mass-media coverage of violent events, such as suicides by celebrities or heavyweight championship boxing matches, increases mortality rates from homicide, suicide, and certain types of accidents, including motor vehicle crashes. This modern variant of the imitation hypothesis has also received limited support in studies by Blumenthal and Bergner (1973), Hankoff (1961), Motto (1967, 1970), Stack (1989) and Wasserman (1984a). Baron and Reiss (1985), however, criticize this body of research for alleged theoretical and methodological shortcomings, and Bailey (1990) finds no support for the proposition that media publicity surrounding executions influences the homicide rate.

3. Indeed, Durkheim's types of suicide were not original. Although Douglas (1967) argues that Durkheim may have coined the term *anomie*, that honor probably goes to Brierre de Boismont (1865). Discussions of both egoistic and anomic suicide appeared on the pages of *Popular Science Monthly* as early as 1880 (Hopkins 1880; Lord 1880).

4. The Belgian astronomer and mathematician Adolphe Quetelet was also instrumental in the development of the cartographic school. Though he, too, wrote about suicide, it was primarily in the context of the stability of rates over time. Quetelet (1831, 1835), like Guerry, used the *Comptes généraux* to investigate regularities in the social distribution of crime. The two corresponded (Quetelet 1835, 6), and their views on violent crime were similar. Indeed, a controversy arose as to which of the two had priority in establishing the stability of crime rates (Quetelet 1835, 96). Lottin (1912) resolves their rival claims in favor of Guerry, but Verkko (1951) favors Quetelet.

5. It is unclear here whether the many references to "fourteen" are an error or a coincidence. Because he later uses the then-conventional way of expressing rates as one suicide per x number of inhabitants, we suspect that Despine means to say that there were fourteen suicides in each of the two groups of fourteen departments.

6. Tarde, though he attended the Congress of Rome, missed the session on suicide and homicide due to a scheduling conflict. Ironically, he sent his paper to the session in Ferri's care.

7. Morselli says "homicide" here. Clearly this is an error in transcription.

8. The reference is to Tarde (1884).

9. Ferri's monograph, *L'Omicidio-suicidio: Responsibililità guiridica*, appeared in five editions, published in Turin in 1883, 1884, 1892, 1895, and 1925 (Sellin 1972). According to Ferri (1925; cf. Verkko 1951, 155), the sections quoted here were added to the third edition to reflect the debate at the Congress of

Rome and remained unchanged in the fourth and fifth editions. The work, which we have been unable to locate in any edition in the original Italian, has apparently never been translated into English, but we have access to the 1934 Spanish translation of the fifth edition by Concha Peña. Our translations are from this source. Although translations of translations are always risky, it seems worthwhile to provide the English-speaking reader with the opportunity to examine Ferri's position in something at least closely resembling his own words. This is especially true in view of Verkko's charge that "Durkheim's assertion that Ferri combined his theory with Morselli's is incorrect" (1951, 155; see note 6 chapter 3). Durkheim used Ferri's fourth edition, which contained the quotations reproduced here. Although Ferri (1925, 280-81) fails to mention Morselli by name, his reference to "the inverse relationship between suicide and homicide . . . that others have demonstrated in its ethnic and geographic aspects" in the context of the Congress of Rome clearly refers to Morselli. It is Verkko rather than Durkheim who is incorrect.

10. Ferri erroneously believed that homicide rates increase with age.

11. Actually, the relationship, as Tarde (1886b) notes, was not complete because both the suicide and the homicide curves were rising: the suicide curve slowly and the one for homicide more rapidly.

12. Although most studies find that both suicide and homicide rates increase during economic recession and depression, Henry and Short (1954) find that crimes against persons rise during prosperity and fall when business is bad.

13. Durkheim does not discuss the relationship between homicide and his fourth type of suicide—fatalistic—which is found only in a footnote (Durkheim 1897, 276). Fatalistic suicide, he claims, is "the opposite of anomic suicide, just as egoistic and altruistic suicide are opposites." Fatalistic suicide is the result of excessive regulation and oppressive discipline, as in the case of slaves as well as "of very young husbands, of the married woman who is childless."

14. For a more detailed treatment of our position on the monograph, see Whitt (1968).

15. These two components of the self, which became clearer in Durkheim's later work (for example, Durkheim 1912), are reminiscent of Freud's concepts of the id (stripped of its instinctually sexual and aggressive connotations) and the superego. There is no evidence in Durkheim's references that he read Freud, but Freud cites *The Elementary Forms of the Religious Life* (Durkheim 1912), where these ideas are well developed, in his *Totem and Taboo* (Freud 1913).

16. Homicide rates generally fall during popular wars. Durkheim (1900) draws his conclusion that they increase from the French experience during the Franco-Prussian War of 1870, which, like Vietnam, was atypical in its unpopularity.

17. Schmid (1928, 1933; cf. Schmid and Van Arsdol 1955) found suicide rates directly correlated with the homicide rates of social areas in Seattle
and Minneapolis. Similar positive relationships were reported for Chicago
by Cavan (1928) and for St. Louis by Queen and Thomas (1939). The areas with
both high suicide and high homicide were those characterized by poverty
and social disorganization. Although lower status areas invariably have high
homicide rates, the relationship between suicide and the economic and social
status of social areas of cities seems to vary. Wendling and Polk (1958) found
a positive relationship between suicide and social class measures in San
Francisco, a negative relationship in the East Bay region, and no relationship in
San Diego. Porterfield (1952a) found very high suicide rates for upper- and
middle-class census tracts in Fort Worth. Whitt (1966), on the basis of a study
of suicide and homicide in Atlanta, suggests that the association between suicide rates and median family income is curvilinear, with the highest rates in
both the poorest and richest tracts. We shall return to these findings later.

CHAPTER 3

1. Wolfgang and Ferracuti (1967) cite a study in the stream of violence tradition by Enrico Altavilla (1932), which we have been unable to locate.

2. Durkheim (1900) thought that homicide rates increase in wartime, but
later research suggests that this is true only if the war divides society—for example, the Franco-Prussian War, which Durkheim studied, and the Vietnam
conflict. Otherwise, there is a consistent diminution in both suicide and homicide rates in combatant nations (cf. chapter 2, note 16).

3. Porterfield's knowledge of Morselli and Ferri is apparently derived entirely from discussions of their work by Durkheim (1897) and Halbwachs (1930).

4. Porterfield's methodological contributions in this same article will be
considered later.

5. Like most of the empirical generalizations discovered during this second, largely American period of interest in the relationship between suicide and
homicide, the social-class patterns observed by Alpert (1950) were well known
to European scholars in the nineteenth century (for example, Despine 1868).
Morselli explicitly pointed out at the Congress of Rome that suicide varies directly and homicide inversely with social class (*Actes du premier congrès . . .*
1886–87, 203). Some of the empirical generalizations advanced at the Congress
have apparently not been addressed in this century. For example, Morselli
(*Actes . . .* 1886–87, 203) suggests that hair color is a factor—blondes tend toward
suicide while brunettes prefer murder.

6. Verkko, no lover of Durkheim, whom he calls "one of the forerunners
of . . . Italian fascism" (1951, 152), charges that both Durkheim and Tarde
(1886a) misrepresented Ferri's position by linking it with Morselli's. According
to Verkko, "It is very condemnable that Durkheim . . . has included a detailed

report of the theories of Italian scientists containing half truths. A great deal of false information has been disseminated to the world in this way" (1951, 155). He argues that "it must be stated that Ferri in particular, but also Morselli, have emerged from the dispute with honour, whereas this cannot, unfortunately, be said of Tarde, and still less of Durkheim" (1951, 162). According to Verkko, "Ferri, while emphasizing annual antagonisms, does not support the dual law of suicides and homicides put forth by Morselli. . . . Ferri has never changed his theory; he has modified it" (1951, 149, 155). We have no idea what this means. Nonetheless, as the quotes from Ferri (1925) in chapter 2 clearly show, it is Verkko rather than Durkheim and Tarde who is incorrect (cf. chapter 2, note 9). Ferri indeed combined his theory with Morselli's as Durkheim and Tarde claimed, and their honor is vindicated. If Durkheim (1897) engaged in half truths, so does Verkko, who claims that he cannot find an article by Tarde cited by Ferri, in the *Revue philosophique*. The article, actually a review of Ferri's monograph, appeared in 1884, not 1893 as Verkko claims. It is signed simply "G. T." (see Tarde 1884).

7. Porterfield, a pioneer in many ways, had already invented a measure that would have accomplished the same purpose, but he failed to place it in a theoretical context. Porterfield's 1949 measure is the ratio of the homicide rate to the suicide rate or vice versa, depending on which of the two rates is higher. Gold's measure is preferable to Porterfield's because it has determinate upper limits and because it has an immediate theoretical interpretation.

8. Gold (1958) originally intended to call his measure the SHR but chose SMR instead to avoid confusion with the SHR (stimulus-habit-response) developed by Clark Hull. A generation and more later, we prefer SHR both because of its greater accuracy and because sociologists today often use SMR as an abbreviation for the journal *Sociological Methods and Research*. The SHR, of course, is a proportion rather than a true ratio like Porterfield's measurement. Calling it the SHR may cause some confusion with the FBI's supplementary homicide reports, but the reference should be clear in context.

9. The sociological and anthropological approaches to the study of suicide and homicide developed along largely separate paths. Because the different tribal societies in New Guinea, India, or Africa tend to occupy similar ecological niches, anthropologists tend to reject the type of macrostructural explanations given by sociologists in favor of interpretations stressing value orientations, individual dispositions (Saran 1974), or the microstructural role relationships associated with suicide and homicide in different tribal societies (Bohannan 1965).

10. Although we have never seen it used, Palmer's 1965 study has implications for the debate on capital punishment.

11. In the United States, as in Europe, suicide-homicide ratios are lower in the South than in the North, but researchers investigating Southern violence in America have ignored a century of European findings. This leaves open the possibility that climate really does have something to do with the choice between homicide and suicide, as many nineteenth-century writers (for example,

Morselli 1879a, 1879b) suggested. Indeed, Lester (1974, 1977) has linked suicide and homicide rates to the incidence of thunderstorms. No definitive crucial test has ever firmly eliminated climatological variables in the direction violence takes, though the work of John Rice Miner (1922) comes close.

12. Hackney's paper was included in the "Graham Report" submitted to the National Commission on the Causes and Prevention of Violence (Graham and Gurr 1969). Many publishers reprinted the volume with varying titles, and in at least one (the Praeger edition) the table reporting Hackney's regression analysis contains errors that render it unintelligible. Caution dictates going to the original source cited in the references at the end of this book.

13. Japan is clearly an exception, but Robert Bellah (1957) links its strong economic growth to religious developments during the Tokugawa period.

CHAPTER 4

1. Daly and Wilson (1988) are not alone in suggesting that mental disorders are attributions or social constructions. Szasz (1974), for example, argues that they are myths created to explain problems of living, while Scheff (1966) maintains that they are labels applied by psychiatry to *residual deviance*—behaviors that seem to an audience to be contrary to fundamental, taken-forgranted assumptions about human nature and the nature of reality.

CHAPTER 5

1. The distinctions drawn by attribution theorists closely parallel the concept of mens rea, or criminal intent, as a test for legal responsibility for crime; and the mitigating environmental influences Heider (1958) identifies are very similar to such legally recognized excuses and justifications as accident, necessity, insanity, or mistake of fact (see, for example, Clark and Marshall 1967).

2. Although attribution theorists tend to think of "others" as concrete individual persons, we suspect that anger can also result from actions attributed to the deity (or the devil), social groups (such as Republican politicians), faceless governmental entities (such as the Internal Revenue Service), or such vague but anthropomorphized entities as "the system."

3. According to Marc Riedel and Margaret A. Zahn (1985), approximately 60 percent of murder victims are either family members or acquaintances of the offender, while less than 15 percent are strangers.

CHAPTER 6

1. The integrated model is, however, completely compatible with the stress-diathesis model, an individual-level psychological theory that includes

suicide as a symptom of hopelessness depression (see chapter 5). Both theories view suicide as the product of a statistical interaction between negative life events and explanatory styles.

2. Whitt (1968) also attempts to show that, from a strictly statistical viewpoint, it is impossible to infer the forms of the relationships of suicide or homicide to forces of production and direction. We now believe that inferences are legitimate when frustration and locus of causality work together and that theoretical (as opposed to statistical) reasoning can be used to infer that the direction and form of the relationship is indeterminate when forces of production and those of direction work at cross purposes.

3. Indeed, a study by Catherine E. Ross (1990; cf. Krause and Stryker 1984) found that internal locus of control is associated with reduced levels of psychological distress, a variable that is conceptually close to perceived frustration.

4. Actually, this interpretation cannot account for Boor's (1976) specific findings. Across the ten nations he studied, the SHR, like the suicide rate, varies with scores on external locus of control. Contrary to what we may seem to be saying, the integrated model cannot account for all conceivable relationships between suicide and homicide rates. Evidence of this sort does appear to contradict the integrated model.

There are, however, problems with Boor's analysis. Generalizing from student samples to total populations is a risky business, and the sample itself is restricted to only a few nations drawn from the economic core of the world system. With two exceptions—Israel and the United States—these nations have very high SHRs. No Third World nations, which typically have much lower SHRs, are included. Again with two exceptions—Sweden and Japan—their mean IE scores fall into the very restricted range of ten to eleven on a twenty-four–point scale. The severe limitations on the variances of both IE scores and the SHR *may* account for Boor's results.

Another way of explaining Boor's findings revolves around the depression paradox (Abramson and Sackheim 1977). While locus of control and the attribution of blame control are sometimes treated as equivalent concepts, it is, as we argued in chapter 5, necessary to draw distinctions. The IE scale measures the generalized expectation that one's efforts can bring about the outcomes one seeks (Rotter 1966; Lefcourt 1983). It says nothing about the attribution of responsibility or blame for negative outcomes. As Boor (1976; cf. Melges and Weisz 1971) suggests, feelings of hopelessness seem to be a common theme underlying suicidal behavior. Hopelessness implies (1) that the individual is frustrated and (2) that he or she has run out of options and can no longer hope to better the situation in the future. It does not imply that he or she is or is not responsible for getting into the hopeless situation in the first place. The helpless or hopeless person may view responsibility for bad events as internal, global, and stable yet hold the expectancy that little or nothing can be done to improve the situation in the future. This is the situation portrayed in the learned helplessness-hopelessness scenario for the development of reactive or hopelessness depression (Abramson, Seligman, and Teasdale 1978; Peterson and Seligman 1984; Alloy, Lipman, and Abramson 1992), and we argue that it applies to suicide as well. The integrated model focuses on the individual's interpretation of why the frustrating situation arose rather than what, if anything, he or she can do about it. If external scores on the IE scale measure the perception of hopelessness or pervasive pessimism (Lamont 1972a, 1972b), then we should not be surprised to see external locus of control positively correlated with suicide rates and the SHR.

5. Durkheim (1897) predicts high suicide rates under conditions of both high and low levels of integration and regulation, with lower rates at intermediate levels. Similarly, Powell (1958) posits two different varieties of anomie to account for high suicide rates at the two ends of the social-status continuum.

6. The idea that the situated meanings used to understand concrete problematic situations differ from general cultural meanings in the abstract has been profitably elaborated by John P. Hewitt and his associates (Hall and Hewitt 1970; Hewitt and Hall 1973; Hewitt and Stokes 1975; Stokes and Hewitt 1976), who correctly point out that persons involved in such situations do not automatically look up the meaning of their situation in a cultural catalog of ready-to-fit meanings. A variety of alternative commonsense quasi-theories are available in the implicit culture to explain the meaning of concrete problematic situations, and some of those that are most likely to be used differ from such officially sanctioned interpretations as the medical model and from the explanations used to interpret situations in which one is not personally involved.

We have no quarrel with Douglas's finding that situated meanings differ from abstract meanings or his suggestion that more work needs to be done on the meanings imputed by persons to problematic situations in which they are directly involved. Indeed, some of our own research (Whitt and Meile 1986) strongly supports this point for persons experiencing what psychiatrists call symptoms of mental illness. We do, however, dispute the implications he draws from this finding.

7. The realization that official statistics on crime and suicide are flawed was by no means new in the 1960s. As early as the 1830s, Guerry (1833) was questioning whether the increasing official suicide rate indicated a real increase or simply better record keeping. Quetelet (1835) produced a surprisingly modern discussion of what is today known as the *dark figure* of crime (the unknown number of crimes that never come to official attention and thus never show up in official statistics).

8. Robert K. Merton's early statement aptly summarizes the situation: "All sociological authorities agree that the statistics of mental illness and suicide, of crime and juvenile delinquency, of prostitution and divorce are subject to all manner of bias" (Merton 1961, 702).

9. This is a direct quote from a review received by Whitt in 1968.

CHAPTER 7

1. If something is rotten in the state of Denmark, it is even more rotten in Greenland, one of its possessions. With a population of slightly less than fifty thousand, Greenland experienced no less than fifty-eight suicides and twenty-four homicides in 1984. The criminal anthropologists would undoubtedly have linked the island's astronomical suicide rate to its forbidding climate, but they would have been baffled by its high homicide rate. We suspect that disputes between persons forced to remain in close proximity may be responsible.

2. Technically, the linear terms define the rate of change in the dependent variable as the independent variable increases by one unit, while the regression coefficients attached to the squared terms show the rate of change in the rate of change.

3. Alternatively, one may calculate the F-ratio associated with the increment in R^2 due to the inclusion of the squared term in the model (Jagodzinski and Weede 1981; Whitt 1986). Thus, for example, the zero-order significance of the nonlinear component of the effect of economic development is given directly by the significance of GNP^2 in model II. An identical result may be obtained by subtracting the R^2 for model I, in which GNP^2 is omitted, from the R^2 for model II, which includes GNP^2, and computing the appropriate F-test. The increment in R^2 gives us a more interpretable measure than the unstable regression coefficient of the importance of the nonlinear component of the relationship. The F-test for non-linearity is given by

$$F_{df = 1, (N - k - 1)} = (N - k - 1)(R^2{}_f - R^2{}_r)/(1 - R^2{}_f),$$

where N is the number of cases, $R^2{}_f$ is the R^2 of the model which includes the squared term (the full model), $R^2{}_r$ is the R^2 of the model which omits the squared term (the restricted model), and k is the number of variables in the full model (Cohen and Cohen 1975).

4. The broad outlines of the shape of the curve may be obtained by inspection of the signs attached to GNP, GNP^2, and GNP^3. The negative slope of GNP indicates that the curve drops at very low levels of development, but because the slope of GNP^2 is positive, it then moves in an increasingly positive direction. The negative slope of GNP^3 indicates that there is a second bend, with a movement back toward a negative relationship between development and income inequality when GNP/capita is high. The three curves defined by the equations in table 7.2 were superimposed on a scatterplot (not shown) relating inequality to development. The quadratic and cubic equations are virtually identical throughout most of their ranges, but the addition of GNP^3 produces slightly lower predicted values of INEQ at very high levels of GNP/capita.

5. The statistical significance of each curve is evaluated by examining the F-ratio associated with its increment in R^2. The formula (Jagodzinski and Weede 1981; Whitt 1986) is

$$F_{df = (k - j), (N - k - 1)} = (N - k - 1) (R^2_f - R^2_r)/(k - j) (1 - R^2_f),$$

where N is the number of cases (i.e., eighty-eight), R^2_f is the R^2 associated with the full model (model VIII), R^2_r is the R^2 associated with the restricted model (not shown) which omits the appropriate curve, j is the number of unstandardized regression coefficients in the restricted model (i.e., four), and k is the number of coefficients in the full model (i.e., six).

6. If b_1 is the slope of GNP and b_2 the slope of GNP^2, the point of inflection is given by evaluating the second derivative of the quadratic equation, or $-b_1/2b_2$ (Budnick 1979). The exact value is $7,612.65.

7. Whitt, Gordon, and Hofley's 1972 analysis of the LVR revealed a statistical interaction between economic development and religious tradition in their sample of forty-seven nations. In Protestant nations, the LVR decreased with the percentage of the economically active male population not engaged in agriculture, but there was no relationship between the two variables in Catholic nations. In the study's data, which center on 1957, the relationship between nonagricultural employment and the LVR shifted to positive for nations outside the Christian tradition.

To check whether something similar might account for our findings, we added to our data set the percent of the economically active population engaged in agriculture (Food and Agriculture Organization 1990) and a set of dummy variables indicating whether the dominant religious tradition was Protestant, Catholic (including Eastern, Russian, and Greek Orthodox), or non-Christian *(Worldmark Encyclopedia of the Nations* 1987). Significant interactions were found between religious tradition and both percent in agriculture and income inequality, but the examination of plots and an influence analysis revealed that a single case, South Africa, with a Cook's D in excess of 60 due to its extremely high LVR, was responsible. When South Africa was removed from the data set, interaction was no longer significant and the results were not materially different from those reported in table 7.6, despite the use of percent non-agriculturally employed rather than GNP/capita to measure development.

CHAPTER 8

1. Patrick O'Carroll and James Mercy (1989) demonstrate that when homicide totals are disaggregated by race, the highest rates are in the West for both blacks and whites. Candice Nelsen, Jay Corzine, and Lin Huff-Corzine (1994) show, however, that the West's lead in white homicides holds only in central cities, while suburban and rural rates are higher in the South. Furthermore, they find that the coefficients of dummy variables for the South and West are both positive and significant in a regression of white homicide rates in SMSAs. With the introduction of percent Hispanic origin into the regression model, however,

the influence of the West is no longer significant while that of the South remains unchanged.

2. Ridge regression techniques (Hoerl and Kennard 1970; Feig 1978) provide a way of correcting for the high levels of multicollinearity that frequently affect research on homicide and other crimes (Fisher and Mason 1981; Light 1984).

3. Few studies on attributional processes have focused on the role of socialization into a cultural environment. However, Joan G. Miller (1984) found subcultural differences independent of socioeconomic status among adults in India.

4. There are obvious similarities between the attributional perspective we adopt and that proposed by Henry and Short (1954), but with one important difference. They view an actor's position in the social structure as determining level of external restraint and propensity toward homicide or suicide. Following Hackney (1969) and Whitt, Gordon, and Hofley (1972), we stress the actor's *perceived* source of control for failures (that is, frustrations) as influencing the direction of aggression. Thus, socialization within a cultural context may affect an individual's attributional tendencies apart from his or her structural position.

5. There is a strong consensus that official statistics are valid indicators of the underlying, or true, number of homicides that occur (Hindelang 1974). Challenges to the use of official records on suicide in statistical analyses (such as Douglas 1967) and renewed support for their employment in research (such as Pescosolido and Mendelsohn 1986) are reviewed in chapter 6.

6. As noted, normalized ridge regression procedures produce estimates with a small amount of bias introduced to increase their efficiency. Coefficients are interpreted in the same manner as those obtained using OLS regression techniques.

7. Researchers have relied too heavily on the examination of correlation matrices to diagnose multicollinearity. If three or more independent variables are collinear, it is possible that the correlations between them will not be very high, even though coefficients obtained from OLS procedures are unstable and not to be trusted (Fisher and Mason 1981). Auxiliary regression procedures provide a more precise measurement of the level and source of multicollinearity in regression models.

8. This is true only if it is younger blacks who are committing greater numbers of suicides in those states with larger black populations in the twenty to thirty-four-year-old age range. While this is certainly a plausible interpretation of the findings, it risks committing the well-known ecological fallacy (Robinson 1950).

CHAPTER 9

1. Dr. Jack Kevorkian, a retired Michigan physician who refers to himself as an "obituarist" and whom critics call "the suicide doctor" or "Dr. Death," has attracted notoriety by using a machine of his own invention to assist a number of victims of severe pain and terminal illnesses to end their own lives. As of this writing, efforts by members of the Michigan legislature to legally redefine Kevorkian's activities as criminal homicide have failed to pass muster in the courts.

References

Abrahamson, Mark, and Valerie J. Carter. 1986. "Tolerance, Urbanism and Region." *American Sociological Review* 51: 287–94.

Abramowitz, S. I. 1969. "Locus of Control and Self-reported Depression among College Students." *Psychological Reports* 25: 149–50.

Abramson, Lyn Y., Lauren B. Alloy, and Gerald I. Metalsky. 1988. "The Cognitive Diathesis Theories of Depression: Toward an Adequate Evaluation of the Theories' Validities." In *Cognitive Processes in Depression*, edited by Lauren B. Alloy, 3–30. New York: Guilford Press.

Abramson, Lyn Y., Gerald I. Metalsky, and Lauren B. Alloy. 1988. "The Hopelessness Theory of Depression: Does the Research Test the Theory?" In *Social Cognition and Clinical Psychology*, edited by Lyn Y. Abramson, 33–65. New York: Guilford Press.

———. 1989. "Hopelessness Depression: A Theory-based Subtype of Depression." *Psychological Review* 96: 358–72.

Abramson, Lyn Y., and Harold A. Sackheim. 1977. "A Paradox in Depression: Uncontrollability and Self-blame." *Psychological Bulletin* 84: 835–51.

Abramson, Lyn Y., Martin E. P. Seligman, and John D. Teasdale. 1978. "Learned Helplessness in Humans: Critique and Reformulation." *Journal of Abnormal Psychology* 87: 49–74.

Actes du premier congrès d'anthropologie criminelle: Biologie et sociologie. 1886–87. Turin: Bocca Frères, Editeurs-Libraires.

Adelman, Irma, and Cynthia Taft Morris. 1973. *Economic Growth and Social Equity in Developing Countries.* Stanford: Stanford University Press.

Ahluwalia, Montek S. 1976. "Income Distribution and Development: Some Stylized Facts." *American Economic Review* 66: 128–35.

Ahmad, S. R. 1991. "USA: Fluoxetine 'Not Linked to Suicide.' " *The Lancet* 338: 875–76.

Allen, H. David, and William B. Bankston. 1981. "Another Look at the Southern Culture of Violence Thesis: The Case of Louisiana." *Southern Studies* 20: 55–66.

Alloy, Lauren B., Lyn Y. Abramson, Gerald I. Metalsky, and Shirley Hartlage. 1988. "The Hopelessness Theory of Depression: Attributional Aspects." *British Journal of Clinical Psychology* 27: 5–21.

Alloy, Lauren B., K. A. Kelly, S. Mineka, and C. M. Clements. 1990. "Comorbidity in Anxiety and Depressive Disorders: A Helplessness/Hopelessness Perspective." In *Comorbidity in Anxiety and Mood Disorders*, edited by J. D. Maser and C. R. Cloninger, 499–543. Washington, D.C.: American Psychiatric Press.

Alloy, Lauren B., Alan J. Lipman, and Lyn Y. Abramson. 1992. "Attributional Style as a Vulnerability Factor in Depression: Validation by Past History of Mood Disorders." *Cognitive Therapy and Research* 16: 391–407.

Alpert, Harry. 1939. *Emile Durkheim and His Sociology*. New York: Russell and Russell.

———. 1950. "Suicides and Homicides." *American Sociological Review* 15: 673.

Altavilla, Enrico. 1932. *Il Suicidio*. Naples: Alberto Morano.

American Psychiatric Association. 1980. *Diagnostic and Statistical Manual of Mental Disorders*. 3d ed. Washington, D.C.: American Psychiatric Association.

Amos, Orley M., Jr. 1988. "Unbalanced Regional Growth and Regional Income Inequality in the Latter Stages of Development." *Regional Science and Urban Economics* 18: 549–66.

Antobrus, P. M. 1973. *Internality, Pride and Humility*. Ph.D. diss. University of Waterloo.

Archer, Dane, and Rosemary Gartner. 1976. "Violent Acts and Violent Times: A Comparative Approach to Postwar Homicide Rates." *American Sociological Review* 41: 937–63.

———. 1984. *Violence and Crime in Cross-National Perspective*. New Haven CT: Yale University Press.

Åsberg, Marie, Peter Thorén, and Lil Träskman. 1976. "Serotonin Depression: A Biochemical Subgroup within the Affective Disorders." *Science* 198: 178–80.

Athens, Lonnie H. 1980. *Violent Criminal Acts and Actors: A Symbolic Interactionist Study*. Boston: Routledge and Kegan Paul.

Augustine. c. 426 A.D. *The City of God*. Translated by Gerald G. Walsh, S.J.; Demetrius B. Zema, S.J.; Grace Monahan, O.S.U.; and Daniel J. Honan. Garden City, N.Y.: Image Books, 1958.

Averill, James R. 1982. *Anger and Aggression*. New York: Springer Verlag.

———. 1983. ""Studies on Anger and Aggression." *American Psychologist* 38: 1145–60.

Bachman, Ronet. 1992. *Death and Violence on the Reservation: Homicide, Family Violence and Suicide in American Indian Populations*. New York: Auburn House.

Bailey, William C. 1984. "Poverty, Inequality, and City Homicide Rates: Some Not So Unexpected Findings." *Criminology* 22: 531–50.

———. 1990. "Murder, Capital Punishment, and Television: Execution Publicity and Homicide Effects." *American Sociological Review* 55: 628–33.

Balkwell, James W. 1990. "Ethnic Inequality and the Rate of Homicide." *Social Forces* 69: 53–70.

Ball, Richard A. 1968. "A Poverty Case: The Analgesic Subculture of the Southern Appalachians." *American Sociological Review* 33: 885–95.

Ballmer-Cao, Thanh-Huyen, and Jurg Scheidegger. 1979. *Compendium of Data for World-system Analyses*. Zurich: Sociologisches Institut der Universität.

Ball-Rokeach, Sandra J., and James F. Short, Jr. 1990. "Collective Violence: The Redress of Grievance and Public Policy." In *Violence: Patterns, Causes, Public Policy*, edited by Neil Alan Weiner, Magaret A. Zahn, and Rita J. Sagi, 187–94. New York: Harcourt Brace Jovanovich.

Banfield, Edward C. 1958. *The Moral Basis of a Backward Society*. New York: Free Press.

Banks, Arthur S. 1971. *Cross-polity Time Series Data*. Cambridge: MIT Press.

Bankston, William B., and Carol Y. Thompson. 1989. "Carrying Firearms for Protection: A Causal Model." *Sociological Inquiry* 59: 75–87.

Baron, James N., and Peter C. Reiss. 1985. "Same Time Next Year: Aggregate Analysis of the Mass Media and Violent Behavior." *American Sociological Review* 50: 347–63.

Baron, Larry, and Murray A. Straus. 1988. "Cultural and Economic Sources of Homicide in the United States." *Sociological Quarterly* 29: 371–90.

Battle, Esther S., and Julian B. Rotter. 1963. "Children's Feelings of Personal Control As Related to Social Class and Ethnic Group." *Journal of Personality* 31: 482–90.

Bebbington, Paul. 1985. "Three Cognitive Theories of Depression." *Psychological Medicine* 15: 759–69.

Beck, Aaron T. 1967. *Depression: Clinical, Experimental, and Theoretical Aspects*. New York: Harper and Row.

————. 1986. "Hopelessness As a Predictor of Eventual Suicide." *Annals of the New York Academy of Sciences* 487: 90–96.

Beck, Aaron T., Gary Brown, Robert J. Berchick, Bonnie L. Stewart, and Robert A. Steer. 1990. "Relationship between Hopelessness and Ultimate Suicide: A Replication with Psychiatric Outpatients." *American Journal of Psychiatry* 147: 190–95.

Beck, Aaron T., Maria Kovacs, and Arlene Weissman. 1975. "Hopelessness and Suicidal Behavior: An Overview." *Journal of the American Medical Association* 234: 1146–49.

Becker, Thomas M., Jonathan M. Samet, Charles L. Wiggins, and Charles R. Key. 1990. "Violent Death in the West: Suicide and Homicide in New Mexico, 1958–1987." *Suicide and Life-threatening Behavior* 20: 324–34.

Beirne, Piers, and James Messerschmidt. 1991. *Criminology*. San Diego: Harcourt Brace Jovanovich.

Bell, Daniel. 1962. "Crime As an American Way of Life." In *The End of Ideology*, 127–50. New York: Free Press.

Bellah, Robert. 1957. *Tokugawa Religion*. Glencoe, IL: Free Press.

Berkowitz, Leonard. 1962. *Aggression: A Social Psychological Analysis*. New York: McGraw-Hill.

————. 1989. "Frustration-Aggression Hypothesis: Examination and Reformulation." *Psychological Bulletin* 100: 59–73.

Berman, Alan L. 1979. "Dyadic Death: Murder-Suicide." *Suicide and Life-threatening Behavior* 9: 15–23.

Black, D. W., and G. Winokur. 1990. "Suicide and Psychiatric Diagnosis." In *Suicide over the Life Cycle*, edited by Susan J. Blumenthal and David J. Kupfer, 135–53. Washington, D.C.: American Psychiatric Press.

Blackstone, Sir William. 1862. *Commentaries on the Laws of England*. 21st ed. 4 vols. New York: Harper and Brothers.

Blau, Judith R., and Peter M. Blau. 1982. "The Cost of Inequality: Metropolitan Structure and Violent Crime." *American Sociological Review* 47: 114–29.

Blau, Peter M., and Reid M. Golden. 1986. "Metropolitan Structure and Criminal Violence." *Sociological Quarterly* 27: 15–26.

Block, Richard. 1979. "Community, Environment, and Violent Crime." *Criminology* 17: 46–57.

Blumenthal, Sol, and Lawrence Bergner. 1973. "Suicide and Newspapers." *American Journal of Psychiatry* 139: 468–71.

Bohannan, Paul, ed. 1965. *African Homicide and Suicide*. Princeton: Princeton University Press.

Boismont, Brierre de. 1865. *De Suicide et de la folie-suicide*. Paris: Germer Bailliere.

Bollen, Kenneth A., and Robert W. Jackman. 1985. "Political Democracy and the Size Distribution of Income." *American Sociological Review* 50: 438–57.

Bollen, Kenneth A., and David A. Phillips. 1981. "Suicidal Motor Vehicle Fatalities in Detroit: A Replication." *American Journal of Sociology* 87: 404–12.

———. 1982. "Imitative Suicides: A National Study of the Effects of Television News Stories." *American Sociological Review* 47: 802–9.

Bollen, Kenneth A., and Sally Ward. 1979. "Ratio Variables in Aggregate Data Analysis: Their Uses, Problems, and Alternatives." *Sociological Methods and Research* 7: 431–50.

Boor, Myron. 1976. "Relationship of Internal-External Control and National Suicide Rates." *Journal of Social Psychology* 100: 143–44.

———. 1982. "Reduction in Deaths by Suicide, Accidents and Homicide Prior to United States Presidential Election." *Journal of Social Psychology* 118: 135–36.

Bowers, W., and G. Pierce. 1980. "Deterrence or Brutalization: What Is the Effect of Executions?" *Crime and Delinquency* 26: 453–84.

Braithwaite, John. 1979. *Inequality, Crime and Public Policy*. Boston: Routledge and Kegan Paul.

Braithwaite, John, and Valerie Braithwaite. 1980. "The Effect of Income Inequality and Social Democracy on Homicide." *British Journal of Criminology* 20: 45–53.

Braun, Denny. 1991a. "Income Inequality and Economic Development: Geographic Divergence." *Social Science Quarterly* 72: 520–36.

———. 1991b. *The Rich Get Richer: The Rise of Income Inequality in the United States and the World*. Chicago: Nelson Hall.

Brearley, H[arrington] C[ooper]. 1932. *Homicide in the United States*. Chapel Hill: University of North Carolina Press.

Brown, George W., and Tirril Harris. 1978. *Social Origins of Depression*. New York: Free Press.

Brown, Gerald L., and Frederick K. Goodwin. 1986. "Cerebrospinal Correlates of Suicide Attempts and Aggression." *Annals of the New York Academy of Sciences* 487: 175–88.

Brown, Serena-Lynn, and Herman M. van Praag. 1991. "Why Study Serotonin in Clinical Psychiatric Research?" In *The Role of Serotonin in Psychiatric Dis-*

orders, edited by Serena-Lynn Brown and Herman M. van Praag, 3–7. New York: Brunner/Mazel.

Brown, Serena-Lynn, Avraham Bleich, and Herman M. van Praag. 1991. "The Monoamine Hypothesis of Depression: The Case of Serotonin." In *The Role of Serotonin in Psychiatric Disorders,* edited by Serena-Lynn Brown and Herman M. van Praag, 91–128. New York: Brunner/Mazel.

Budnick, Frank S. 1979. *Applied Mathematics for Business, Economics, and the Social Sciences.* New York: McGraw-Hill.

Bulcock, Jeffrey W., and Wan Fung Lee. 1983. "Normalization Ridge Regression in Practice." *Sociological Methods and Research* 1: 259–303.

Calhoun, Lawrence G., Thomas Cheney, and A. Stephen Dawes. 1974. "Locus of Control, Self-reported Depression, and Perceived Causes of Depression." *Journal of Consulting and Clinical Psychology* 42: 736.

Cavan, Ruth Shonle. 1928. *Suicide.* Chicago: University of Chicago Press.

Charnov, E. L. 1982. *The Theory of Sex Allocation.* Princeton: Princeton University Press.

Chavez, L., Thomas M. Becker, Charles L. Wiggins, and Jonathan M. Samet. 1989. "Alcohol-related Mortality in New Mexico's Hispanics, American Indians, and Non-Hispanic Whites, 1958–1982." Paper presented at the Western Section of the American Federation for Clinical Research.

Chenery, Hollie, and Moises Syrquin. 1975. *Patterns of Development, 1950–1970.* New York: Oxford University Press.

Chesnais, Jean-Claude. 1992. "The History of Violence: Homicide and Suicide through the Ages." *International Social Science Journal* 44: 217–34.

Chilton, Roland. 1982. "Analyzing Urban Crime Data: Deterrence and the Limitations of Arrests per Offense Ratios." *Criminology* 19: 590–607.

Cicourel, Aaron V. 1968. *The Social Organization of Juvenile Justice.* New York: John Wiley and Sons.

Clark, Terry N. 1969. Introduction. In *Gabriel Tarde on Communication and Social Influence,* edited by Terry N. Clark, 1–69. Chicago: University of Chicago Press.

Clark, William L., and William L. Marshall. 1967. *A Treatise on the Law of Crimes.* 7th ed. Chicago: Callaghan and Company.

Cockerham, William C. 1981. *Sociology of Mental Disorder.* Englewood Cliffs, N.J.: Prentice-Hall.

Cohen, Albert K. 1955. *Delinquent Boys: The Culture of the Gang.* New York: Free Press.

————. 1959. "The Study of Social Disorganization and Deviant Behavior." In *Sociology Today*, edited by Robert K. Merton, Leonard Broom, and Leonard S. Cottrell, 461–84. New York: Harper and Row.

Cohen, Jacob, and Patricia Cohen. 1975. *Applied Multiple Regression/Correlation Analysis for the Behavioral Sciences*. New York: Halsted.

Conklin, George H., and Miles E. Simpson. 1985. "A Demographic Approach to the Cross-national Study of Homicide." *Comparative Social Research* 8: 171–85.

Cook, R. Dennis. 1977. "Detection of Influential Observations in Linear Regression." *Technometrics* 19: 15–18.

Cook, R. Dennis, and Stanford Weisberg. 1982. "Criticism and Influence Analysis in Regression." In *Sociological Methodology, 1982*, edited by Samuel Leinhardt, 313–61. San Francisco: Jossey-Bass.

Coser, Lewis. 1956. *The Functions of Social Conflict*. Glencoe, Ill.: Free Press.

Crandall, V. C., W. Katkovsky, and V. J. Crandall. 1965. "Children's Beliefs in Their Reinforcements in Intellectual Academic Achievement Behaviors." *Child Behavior* 36: 91–109.

Crenshaw, Edward. 1992. "Cross-national Determinants of Income Inequality: A Replication and Extension Using Ecological-Evolutionary Theory." *Social Forces* 71: 339–63.

Daly, Martin, and Margo Wilson. 1988. *Homicide*. New York: Aldine de Gruyter.

Davis, Kingsley. 1949. *Human Society*. Rev. ed. New York: Macmillan.

————. 1961. "Prostitution." In *Contemporary Social Problems*. 3d ed., edited by Robert K. Merton and Robert Nisbet, 262–88. New York: Harcourt Brace and Jovanovich.

Day, Lincoln H. 1984. "Death From Non-war Violence: An International Comparison." *Social Science and Medicine* 19: 917–27.

Denver Post. 1992a. "Jail Suicide." 22 March, p. 3C.

————. 1992b. "Was Death in Day Care Preventable?" 22 March, p. 4C.

Depue, Richard A., and Michele R. Sproont. 1986. "Conceptualizing a Serotonin Trait: A Behavioral Dimension of Constraint." *Annals of the New York Academy of Sciences* 487: 47–62.

Despine, Prosper. 1868. *Psychologie naturelle*. 3 vols. Paris: F. Savy.

DeVellis, Brenda McEvoy, and Susan J. Blalock. 1992. "Illness Attributions and Hopelessness Depression: The Role of Hopelessness Expectancy." *Journal of Abnormal Psychology* 101: 257–64.

Doerner, William G. 1978. "The Index of Southernness Revisited: The Influence of Wherefrom on Whodunit." *Criminology* 16: 47–56.

———. 1983. "Why Does Johnny Reb Die When Shot? The Impact of Medical Resources upon Lethality." *Sociological Inquiry* 53: 1–15.

Doerner, William G., and John C. Speir. 1986. "Stitch and Sew: The Impact of Medical Resources on Criminally Induced Lethality." *Criminology* 24: 319–30.

Dohrenwend, Bruce. 1959. "Egoism, Altruism, Anomie and Fatalism: A Conceptual Analysis of Durkheim's Types." *American Sociological Review* 24: 466–73.

Dollard, John, Leonard W. Doob, Neal E. Miller, O. H. Mowrer, and Robert R. Sears. 1939. *Frustration and Aggression*. New Haven: Yale University Press.

Douglas, Jack D. 1967. *The Social Meanings of Suicide*. Princeton: Princeton University Press.

DuCette, Joseph, Stephen Wolk, and Sarah Friedman. 1972. "Locus of Control and Creativity in Black and White Children." *Journal of Social Psychology* 88: 297–98.

DuCette, Joseph, Stephen Wolk, and E. Soucar. 1972. "Atypical Pattern in Locus of Control and Nonadaptive Behavior." *Journal of Personality* 40: 287–97.

Dulit, Rebecca A., and Robert Michaels. 1992. "Psychodynamics and Suicide." In *Suicide and Clinical Practice*, edited by Douglas Jacobs, 43–53. Washington, D.C.: American Psychiatric Press.

Durkheim, Emile. 1893. *The Division of Labor in Society*. Translated by George Simpson. London: Macmillan, 1933.

———. 1894. *The Rules of the Sociological Method*. Translated by W. D. Halls. New York: Macmillan, 1982.

———. 1897. *Suicide: A Study in Sociology*. Translated by John A. Spaulding and George Simpson. Glencoe, IL: Free Press, 1951.

———. 1900. *Professional Ethics and Civic Morals*. Translated by Cornelia Brookfield. London: Routledge and Kegan Paul.

———. 1912. *The Elementary Forms of the Religious Life*. Translated by John Ward Swain. New York: Free Press, 1947.

Eister, Allen W. 1972. "An Outline of a Structural Theory of Cults." *Journal for the Scientific Study of Religion* 11: 319–33.

Ellner, Melvyn. 1977. "Research on International Suicide." *International Journal of Social Psychiatry* 23: 187–94.

Elmer, E. C. 1933. "Century-old Ecological Studies in France." *American Journal of Sociology* 39: 63–70.

Elwin, Verrier. 1950. *Maria Murder and Suicide.* 2d ed. London: Oxford University Press.

Faris, Robert E. L. 1955. *Social Disorganization.* New York: Roland Press Company.

Feierabend, Ivo K., and Rosalind L. Feierabend. 1966. "Aggressive Behavior within Polities, 1948–62: A Cross-national Study." *Journal of Conflict Resolution* 10: 249–71.

———. 1972. "Systemic Conditions of Political Aggression: An Application of Frustration-Aggression Theory." In *Anger, Violence and Politics*, edited by Ivo K. Feierabend, Rosalind L. Feierabend, and Ted Robert Gurr, 136–83. Englewood Cliffs, N.J.: Prentice-Hall.

Feig, Douglas G. 1978. "Ridge Regression: When Biased Estimation Is Better." *Social Science Quarterly* 58: 708–16.

Feinberg, William E., and Joseph R. Trotta. 1984. "Inferences about Economies of Scale DO Depend on the Form of Statistical Analysis." *Social Forces* 62: 1040–58.

Fennessey, James, and Ronald J. D'Amico. 1980. "Collinearity, Ridge Regression, and Investigator Judgment." *Sociological Methods and Research* 8: 309–40.

Ferdinand, Theodore. 1967. "The Criminal Patterns of Boston since 1849." *American Journal of Sociology* 73: 84–99.

Ferri, Enrico. 1883–84. *Omicidio-Suicidio.* 1st ed. Turin: Fratelli Brocca.

———. 1894. *Omicidio-Suicidio.* 3d ed. Turin: Fratelli Brocca.

———. 1895. *Omicidio-Suicidio.* 4th ed. Turin: Fratelli Brocca.

———. 1925. *Omicidio-Suicidio.* 5th ed. Translated from the Italian to the Spanish by Concha Peña. Madrid: Editorial Review, 1934.

———. 1926. "Un secolo di omicidii e di suicidii in Europa." *Bulletin de l'institut international de statistique* 22: 419–20.

Fields, Gary S. 1980. *Poverty, Inequality and Development.* Cambridge: Cambridge University Press.

Firebaugh, Glenn, and Jack P. Gibbs. 1985. "User's Guide to Ratio Variables." *American Sociological Review* 50: 713–22.

Fischer, Claude S. 1975. "Toward a Subcultural Theory of Urbanism." *American Journal of Sociology* 80: 1319–41.

Fisher, Joseph C., and Robert L. Mason. 1981. "The Analysis of Multicollinear Data in Criminology." In *Methods in Quantitative Criminology*, edited by James Alan Fox, 99–125. New York: Academic Press.

Food and Agriculture Organization. 1990. *Production Yearbook, 1989*. Rome: United Nations.

Franke, R. H., E. W. Thomas, and A. J. Queenen. 1977. "Suicide and Homicide: Common Sources and Consistent Relationships." *Social Psychiatry* 12: 149–56.

Freeman, John Henry, and Jerrold E. Kronenfeld. 1973. "Problems of Definitional Dependency: The Case of Administrative Intensity." *Social Forces* 52: 108–21.

Freidson, Eliot. 1970. *The Profession of Medicine*. New York: Dodd, Mead.

Freud, Sigmund. 1913. *Totem and Taboo*. Vol. 13 in *The Standard Edition of the Complete Psychological Works of Sigmund Freud*, translated under the general editorship of James Strachey, 1–162. London: Hogarth Press, 1961.

———. 1915. "Instincts and Their Vicissitudes." Vol. 14 in *The Standard Edition of the Complete Psychological Works of Sigmund Freud*, translated under the general editorship of James Strachey, 117–40. London: Hogarth Press, 1961.

———. 1917. "Mourning and Melancholia." Vol. 14 in *The Standard Edition of the Complete Psychological Works of Sigmund Freud*, translated under the general editorship of James Strachey, 243–58. London: Hogarth Press, 1961.

———. 1920. *Beyond the Pleasure Principle*. Vol. 18 in *The Standard Edition of the Complete Psychological Works of Sigmund Freud*, translated under the general editorship of James Strachey, 7–64. London: Hogarth Press, 1961.

———. 1923. *The Ego and the Id*. Translated by Joan Riviere. London: Hogarth Press, 1927.

———. 1929. *Civilization and Its Discontents*. Vol. 21 in *The Standard Edition of the Complete Psychological Works of Sigmund Freud*, translated under the general editorship of James Strachey, 64–145. London: Hogarth Press, 1961.

Gastil, Raymond D. 1971 "Homicide and a Regional Culture of Violence." *American Sociological Review* 36: 412–27.

Gibbs, Jack P. 1961. "Suicide." In *Contemporary Social Problems*, edited by Robert K. Merton and Robert A. Nisbet, 222–61. New York: Harcourt Brace and World.

Gibbs, Jack P., ed. 1968. *Suicide*. New York: Harper and Row.

Gibbs, Jack P., and Walter T. Martin. 1964. *Status Integration and Suicide: A Sociological Study*. Eugene: University of Oregon Books.

Gibbs, Jack P., and Austin L. Porterfield. 1960. "Occupational Prestige and Social Mobility of Suicides in New Zealand." *American Journal of Sociology* 66: 147–52.

Giddens, Anthony. 1965. "The Suicide Problem in French Sociology." *British Journal of Sociology* 16: 3–18.

———. 1970. Introduction. In *Suicide and the Meaning of Civilization*, by Thomas G. Masaryk. Chicago: University of Chicago Press.

Gold, Martin. 1958. "Suicide, Homicide, and the Socialization of Aggression." *American Journal of Sociology* 63: 651–61.

Goldblatt, Mark, and Alan Schatzberg. 1992. "Medication and the Suicidal Patient." In *Suicide and Clinical Practice*, edited by Douglas Jacobs, 23–41. Washington, D.C.: American Psychiatric Press.

Goldstein, Jeffrey H. 1986. *Aggression and Crimes of Violence*. 2d ed. New York: Oxford University Press.

Goodwin, Frederick K., and K. R. Jamison. 1990. *Manic-Depressive Illness*. New York: Oxford University Press.

Goodwin, Frederick K., and Bette L. Runck. 1992. "Suicide Intervention: Integration of Psychosocial, Clinical, and Biomedical Traditions." In *Suicide and Clinical Practice*, edited by Douglas Jacobs, 1–21. Washington, D.C.: American Psychiatric Press.

Graham, Hugh Davis, and Ted Robert Gurr, eds. 1969. *The History of Violence in America: Historical and Comparative Perspectives*. New York: Frederick A. Praeger.

Grasmick, Harold G., Elizabeth Davenport, Mitchell B. Chamlin, and Robert J. Bursik, Jr. 1992. "Protestant Fundamentalism and the Retributive Doctrine of Punishment." *Criminology* 30: 21–45.

Grasso, Patrick G., and Ira Sharansky. 1980. "Economic Development and the Distribution of Income in the American States." *Social Science Quarterly* 61: 446–57.

Greenberg, Michael R., George W. Carey, and Frank J. Popper. 1987. "Violent Death, Violent States and American Youth." *The Public Interest* 87: 38–48.

Gregory, W. Larry. 1978. "Locus of Control for Positive and Negative Outcomes." *Journal of Personality and Social Psychology* 36: 840–49.

Griffith, Ezra E. H., and Carl C. Bell. 1989. "Recent Trends in Suicide and Homicide among Blacks." *Journal of the American Medical Association* 262: 2265–69.

Grollman, Earl A. 1971. *Suicide: Prevention, Intervention, Postvention*. Boston: Beacon Press.

Guerry, Andre Michel. 1833. *Essai sur la statistique morale de la France*. Paris: Crochard.

Guimond, Serge, Guy Begin, and Douglas L. Palmer. 1989. "Education and Causal Attributions: The Development of 'Person-Blame' and 'System-Blame' Ideology." *Social Psychology Quarterly* 52: 126–40.

Gurr, Ted Robert. 1980. *Handbook of Political Conflict*. New York: Free Press.

Hackney, Sheldon. 1969. "Southern Violence." *American Historical Review* 39: 906–25.

Halbwachs, Maurice. 1930. *Les Causes du suicide*. Paris: Felix Alcan.

Hall, Peter M., and John P. Hewitt. 1970. "The Quasi-theory of Communication and the Management of Dissent." *Social Problems* 18: 17–27.

Hamilton, W. D. 1964. "The Genetical Evolution of Social Behaviour, I." *Journal of Theoretical Biology* 7: 1–16.

Hankoff, Leon D. 1961. "An Epidemic of Attempted Suicide." *Comprehensive Psychiatry* 2: 294–98.

Hansmann, Henry B., and John M. Quigley. 1982. "Population Heterogeneity and the Sociogenesis of Homicide." *Social Forces* 61: 206–24.

Harrison, Bennet, and Barry Bluestone. 1988. *The Great U-Turn: Corporate Restructuring and the Polarizing of America*. New York: Basic Books.

Harvey, J. H., and G. Weary. 1981. *Perspectives on Attributional Processes*. Dubuque, IA: William C. Brown.

Heider, Fritz. 1958. *The Psychology of Interpersonal Relations*. New York: Wiley.

Heinicke, C. M. 1953. *Some Antecedents and Correlates of Guilt and Fear in Young Boys*. Ph.D. diss., Harvard University.

Heise, David R. 1969. "Separating Reliability and Stability in Test-Retest Correlation." *American Sociological Review* 34: 93–101.

———. 1971. "Employing Nominal Variables, Induced Variables, and Block Variables in Path Analysis." *Sociological Methods and Research* 1: 147–73.

Hendin, Herbert. 1964. *Suicide and Scandinavia*. Garden City, N.Y.: Anchor.

———. 1969a. *Black Suicide*. New York: Harper Colophon.

———. 1969b. "Black Suicide." *Archives of General Psychiatry* 21: 401–22.

Henry, Andrew F., and James F. Short, Jr. 1954. *Suicide and Homicide: Some Economic, Sociological, and Psychological Aspects of Aggression*. London: Free Press of Glencoe.

———. 1957. "The Sociology of Suicide." In *Clues to Suicide*, edited by Edwin S. Shneidman and Norman L. Farborow, 58–69. New York: McGraw-Hill.

Hewitt, John P., and Peter M. Hall. 1973. "Social Problems, Problematic Situations, and Quasi-theories." *American Sociological Review* 38: 367–74.

Hewitt, John P., and Randall Stokes. 1975. "Disclaimers." *American Sociological Review* 40: 1–11.

Hey, Richard. 1785. *A Dissertation on Suicide*. London: Archdeacon.

Hill, Kerrie J., and Lisa M. Larson. 1992. "Attributional Style in the Reformulated Learned Helplessness Model of Depression: Cognitive Processes and Measurement Implications." *Cognitive Therapy and Research* 16: 83–94.

Himmelhoch, Jonathan M. 1988. "What Destroys Our Restraints Against Suicide?" *Journal of Clinical Psychiatry* 49 (9, supplement): 46–52.

Hindelang, Michael J. 1974. "The Uniform Crime Reports Revisited." *Journal of Criminal Justice* 2: 1–17.

Hiroto, Donald S. 1974. "Locus of Control and Learned Helplessness." *Journal of Experimental Psychology* 102: 187–93.

Hiroto, Donald S., and Martin E. P. Seligman. 1975. "Generality of Learned Helplessness in Man." *Journal of Personality and Social Psychology* 31: 311–27.

Hitson, Hazel M., and Daniel H. Funkenstein. 1959. "Family Pattern and Paranoidal Personality Structure in Boston and Burma." *International Journal of Social Psychiatry* 5: 182–90.

Hoerl, Arthur E., and Robert W. Kennard. 1970. "Ridge Regression: Biased Estimation for Nonorthogonal Problems." *Technometrics* 12: 55–67.

Holinger, Paul C. 1979. "Violent Deaths among the Young: Recent Trends in Suicide, Homicide, and Accidents." *American Journal of Psychiatry* 136: 1144–47.

———. 1980. "Violent Deaths As a Leading Cause of Mortality: An Epidemiologic Study of Suicide, Homicide and Accidents." *American Journal of Psychiatry* 137: 472–76.

———. 1987. *Violent Deaths in the United States: An Epidemiologic Study of Suicide, Homicide, and Accidents*. New York: Guilford.

Hoover, Greg A. 1989. "Intranational Inequality: A Cross-national Dataset." *Social Forces* 67: 1008–26.

Hopkins, J. H. 1880. "A Consideration of Suicide." *Popular Science Monthly* 16: 798–803.

Hudson, R. Page, John A. Humphrey, and Harriet J. Kupferer. 1980. "Regional Variations in the Characteristics of Victims of Violence." *International Journal of Social Psychiatry* 26: 300–20.

Huff-Corzine, Lin, Jay Corzine, and David C. Moore. 1986. "Southern Exposure: Deciphering the South's Influence on Homicide Rates." *Social Forces* 64: 906–24.

———. 1991. "Deadly Connections: Culture, Poverty and the Direction of Lethal Violence." *Social Forces* 69: 715–32.

Humphrey, John A., and Harriet Kupferer. 1977. "Pockets of Violence: An Exploration of Homicide and Suicide." *Diseases of the Nervous System* 38: 883–97.

———. 1982. "Homicide and Suicide among the Cherokee and Lubee Indians of North Carolina." *International Journal of Social Psychiatry* 28: 121–28.

Hurlbert, Jeanne S. 1989. "The Southern Region: An Empirical Test of the Hypothesis of Cultural Distinctiveness." *Sociological Quarterly* 30: 245–66.

Jacobs, Douglas. 1992. "Evaluating and Treating Suicidal Behavior in the Borderline Patient." In *Suicide and Clinical Practice*, edited by Douglas Jacobs, 101–30. Washington, D.C.: American Psychiatric Press.

Jagodzinski, Wolfgang, and Erich Weede. 1981. "Testing Curvilinear Propositions by Polynomial Regression with Particular Reference to the Interpretation of Standardized Solutions." *Quality and Quantity* 15: 447–63.

Jain, Shail. 1975. *Size Distribution of Income: A Compilation of Data.* Washington, D.C.: World Bank.

Janoff-Bulman, Ronnie. 1979. "Characterological Versus Behavioral Self-blame: Inquiries into Depression and Rape." *Journal of Personality and Social Psychology* 37: 1798–1809.

Jenkins, Phillip. 1988. "Myth and Murder: The Serial Killer Panic of 1983–1985." *Criminal Justice Research Bulletin* 3: 112–30.

Jirovec, Ronald. 1984. "Documenting the Impact of Reaganomics on Social Welfare Recipients." *Arete* 9: 36–47.

Johnson, Barclay D. 1965. "Durkheim's One Cause of Suicide." *American Sociological Review* 30: 556–64.

Kansas City Star. 1992. "Six Dead in Murder-Suicide." 22 March, pp. 1A, 10A.

Kasarda, John D., and Patrick D. Nolan. 1979. "Ratio Measurement and Theoretical Inference in Social Research." *Social Forces* 58: 212–27.

Kelley, Harold H. 1967. "Attribution Theory in Social Psychology." In *Nebraska Symposium on Motivation. Vol. 15*, edited by David Levine, 192–240. Lincoln: University of Nebraska Press.

Kitsuse, John I., and Aaron V. Cicourel. 1963. "A Note on the Uses of Statistics." *Social Problems* 11: 131–39.

Kivela, S. L. 1985. "Relationship between Suicide, Homicide, and Accidental Deaths among the Aged in Finland in 1951–1979." *Acta Psychiatrica Scandinavica* 72: 155–60.

Klebba, A. John. 1981. "Comparison of Trends for Suicide and Homicide in the United States, 1900-1976." In *Violence and the Violent Individual*, edited by J. Ray Hays, Thomas K. Roberts, and Kenneth S. Solway, 127–48. Jamaica, N.Y.: Spectrum Publications.

Kmenta, Jan. 1971. *Elements of Econometrics*. New York: Macmillan.

Kohn, Melvin L. 1989. *Cross-national Research in Sociology*. Newbury Park, CA: Sage.

Krahn, Harvey, Timothy F. Hartnagel, and John W. Gartrell. 1986. "Income Inequality and Homicide Rates: Cross-national Data and Criminological Theories." *Criminology* 24: 269–95.

Krause, Neal, and Sheldon Stryker. 1984. "Stress and Well-being: The Buffering Role of Locus of Control Beliefs." *Social Science and Medicine* 18: 783–90.

Kreitman, Norman. 1988. "The Two Traditions in Suicide Research (The Dublin Lecture)." *Suicide and Life-threatening Behavior* 18: 67–72.

Krohn, Marvin. 1976. "Inequality, Unemployment and Crime: A Cross-national Examination." *Sociological Quarterly* 17: 303–13.

———. 1978. "A Durkheimian Analysis of International Crime Rates." *Social Forces* 57: 654–70.

Kuhn, Thomas S. 1970. *The Structure of Scientific Revolutions*. 2d ed. Chicago: University of Chicago Press.

Kupferer, Harriet J., and John A. Humphrey. 1975. "Fatal Indian Violence in North Carolina." *Anthropological Quarterly* 48: 236–44.

Kuznets, Simon. 1957. "Quantitative Aspects of the Economic Growth of Nations, II: Industrial Distribution of National Product and Labor Force." *Economic Development and Cultural Change* 5: supplement.

———. 1963. "Quantitative Aspects of the Economic Growth of Nations, VII: Distribution and Income by Size." *Economic Development and Cultural Change* 11: supplement.

Labovitz, Sanford, and Merlin Brinkerhoff. 1977. "Structural Changes and Suicide in Canada." *International Journal of Comparative Sociology* 18: 254–67.

LaCapra, Dominick. 1972. *Emile Durkheim: Sociologist and Philosopher*. Chicago: University of Chicago Press, 1985.

Lamont, John. 1972a. "Item Mood-level As a Determinant of IE Test Response." *Journal of Clinical Psychology* 28: 190.

———. 1972b. "Depression, Locus of Control and Mood Response Set." *Journal of Clinical Psychology* 28: 342–45.

Lane, Roger. 1979. *Violent Death in the City: Suicide, Accident, and Murder in Nineteenth-century Philadelphia.* Cambridge: Harvard University Press.

Lecaillon, Jacques, Felix Paukert, Christian Morrison, and Dimitri Germidis. 1984. *Income Distribution and Economic Development.* Geneva: International Labour Office.

Lefcourt, Herbert M. 1982. *Locus of Control: Current Trends in Theory and Research.* 2d ed. Hillsdale, N.J.: Lawrence Erlbaum.

———. 1983. *Research with the Locus of Control Construct.* 3 vols. New York: Academic Press.

Lemert, Edwin M. 1962. "Paranoia and the Dynamics of Exclusion." *Sociometry* 25: 2–25.

Lenski, Gerhard E. 1966. *Power and Privilege: A Theory of Social Stratification.* New York: McGraw-Hill.

Lester, David. 1972. *Why People Kill Themselves.* Springfield, IL: Charles C. Thomas.

———. 1974. "A Cross-national Study of Suicide and Homicide." *Behavior Science Research* 9: 307–18.

———. 1977. "The Prediction of Suicide and Homicide Rates Cross-nationally by Means of Step-wise Multiple Regression." *Behavior Science Research* 12: 61–69.

———. 1983. *Why People Kill Themselves: A 1980's Summary of Research Findings on Suicidal Behavior.* Springfield, IL: Charles C. Thomas.

———. 1987. "Cross-national Correlations among Religion, Suicide and Homicide." *Sociology and Social Research* 71: 103–4.

———. 1988a. "A Regional Analysis of Suicide and Homicide Rates in the USA: Search for Broad Cultural Patterns." *Social Psychiatry and Psychiatric Epidemiology* 23: 202–5.

———. 1988b. "Strikes, Suicide and Homicide: A Cross-national Analysis." *International Journal of Contemporary Sociology* 25: 9–14.

———. 1989a. "National Suicide and Homicide Rates: Correlates Versus Predictors." *Social Science and Medicine* 29: 1249–52.

———. 1989b. "A Depression Paradox Theory of Suicide." *Personality and Individual Differences* 10: 1103–4.

————. 1990a. "Suicide, Homicide and the Quality of Life in Various Countries." *Acta Psychiatrica Scandinavica* 81: 332–34.

————. 1990b. "Capital Punishment, Gun Control, and Personal Violence (Suicide and Homicide)." *Psychological Reports* 66: 122.

————. 1990–91. "Mortality from Suicide and Homicide for African Americans in the USA: A Regional Analysis." *Omega* 22: 219–26.

————. 1991a. "A Test of Lester's Depression Paradox Theory of Suicide." *Psychological Reports* 68: 1254.

————. 1991b. "Totalitarianism and Fatalistic Suicide." *Journal of Social Psychology* 131: 129–30.

Levey, Jerrold. 1965. "Navajo Suicide." *Human Organization* 24: 308–18.

Levi, Ken. 1982. "Homicide and Suicide: Structure and Process." *Deviant Behavior* 3: 91–115.

Lidberg, L., J. R. Tuck, M. Åsberg, G. P. Scalia-Tomba, and L. Bertilsson. 1985. "Homicide, Suicide and CSF 5-HIAA." *Acta Psychiatrica Scandinavica* 71: 230–36.

Light, Stephen C. 1984. "Multicollinearity in a Study of Regional Variations in Homicide Rates: A Comment on Smith and Parker." *Social Forces* 62: 800–803.

Loftin, Colin, and Robert H. Hill. 1974. "Regional Subculture and Homicide: An Examination of the Gastil-Hackney Thesis." *American Sociological Review* 39: 714–24.

Loftin, Colin, and Robert Nash Parker. 1985. "An Error-in-Variable Model of the Effect of Poverty on Urban Homicide Rates." *Criminology* 23: 269–87.

Logan, Charles H. 1982. "Problems in Ratio Correlation: The Case of Deterrence Research." *Social Forces* 60: 791–810.

Long, Susan B. 1979. "The Continuing Debate over the Use of Ratio Variables: Facts and Fiction." In *Sociological Methodology, 1980*, edited by Karl F. Schuessler, 37–67. San Francisco: Jossey-Bass.

Lord, W. W. 1880. "A Consideration of Suicide." *Popular Science Monthly* 17: 120–21.

Lottin, Joseph. 1912. *Quetelet: Statisticien et sociologue.* New York: Burt Franklin.

Lukes, Steven. 1973. *Emile Durkheim: His Life and Work.* Stanford: Stanford University Press, 1985.

Lunden, Walter A. 1932. *Statistics on Crime and Criminals.* Pittsburgh: Stevenson and Foster.

————. 1955. *Crimes and Criminals*. Ames: Iowa State University Press.

Lupfer, Michael, Patricia J. Hopkinson, and Patricia Kelley. 1988. "An Exploration of the Attributional Styles of Christian Fundamentalists and Authoritarians." *Journal of the Scientific Study of Religion* 27: 389–98.

Lydall, H. 1977. "Income Distribution during the Process of Development." *World Employment/Working Paper No. WP52*. Geneva: International Labor Office.

MacArthur, Douglas A. 1951. "Farewell Address, Joint Session of Congress, Washington, D.C., April 19, 1951." In *Great Speeches for Criticism and Analysis*. 2d ed., edited by Lloyd E. Rohrer and Roger Cook, 145–50. Greenwood, Ind.: Alistair Press, 1993.

Mann, J. John, and Michael Stanley, eds. 1986. *Psychobiology of Suicidal Behavior*. New York: New York Academy of Sciences.

Marshall, James R. 1981. "Political Integration and the Effect of War on Suicide: United States, 1933–1976." *Social Forces* 59: 771–85.

Marx, Karl. 1853. "Capital Punishment.—Mr. Cobden's Pamphlet.—Regulations of the Bank of England." Vol. 11 in *Collected Works*, by Karl Marx and Frederick Engels, 495–501. New York: International Publishers, 1975.

Masaryk, Thomas G. 1881. *Suicide and the Meaning of Civilization*. Translated by William B. Weist and Robert G. Batson. Chicago: University of Chicago Press, 1970.

Maury, Alfred. 1860. "Du Mouvement moral des sociétés: D'après les derniers résultats de la statistique." *Revue des Deux Mondes* (September-October): 456–84.

Mawson, Anthony R., and K. W. Jacobs. 1978. "Corn Consumption, Tryptophan, and Cross-national Homicide Rates." *Journal of Orthomolecular Psychiatry* 7: 227–30.

McClelland, David. 1961. *The Achieving Society*. Princeton: Van Nostrand.

McClure, G. M. 1984. "Trends in Suicide for England and Wales, 1975–80." *British Journal of Psychiatry* 144: 119–26.

McCord, William, and Joan McCord. 1956. *Psychopathy and Delinquency*. New York: Grune and Stratton.

————. 1964. *The Psychopath*. Princeton: Van Nostrand.

McDonald, Lynn. 1976. *The Sociology of Law and Order*. Boulder, CO: Westview Press.

McGinnies, Elliott, Lena A. Nordholm, Charles D. Ward, and Duangduen L. Bhanthumnavin. 1974. "Sex and Cultural Differences in Perceived Locus of Control among Students in Five Countries." *Journal of Consulting and Clinical Psychology* 42: 451–55.

Mead, Margaret. 1935. *Sex and Temperament in Three Primitive Societies.* New York: Morrow.

Melges, F. T., and A. E. Weisz. 1971. "The Personal Future and Suicidal Ideation." *Journal of Nervous and Mental Disease* 153: 244–50.

Menard, Scott. 1986. "A Research Note on International Comparisons of Inequality of Income." *Social Forces* 64: 778–93.

Menninger, Karl. 1938. *Man against Himself.* New York: Harcourt Brace and World.

Merritt, Richard L., and Stein Rokkan. 1966. *Comparing Nations.* New Haven: Yale University Press.

Merton, Robert K. 1938. "Social Structure and Anomie." *American Sociological Review* 3: 672–82.

———. 1957. *Social Theory and Social Structure.* Rev. ed. Glencoe, IL: Free Press.

———. 1961. "Social Problems and Sociological Theory." In *Contemporary Social Problems,* edited by Robert K. Merton and Robert A. Nisbet, 697–737. New York: Harcourt Brace and World.

Messner, Steven F. 1980. "Income Inequality and Murder Rates: Some Cross-national Findings." *Comparative Social Research* 3: 185–98.

———. 1982a. "Social Development, Social Equality and Homicide: A Cross-national Test of a Durkheimian Model." *Social Forces* 61: 225–40.

———. 1982b. "Poverty, Inequality, and the Urban Homicide Rate." *Criminology* 20: 103–14.

———. 1983. "Regional and Racial Effects on the Urban Homicide Rate." *American Journal of Sociology* 88: 997–1007.

Messner, Steven F., and Kenneth Tardiff. 1986. "Economic Inequality and Levels of Homicide: An Analysis of Urban Neighborhoods." *Criminology* 24: 297–317.

Miller, Dale T., and Carol A. Porter. 1988. "Errors and Biases in the Attribution Process." In *Social Cognition and Clinical Psychology,* edited by Lyn Y. Abramson, 3–30. New York: Guilford Press.

Miller, Daniel R., and Guy E. Swanson. 1960. *Inner Conflict and Defense.* New York: Henry Holt.

Miller, Joan G. 1984. "Culture and the Development of Everyday Social Explanation." *Journal of Personality and Social Psychology* 46: 961–78.

Miller, Neal E., Robert R. Sears, O. H. Mowrer, Leonard W. Doob, and John Dollard. 1941. "The Frustration-Aggression Hypothesis." *Psychological Review* 48: 337–42.

Miller, Walter B. 1958. "Lower-Class Culture As a Generating Milieu of Gang Delinquency." *Journal of Social Issues* 14: 5–19.

Miller, William R., and Martin E. P. Seligman. 1973. "Depression and the Perception of Reinforcement." *Journal of Abnormal Psychology* 84: 228–38.

Miner, John Rice. 1922. "Suicide and Its Relation to Other Factors." *American Journal of Hygiene, Monographic Series* 2: 72–112.

Mischel, W., R. Zeiss, and R. Zeiss. 1974. "An Internal-External Control Test for Young Children." *Journal of Personality and Social Psychology* 29: 265–78.

Morris, Terence. 1958. *The Criminal Area*. London: Routledge and Kegan Paul.

Morselli, Henry [Enrico]. 1879a. *Suicide: An Essay in Comparative Moral Statistics*. Abridged edition. New York: Appleton, 1882.

———. 1879b. *Suicide*. New York: Appleton, 1903.

Motto, Jerome A. 1967. "Suicide and Suggestibility." *American Journal of Psychiatry* 124: 252–56.

———. 1970. "Newspaper Influence on Suicide." *Archives of General Psychiatry* 23: 146–48.

Muller, Edward N. 1988. "Democracy, Economic Development and Income Inequality." *American Sociological Review* 53: 50–68.

Murphy, G. E., and R. D. Wetzel. 1990. "The Lifetime Risk of Suicide in Alcoholism." *Archives of General Psychiatry* 47: 383–92.

Murphy, G. K. 1979. "The 'Undetermined' Ruling: A Medicolegal Dilemma." *Journal of Forensic Sciences* 24: 483–91.

National Center for Health Statistics. 1974a. *Vital Statistics of the United States, 1969*. Washington, D.C.: Government Printing Office.

———. 1974b. *Vital Statistics of the United States, 1970*. Washington, D.C.: Government Printing Office.

———. 1974c. *Vital Statistics of the United States, 1971*. Washington, D.C.: Government Printing Office.

———. 1992. *Vital Statistics of the United States, 1989*. Washington, D.C.: Government Printing Office.

Neifield, M. R. 1927. "A Study of Spurious Correlation." *Journal of the American Statistical Association* 22: 331–38.

Nelsen, Candice, Jay Corzine, and Lin Huff-Corzine. 1994. "The Violent West Reexamined: A Research Note on Regional Homicide Rates." *Criminology.* 32:149–161.

Ness, Gayl D. 1985. "Managing Not-so-small Numbers: Between Comparative and Statistical Methods." *International Journal of Comparative Sociology* 26: 1–13.

Newman, Graeme. 1979. *Understanding Violence.* New York: Harper and Row.

Nisbett, Richard E. 1993. "Violence and U.S. Regional Culture." *American Psychologist* 48: 441–49.

O'Carroll, Patrick W. 1989. "A Consideration of the Validity and Reliability of Suicide Mortality Data." *Suicide and Life-threatening Behavior* 19: 1–16.

O'Carroll, Patrick W., and James A. Mercy. 1989. "Regional Variation in Homicide Rates: Why Is the *West* So Violent." *Violence and Victims* 4: 17–25.

Ortega, Suzanne T., Jay Corzine, Cathleen Burnett, and Tracey Poyer. 1992. "Modernization, Age Structure, and Regional Context: A Cross-national Study of Crime." *Sociological Spectrum* 12: 257–77.

Osler, Sir William. 1922. *The Evolution of Modern Medicine.* New Haven: Yale University Press.

Overmier, J. B., and Martin E. P. Seligman. 1967. "Effects of Unavoidable Shock upon Subsequent Escape and Avoidance Learning." *Journal of Comparative and Physiological Psychology* 63: 23–33.

Palmer, Stuart. 1965. "Murder and Suicide in Forty Non-literate Societies." *Journal of Criminal Law, Criminology and Police Science* 56: 320–24.

———. 1972. *The Violent Society.* New Haven: College and University Press.

Palmer, Stuart, and Arnold S. Linsky, eds. 1972. *Rebellion and Retreat.* Columbus, Ohio: Merrill.

Parker, Robert N. 1989. "Poverty, Subculture of Violence, and Type of Homicide." *Social Forces* 67: 983–1007.

Parker, Robert N., and M. Dwayne Smith. 1979. "Deterrence, Poverty, and Type of Homicide." *American Journal of Sociology* 85: 614–24.

Parsons, Oscar A., and John M. Schneider. 1974. "Locus of Control in University Students from Eastern and Western Societies." *Journal of Consulting and Clinical Psychology* 42: 456–61.

Parsons, Talcott. 1937. *The Structure of Social Action.* New York: McGraw-Hill.

Pastore, Nicholas. 1952. "The Role of Arbitrariness in the Frustration-Aggression Hypothesis." *Journal of Abnormal and Social Psychology* 47: 728–32.

Paukert, Felix. 1973. "Income Distribution at Different Levels of Development: A Survey of Evidence." *International Labour Review* 18: 97–125.

Pearson, Karl. 1897. "Mathematical Contributions to the Theory of Evolution: On a Form of Spurious Correlation Which May Arise When Indices Are Used in the Measurement of Organs." *Proceedings of the Royal Society of London* 60: 489–98.

Pendleton, Brian F. 1984. "Correcting for Ratio Variable Correlation: Examples Using Models of Mortality." *Social Science Research* 13: 268–86.

Pescosolido, Bernice A., and Robert Mendelsohn. 1986. "Social Causation or Social Construction of Suicide? An Investigation into the Social Organization of Official Rates." *American Sociological Review* 51: 80–101.

Peterson, Christopher, and Martin E. P. Seligman. 1984. "Causal Explanations As a Risk Factor in Depression: Theory and Evidence." *Psychological Review* 91: 347–74.

Pfohl, Stephen J. 1985. *Images of Deviance and Social Control*. New York: McGraw-Hill.

Phillips, David P. 1974. The Influence of Suggestion on Suicide: Substantive and Theoretical Implications of the Werther Effect." *American Sociological Review* 39: 340–54.

———. 1977. "Motor Vehicle Accidents Increase Just after Publicized Suicide Stories." *Science* 196: 1464–65.

———. 1978. "Airplane Accidents Increase Just after Newspaper Stories about Murder and Suicide." *Science* 201: 748–50.

———. 1979. "Suicide, Motor Vehicle Fatalities and the Mass Media: Evidence toward a Theory of Suggestion." *American Journal of Sociology* 84: 1150–74.

———. 1980. "Airplane Accidents, Murder, and the Mass Media: Towards a Theory of Imitation and Suggestion." *Social Forces* 58: 1001–24.

———. 1983. "The Impact of Mass Media Violence on U.S. Homicides." *American Sociological Review* 48: 560–68.

Phillips, David P., and Kenneth A. Bollen. 1985. "Same Time, Last Year: Selective Data Dredging for Negative Findings." *American Sociological Review* 50: 364–71.

Phillips, Leslie. 1968. *Human Adaptation and Its Failures*. New York: Academic Press.

Pincus, Jonathan H., and Gary J. Tucker. 1978. *Behavioral Neurology*. 2d ed. New York: Oxford University Press.

Planck, Max. 1949. *Scientific Autobiography and Other Papers*. Translated by F. Gaynor. New York: Greenwood Press.

Plutchik, Robert, and Herman M. van Praag. 1990. "Psychosocial Correlates of Suicide and Violent Risk." In *Violence and Suicidality: Perspectives in Clinical and Psychobiological Research*, edited by Herman M. van Praag, Robert Plutchik, and Alan Apter, 37–65. New York: Brunner/Mazel.

Porterfield, Austin L. 1949. "Indices of Suicide and Homicide by States and Cities: Some Southern–Non-Southern Contrasts with Implications for Research." *American Sociological Review* 14: 481–90.

————. 1952a. "Suicide and Crime in the Social Structure of an Urban Setting: Fort Worth, 1930–1950." *American Sociological Review* 17: 341–49.

————. 1952b. "Suicide and Crime in Folk and Secular Society." *American Journal of Sociology* 57: 331–38.

————. 1960. "Traffic Fatalities, Suicide, and Homicide." *American Sociological Review* 25: 897–901.

Porterfield, Austin L., and Robert H. Talbert. 1948. *Suicide, Crime and Social Wellbeing in Your City and State*. Fort Worth: Leo Potisham Foundation.

Powell, Elwin H. 1958. "Occupation, Status, and Suicide: Toward a Redefinition of Anomie." *American Sociological Review* 32: 131–39.

Prudhomme, Charles. 1938. "The Problem of Suicide in the American Negro." *Psychoanalytic Review* 25: 187–204, 372–91.

Przworski, Adam, and Fernanda Cortes. 1977. "Comparing Partial and Ratio Regression Models." *Political Methodology* 4: 63–75.

Queen, Stuart A., and Lewis F. Thomas. 1939. *The City*. New York: McGraw-Hill.

Quetelet, Adolphe. 1831. *Research on the Propensity for Crime at Different Ages*. Translated by Sawyer Sylvester. Cincinnati: Anderson, 1984.

————. 1835. *A Treatise on Man*. Translated by R. Knox and T. Smibert. Edinburgh: Chambers.

Quinney, Richard C. 1965. "Suicide, Homicide, and Economic Development." *Social Forces* 43: 401–6.

Ragin, Charles C. 1987. *The Comparative Method: Moving Beyond Qualitative and Quantitative Strategies*. Berkeley: University of California Press.

Redfield, H. V. 1880. *Homicide, North and South*. Philadelphia: Lippincott.

Reed, John Shelton. 1972. *The Enduring South: Subcultural Persistence in Mass Society*. Lexington, MA: Heath.

————. 1982. *One South: An Ethnic Approach to Regional Culture*. Baton Rouge: Louisiana State University Press.

Reiss, Albert J., Jr., and Jeffrey A. Roth, eds. 1993. *Understanding and Preventing Violence*. Washington, D.C.: National Academy Press.

Riedel, Marc, and Margaret A. Zahn. 1985. *The Nature and Patterns of American Homicide*. Washington, D.C.: Government Printing Office.

Roberti, P. 1974. "Income Distribution: A Time Series and Cross-sectional Study." *Economic Journal* 84: 629–38.

Robinson, William S. 1950. "Ecological Correlation and the Behavior of Individuals." *American Sociological Review* 15: 351–57.

Rockett, Ian R. H., and Gordon S. Smith. 1989. "Homicide, Suicide, Motor Vehicle Crash, and Fall Mortality: U.S.'s Experience in Comparative Perspective." *American Journal of Public Health* 79: 1396–1400.

Ross, Catherine E. 1990. "Emotional Consequences of Various Attributions of Success." *Sociological Focus* 23: 101–13.

Rotter, Julian B. 1966. "Generalized Expectancies for Internal Versus External Control of Reinforcements." *Psychological Monographs* 80: 1–29.

Rotter, Julian B., Stanley Liverant, and Melvin Seeman. 1962. "Internal Versus External Control of Reinforcement: A Major Variable in Behavior Theory." Vol. 2 in *Decisions, Values and Groups*, edited by N. Washburne, 473–516. London: Pergamon.

Saigo, Roy H. 1989. "The Barriers of Racism: Righting the Wrongs of Past and Present." *Change Magazine*, November-December, pp. 8–10.

Sainsbury, Peter. 1956. *Suicide in London*. New York: Basic Books.

Sainsbury, Peter, and S. J. Jenkins. 1982. "The Accuracy of Officially Reported Suicide Statistics for Purposes of Epidemiological Research." *Journal of Epidemiology and Community Health* 36: 43–48.

Saran, Anirudha Bahari 1974. *Murder and Suicide among the Munda and the Oraon*. New Delhi: National.

Sawyer, Malcolm. 1976. "Income Distribution in OECD Countries." *OECD Economic Outlook: Occasional Studies*: 3–36.

Scheff, Thomas J. 1966. *Being Mentally Ill: A Sociological Theory*. Chicago: Aldine.

Schmid, Calvin S. 1928. *Suicides in Seattle, 1914 to 1928*. Seattle: University of Washington Press.

————. 1933. "Suicide in Minneapolis, 1928–1932." *American Journal of Sociology* 39: 30–48.

Schmid, Calvin S., and Maurice D. Van Arsdol. 1955. "Completed and At-tempted Suicides: A Comparative Analysis." *American Sociological Review* 20: 273–83.

Schmidt, Rolf W., Helmut Lamm, and Gisela Trommsdorff. 1978. "Social Class and Sex As Determinants of Future Orientation (Time Perspective) in Adults." *European Journal of Social Psychology* 8: 71–90.

Schrauzer, Gerhard N., and Krishna P. Shrestha. 1990. "Lithium in Drinking Water and the Incidences of Crimes, Suicides, and Arrests Related to Drug Addictions." *Biological Trace Element Research* 25: 105–14.

Schuessler, Karl. 1973. "Ratio Variables and Path Models." In *Structural Equa-tion Models in the Social Sciences*, edited by Arthur S. Goldberger and Otis Dudley Duncan, 201–28. New York: Seminar Press.

———. 1974. "Analysis of Ratio Variables: Opportunities and Pitfalls." *Ameri-can Journal of Sociology* 80: 379–96.

Schwartz, D. A. 1964. "The Paranoid-depressive Existential Continuum." *Psy-chiatric Quarterly* 38: 690–706.

Sears, Robert R., Eleanor E. Maccoby, and Harry Levin. 1957. *Patterns of Child Rearing*. Evanston, IL: Row, Peterson.

Seeman, Melvin. 1959. "On the Meaning of Alienation." *American Sociological Review* 24: 783–91.

———. 1975. "Alienation Studies." *Annual Review of Sociology* 1: 91–123.

Seiden, Richard H., and Raymond P. Freitas. 1980. "Shifting Patterns of Deadly Violence." *Suicide and Life-threatening Behavior* 10: 195–209.

Seligman, Martin E. P. 1972. "Learned Helplessness." *Annual Review of Medicine* 23: 407–12.

———. 1974. "Depression and Learned Helplessness." In *The Psychology of De-pression: Contemporary Theory and Research*, edited by J. R. Friedman and M. M. Katz, 83–113. Washington, D.C.: Winston.

———. 1975. *On Depression, Development, and Death*. San Francisco: Freeman.

Seligman, Martin E. P., and S. F., Maier. 1967. "Failure to Escape Traumatic Shock." *Journal of Experimental Psychology* 74: 1–9.

Seligman, Martin E. P., S. F. Maier, and J. Geer. 1968. "The Alleviation of Learned Helplessness in the Dog." *Journal of Abnormal and Social Psychol-ogy* 73: 256–62.

Selkin, J. 1978. "Rescue Fantasies in Homicide-Suicide." *Suicide and Life-threatening Behavior* 6: 79–85.

Sellin, Thorsten. 1972. "Enrico Ferri, 1856-1929." In *Pioneers in Criminology*. 2d ed., edited by Hermann Mannheim, 361–384. Montclair, N.J.: Patterson Smith.

Selvin, Hanan. 1958. "Durkheim's *Suicide* and Problems of Empirical Research." *American Journal of Sociology* 63: 607–19.

Shannon, Lyle W. 1954. "The Spatial Distribution of Criminal Offenses by States." *The Journal of Criminal Law, Criminology and Police Science* 45: 264–73.

Shields, Nancy M., and Christine R. Hanneke. 1983. "Attribution Processes in Violent Relationships: Perceptions of Violent Husbands and Their Wives." *Journal of Applied Social Psychology* 13: 515–27.

Shneidman, Edwin S. 1980. *Voices of Death*. New York: Harper and Row.

Shneidman, Edwin S., and Norman L. Farberow, eds. 1957. *Clues to Suicide*. New York: McGraw-Hill.

Simpson, Miles. 1990. "Political Rights and Income Inequality: A Cross-national Test." *American Sociological Review* 55: 682–93.

Sorokin, Pitirim A. 1937–41. *Social and Cultural Dynamics*. 4 vols. New York: American Book Company.

South, Scott J. 1984. "Unemployment and Social Problems in the Post-war United States." *Social Indicators Research* 15: 391–416.

Stack, Steven. 1978. "Suicide: A Comparative Analysis." *Social Forces* 57: 644–53.

———. 1982. "Suicide: A Decade Review of the Literature." *Deviant Behavior* 4: 41–66.

———. 1983. "The Effect of Religious Commitment on Suicide: A Cross-national Analysis." *Journal of Health and Social Behavior* 24: 362–74.

———. 1985. "Economic Development, Religion, and Lethal Aggression—A Reply to Whitt." *Deviant Behavior* 6: 233–36.

———. 1987. "The Sociological Study of Suicide: Methodological Issues." *Suicide and Life-threatening Behavior* 17: 133–50.

———. 1988. "Review of *Violent Deaths in the United States*, by Paul Holinger." *Contemporary Sociology* 17: 691–92.

———. 1989. "The Effect of Publicized Mass Murders and Murder Suicides on Lethal Violence, 1968–1980." *Social Psychiatry and Psychiatric Epidemiology* 24: 202–8.

Stafford, Mark C., and Ralph A. Weisheit. 1988. "Changing Age Patterns of U.S. Male and Female Suicide Rates, 1934–1983." *Suicide and Life-threatening Behavior* 18: 149–63.

Stanley, Michael, and Barbara Stanley. 1990. "Portmortem Evidence for Serotonin's Role in Suicide." *Journal of Clinical Psychiatry* 51: 22–28.

Stewart, Omer. 1964. "Questions Regarding Indian Criminality." *Human Organization* 23: 61–66.

Stimson, James A., Edward G. Carmines, and Richard A. Zeller. 1976. "Interpreting Polynomial Regression." *Sociological Methods and Research* 6: 515–23.

Stokes, Randall, and John P. Hewitt. 1976. "Aligning Actions." *American Sociological Review* 41: 838–49.

Stone, Richard. 1992. "HHS 'Violence Initiative' Caught in a Cross-fire." *Science* 258: 212–13.

Straus, Jacqueline H., and Murray A. Straus. 1953. "Suicide, Homicide, and Social Structure in Ceylon." *American Journal of Sociology* 58: 461–69.

Sullivan, Harry Stack. 1956. *Clinical Studies in Psychiatry*. New York: W. W. Norton.

Swanson, Guy E. 1960. "Determinants of the Individual's Defenses against Inner Conflict. In *Parental Attitudes and Child Behavior*, edited by John Glidewell, 5–41. Springfield, IL: Charles C. Thomas.

Swidler, Ann. 1986. "Culture in Action." *American Sociological Review* 51: 273–86.

Sykes, Gresham, and David Matza. 1957. "Techniques of Neutralization: A Theory of Delinquency." *American Sociological Review* 22: 664–70.

Szasz, Thomas S. 1974. *The Myth of Mental Illness: Foundations of a Theory of Personal Conduct*. New York: Harper and Row.

Sztompka, Piotr. 1988. "Conceptual Frameworks in Comparative Inquiry: Divergent or Convergent?" *International Sociology* 3: 207–18.

Tangney, June Price, Patricia Wagner, and Richard Gramzow. 1992. "Proneness to Shame, Proneness to Guilt, and Psychopathology." *Journal of Abnormal Psychology* 101: 469–78.

Tarde, Gabriel. 1883. "Quelques criminalistes italiens de la nouvelle école." *Revue Philosophique* 15: 658–69.

———[G. T.]. 1884. "E. Ferri—L'Omicidio-suicidio. *L'Homicide-suicide*. Torino, Fratelli Brocca, 1884." *Revue Philosophique* 17: 688–90.

———. 1886a. *La criminalité comparée*. Paris: Felix Alcan.

———. 1886b. "Problèmes de criminalité." *Revue Philosophique* 21: 1–23, 122–43.

———. 1890. *Penal Philosophy*. Translated by Rapelje Howell. Boston: Little, Brown, and Company, 1912.

Taubes, Gary. 1992. "Violence Epidemiologists Test the Hazards of Gun Ownership." *Science* 258: 213–15.

Teicher, Martin H., Carol Glod, and Jonathan O. Cole. 1990. "Emergence of Intense Suicidal Preoccupation during Fluoxetine Treatment." *American Journal of Psychiatry* 147: 207–10.

Tennen, Howard, and Glenn Affleck. 1990. "Blaming Others for Threatening Events." *Psychological Bulletin* 108: 209–32.

Tiryakian, Edward A. 1962. *Sociologism and Existentialism*. Englewood Cliffs, N.J.: Prentice-Hall.

Travis, Robert. 1990. "Suicide in Cross-cultural Perspective." *International Journal of Comparative Sociology* 31: 237–48.

United Nations. 1971–90. *Demographic Yearbook*. New York: United Nations.

United States Bureau of the Census. 1973. *United States Census of Population, 1970*. Washington, D.C.: Government Printing Office.

Unnithan, N. Prabha. 1983. *Homicide and the Social Structure: A Cross-national Analysis of Lethal Violence Rates, 1950–1970*. Ph.D. diss., University of Nebraska-Lincoln.

Unnithan, N. Prabha, and Hugh P. Whitt. 1992. "Inequality, Economic Development and Lethal Violence: A Cross-national Analysis of Suicide and Homicide." *International Journal of Comparative Sociology* 33: 182–95.

Uslaner, Eric M. 1976. "The Pitfalls of Per Capita." *American Journal of Political Science* 20: 125–33.

———. 1977. "Straight Lines and Straight Thinking: Can All of Those Econometricians Be Wrong?" *American Journal of Political Science* 21: 183–91.

Vance, Rupert B. 1935. *Human Geography of the South: A Study in Regional Resources and Human Adequacy*. Chapel Hill: University of North Carolina Press.

Vanderbok, William G. 1977. "On Improving the Analysis of Ratio Data." *Political Methodology* 4: 171–84.

van Praag, Herman M., and Robert Plutchik. 1986. "An Empirical Study of the 'Cathartic Effect' of Attempted Suicide." *Psychiatry Research* 16: 123–30.

Verkko, Veli. 1951. *Homicides and Suicides in Finland and Their Dependence on National Character*. Copenhagen: G. E. C. Gads Forlag.

Virkkunen, Matti. 1974. "Suicide Linked to Homicide." *Psychiatric Quarterly* 48: 276–82.

von Hentig, Hans. 1948. *The Criminal and His Victim*. New Haven: Yale University Press.

Wallwork, Ernest. 1972. *Durkheim: Morality and Milieu*. Cambridge: Harvard University Press.

Wasserman, Ira M. 1984a. "Imitation and Suicide: A Reexamination of the Werther Effect." *American Sociological Review* 49: 427–36.

————. 1984b. "The Linkage of United States Presidential Elections, Unemployment Changes, and Reductions in Suicide, Accident, and Homicide Rates." *The Journal of Social Psychology* 124: 115–17.

Weber, Max. 1906. *The Protestant Ethic and the Spirit of Capitalism*. New York: Charles Scribner, 1958.

Weede, Erich. 1980. "Beyond Misspecification in Sociological Analyses of Income Inequality." *American Sociological Review* 45: 497–501.

————. 1989. "Democracy and Income Inequality Reconsidered." *American Sociological Review* 54: 865–68.

Weiden, Peter, and Alec Roy. 1992. "General Versus Specific Risk Factors for Suicide in Schizophrenia." In *Suicide and Clinical Practice*, edited by Douglas Jacobs, 75–100. Washington, D.C.: American Psychiatric Press.

Weiner, Bernard. 1972. *Theories of Motivation: From Mechanism to Cognition*. Chicago: Rand McNally.

————. 1974. *Achievement Motivation and Attribution Theory*. Morristown, N.J.: General Learning Press.

————. 1980. "The Role of Affect in Rational (Attributional) Approaches to Human Motivation." *Educational Researcher* 9: 4–11.

————. 1985. "An Attributional Theory of Achievement Motivation and Emotion." *Psychological Review* 92: 548–73.

————. 1986. *An Attributional Theory of Motivation and Emotion*. New York: Springer Verlag.

————. 1988. "Attribution Theory and Attributional Therapy: Some Theoretical Observations and Suggestions." *British Journal of Clinical Psychology* 27: 93–104.

Weiner, Bernard, Sandra Graham, and Carla Chandler. 1982. "Causal Antecedents of Pity, Anger and Guilt." *Personality and Social Psychology Bulletin* 8: 226–32.

Weiner, Bernard, Dan Russell, and David Lerman. 1979. "The Cognition-Emotion Process in Achievement-related Contexts." *Journal of Personality and Social Psychology* 37: 1211–20.

Weiss, Noel S. 1976. "Recent Trends in Violent Deaths among Young Adults in the United States." *American Journal of Epidemiology* 103: 416–22.

Weiss, Roger D., and Peggy S. Stephens. 1992. "Substance Abuse and Suicide." In *Suicide and Clinical Practice*, edited by Douglas Jacobs, 101–14. Washington, D.C.: American Psychiatric Press.

Weissman, M. M., G. L. Klerman, and J. S. Markowitz. 1989. "Suicidal Ideation and Suicide Attempts in Panic Disorder and Attacks." *New England Journal of Medicine* 321: 1210–14.

Wendling, Aubrey, and Kenneth Polk. 1958. "Suicide and Social Areas." *Pacific Sociological Review* 1: 50–53.

West, D[onald] J. 1967. *Murder Followed by Suicide*. Cambridge: Harvard University Press.

Westcott, William Wynn. 1885. *Suicide, Its History, Literature, Jurisprudence, Causation and Prevention*. London: H. K. Lewis.

Whiting, John W. M., and Irvin L. Child. 1953. *Child Training and Personality*. New Haven: Yale University Press.

Whitt, Hugh P. 1966. *Suicide and Hierarchical Residential Status in Atlanta*. M.A. thesis, University of North Carolina at Chapel Hill.

————. 1968. *The Lethal Aggression Rate and the Suicide-Murder Ratio*. Ph.D. diss., University of North Carolina at Chapel Hill.

————. 1985. "Comments on Steven Stack's paper 'Suicide: A Decade Review of the Sociological Literature.' " *Deviant Behavior* 6: 229–31.

————. 1986. "The Sheaf Coefficient: A Simplified and Expanded Approach." *Social Science Research* 15: 174–89.

Whitt, Hugh P., Charles C. Gordon, and John R. Hofley. 1972. "Religion, Economic Development and Lethal Aggression." *American Sociological Review* 37: 193–201.

Whitt, Hugh P., and Richard L. Meile. 1985. "Alignment, Magnification and Snowballing: Processes in the Definition of Mental Illness." *Social Forces* 63: 682–97.

Wilbanks, William. 1984. *Murder in Miami*. Lanham, MD: University Press of America.

Williams, Kirk R. 1984. "Economic Sources of Homicide: Reestimating the Effects of Poverty and Inequality." *American Sociological Review* 49: 283–89.

Williams, Robin. 1970. *American Society*, 3d ed. New York: Knopf.

Wilson, Margo, and Martin Daly. 1985. "Competitiveness, Risk Taking, and Violence: The Young Male Syndrome." *Ethology and Sociobiology* 6: 59–73.

Winslow, Robert W. 1970. *Society in Transition: A Social Approach to Deviancy*. New York: Free Press.

Wolfgang, Marvin E. 1958a. "An Analysis of Homicide-Suicide." *Journal of Clinical and Experimental Psychopathology* 19: 208–18.

————. 1958b. *Patterns in Criminal Homicide.* Philadelphia: University of Pennsylvania Press.

————. 1959. "Suicide by Means of Victim-precipitated Homicide." *Journal of Clinical and Experimental Psychopathology* 20: 335–49.

Wolfgang, Marvin E., and Franco Ferracuti. 1967. *The Subculture of Violence.* London: Tavistock.

Wood, Arthur J. 1961a. "A Socio-structural Analysis of Murder, Suicide, and Economic Crime in Ceylon." *American Sociological Review* 26: 744–53.

————. 1961b. "Crime and Aggression in Changing Ceylon: A Sociological Analysis of Homicide, Suicide, and Economic Crime." *Proceedings of the American Philosophical Society* 51: part 8.

Wood, Keith, and Alec Coppen. 1980. "Biochemical Abnormalities in Depressive Illness: Tryptophan and 5-hydroxytryptamine." In *The Biochemistry of Psychiatric Disorders*, edited by G. Curzon, 13–34. New York: John Wiley and Sons.

World Almanac and Book of Facts. 1993. New York: World Almanac.

World Bank. 1979–85, 1991. *World Development Report.* Oxford: Oxford University Press.

World Health Organization. 1971–91. *World Health Statistics Annual.* Geneva: World Health Organization.

Worldmark Encyclopedia of the Nations. 7th ed. 1987. New York: John Wiley and Sons.

Worley, Paul F., William A. Heller, Solomon H. Snyder, and Jay M. Baraban. 1988. "Lithium Blocks a Phosphoinositide-mediated Cholinergic Response in Hippocampic Slices." *Science* 239: 1428–29.

Yang, Bijou, and David Lester. 1988. "The Participation of Females in the Labor Force and Rates of Personal Violence (Suicide and Homicide)." *Suicide and Life-threatening Behavior* 18: 270–78.

Yap, P[ow] M[eng]. 1958. *Suicide in Hong Kong.* Hong Kong: Hong Kong University Press.

Young, Simon N. 1990. "Factors Influencing the Effect of Tryptophan in Affective Disorders, Sleep, Aggression and Pain." In *Amino Acids in Psychiatric Disease*, edited by Mary Ann Richardson, 49–75. Washington, D.C.: American Psychiatric Press.

Young, Thomas J. 1990. "Poverty, Suicide, and Homicide among Native Americans." *Psychological Reports* 67: 1153–54.

Zilboorg, Gregory. 1936. "Differential Diagnostic Types of Suicide." *Archives of Neurology and Psychiatry* 35: 270–91.

———. 1937. "Considerations on Suicide, with Particular Reference to that of the Young." *American Journal of Orthopsychiatry* 7: 15–31.

Zimmern, Helen. 1896. "Enrico Ferri on Homicide." *Popular Science Monthly* 49: 678–84, 828–37.

INDEX